Death in the Midnight Sky:

Flying the Mighty Gunship in Combat

A Memoir

by

Joe Berardino

DORRANCE
PUBLISHING CO
EST. 1920
PITTSBURGH, PENNSYLVANIA 15238

Dorrance Publishing Co
585 Alpha Drive
Suite 103
Pittsburgh, PA 15238
Visit our website at *www.dorrancebookstore.com*

ISBN: 978-1-4809-3651-5
eISBN: 978-1-4809-3674-4

ACKNOWLEDGMENTS

The author wishes to thank the following people: Heather Calabrese who performed a difficult first edit and her husband Matt Calabrese my first beta reader. Gloria Schmitten helped rewrite that first manuscript.

In addition, my family was very supportive in this entire effort: Cindy, Lucy and John Berardino as well as Tiffany Obenhein. Melissa and Scott were wonderful. Further, my step family have been enormously supportive: Tracy, Michael, Justin and Logan.

Thank you Inkbloods Writer's Critique group for your many years of dedicated help: Dwight Marshallack, Jeannie Kraus, George Pocs, Sue Allstott, Pat Crumpler, Sharon Marsten, Shelly Olskansky, Roslyn Fishman, Christina Craig, Dick Beerman, Manfred Brecker and Steve Le Bray.

Thank you for your inspiration my band of Colonels: Mike Freidline, Tom Hill, Tom Nett and Don Woodworth, you are the best.

My lifetime appreciation to the Gunship Generals Jack Cole and Monte Montgomery.

Deep appreciation to my other band of writers in my Boca Group; Pat Williams, Bunny Shulman, Carren Strock, Lee Ravine, Michelle Putnam, Bea Lewis, Barbara Brixon, and Lea Becker.

I had a number of incredible writing instructors; Ann Hood, Denis Lahane, and Dr. James W. Hall, my deepest appreciation.

The Broward County Library system has been immensely helpful in providing meeting rooms and research facilities. The Palm Beach Library has been of invaluable service to this entire effort.

The author can be reached at Joeberardino1@juno.com.

DEDICATION

This book is dedicated to the men and women of the 4th Air
Commando Squadron, the 1st Air Commando Wing and
all people who flew Puff, Spooky, Shadow, Stinger and Spectre.

A portion of proceeds from this book will be donated to the
Spooky Brotherhood.

My life and work are dedicated to my children, Cindy, John
and Tiffany; and to my grandchildren, Jacob (Jake), Chloe, Maya,
Claire, Jack and Joshua.

TABLE OF CONTENTS

CHAPTER I

FEBRUARY 1967

"Marines are dying." My pulse raced as the twin engines of my airplane thundered into attack.

Scores of fathers would be in body bags tonight, but not me. I needed to kill and survive to take care of my sick baby Cindy back home.

"Da Nang Tower, go ahead, this is Spooky Three," Ace shot back.

"Spooky One is calling for you to fly to the Marine outpost, Tricky Misfit to relieve them. They're losing a bad ass fight!"

"Joe, arm the guns." I prepared myself for battle at the Marine outpost.

"Roger, sir."

I had to do my job and save the Marines so they could go home to their babies. The clean, sweet smell of gun oil reminded me that I held the agents of death in my hands: fifteen hundred copper clad bullets. I fought to raise my chin through the weight of the helmet.

Ace slammed the throttles to full power. The engines screamed. Like an eagle spotting its kill, we streaked south. I paced around the airplane. I felt all twitchy. *Ron and his crew were already there. This must be one dangerous battle, but we're safe up here.*

"Sparks, call the other airplane. Find out the situation," Ace said.

Sparks spit back, in rapid fire staccato. "Viet Cong ambushed a 159 truck convoy in front of Tricky Misfit. They're shooting the Marines with our own 50-caliber guns. Spooky One has two malfunctioning guns needing repair. He wants us to go on target and shoot the VC on the trucks," he said. Ace turned our war bird toward the fight. I knew my best friend Ron would be fixing the guns fast enough to kill the enemy. *Ron is safe.*

In less time than it takes a soldier to say a prayer, Ace came back on the radio, "Joe, we're two minutes out, get ready. The Viet Cong are trying to go over the fence by the convoy." I thought *they're bold now because Spooky One's guns broke a half an hour ago. We have a surprise for The Cong!*

I watched through the blacked out cargo compartment. Fires on the ground were a beacon to where an ambush was cutting Tricky Misfit to pieces.

"Guns Hot, Pilot," I called. "Give him all the firepower at once."

"It's okay, Joe, the VC is all over the trucks, I want to catch them off guard." I heard the engines grow quiet and the vibrations stop. "We're going in stealthily," Ace said as we silently glided like a deadly nighthawk to the target.

I could barely hear the engines as the left wing tilted down thirty degrees into firing position. I tensed up, puckered my sphincter and stared at my gun, waiting for it to fire.

RHOOOMMMM, my gun screamed. RHOOOMMMM, the sound of death roared and my heart soared. I grinned, felt lightheaded and stared at the tracers flying down to the enemy.

BOOOMM! I heard an intense blast. This new sound and cloud of smoke startled me. I tasted the metallic bitter gunpowder. A gun had exploded. I lurched over to gun number one and saw a bent round of ammo, so I grabbed my screwdriver and pried it until the round came out. There was screaming over the radio from the Marines, "Medic!" I cycled the gun. It seemed to work fine. More screaming over the radio, "By the wire to the east!"

I re-armed the gun, looked over at Tex and saw he was almost done loading.

RHOOOOOM! It sang out a five second burst.

Tex stood there, staring out of the small square window between the guns, watching the battle. I yelled at him, "Tex, don't look out. Keep your head in the airplane and take care of your guns. You can't help the Marines if you're looking outside!" *Man, I sounded like Ron.*

Tex had a startled look on his face as he stumbled forward to the line of ammo cans, with 1,500 rounds in each, unstrapped a can and carried it to the front gun and began loading.

RHOOOMMMM, BLAAAASSST.

Damn— another malfunction. This is going to be impossible to repair.

"Number two is hard broke," I had a sinking feeling in the pit of my stomach, "I'm on it. It looks bad," I yanked off the feeder and pulled out the bent bullets.

"Hot shit," Sparks shouted, "Tricky Misfit says we smashed the VC. They didn't know we were here and we shot the shit out of them. Go east, they're massing to attack."

"Roger Sparks, we're on it," Ace said.

I stared out and could see the other side of the fort, two hundred and fifty yards to the east. There were a couple of bright orange fires burning and sporadic red tracers shooting out. The long, bright blood red tracers looked like thin neon lights pointing at the enemy. The fort was pitch black and only lighted by bursts of orange fires, muzzle flashes, and an intense, white flare hanging in the sky like an eerily lit ghost.

Neon red tracers also fired from the convoy into Tricky. Blood red fire pointed back at the Marines. Felt like a finger pushed into my chest. *It must be terrifying, cornered in that hellhole. You boys must feel like wild horses trapped in a death corral. We will never leave you.*

The darkness and the jungle hid the massing VC. Even under the best conditions, it was impossible to see individuals—it was all a haze, like trying to sight a gun with old glasses.

We circled around to the east of the compound, entered our thirty-degree left bank, and fired a short burst until the gun spun freely. Tex ran over and started loading as fast as he could; I turned

3

on number three and started to get another can of ammo. BLAAAAASSST. The damned gun malfunctioned *again*.

"Son of a bitch," I shouted. I ran over to it and began taking it apart.

Ace answered, "That's okay, Joe; Spooky One has their weapons fixed and is ready to come down and fight. We'll go up to six thousand feet where you can fix the guns." I thought of good Ron up there readying to get back in the fight. It made me smile.

"Help me watch out the right side of the airplane," Ace said. "Spooky One is going to pass by us on his way down, and we can't stand a midair collision." I shuddered remembering that blacked out airplanes crashed together all the time. Certain death was the result.

I stared out the small window. I was a brother to everyone on the plane. Part of me was in that plane. My heart was in that plane and most of my bravery. Ron, my best friend was the lead gunner. Everyone called Ron Teacher, or Teach. He had been my instructor, my colleague, my brother, and mentor in Vietnam and so I had the deepest feelings of camaraderie, love and respect for him. My chest filled up as I thought of him.

Where are they?

"There they are, three o'clock, descending through our altitude!" yelled copilot Zoomie.

My eyes fixed on the black outline of a C-47 over the horizon, barely visible about 1,500 yards to the right of us. "They're clear," Ace said.

I started to turn towards number two gun when an intense flash of light caught my right eye and I saw a stream of red tracers climb up from the ground below.

"Tracers at four o'clock. Don't turn on the lights. Someone is shooting at us," I shouted. In slow motion, a stream of them lit up the coal black sky. Like car brake lights in a time elapse picture, long streaks of blood-red ribbons shot into the sky. Out of nowhere, a flash of sun bright white light lit up the night. I stared out for a few seconds.

"Spooky, Spooky, this is Tricky Misfit, are you hit?"

"Tricky Misfit, this is Spooky Three, we're fine. Just tracers fired at us and missed by a mile," answered Sparks.

"Negative Three. There's a spooky bird crashed on the ground… We thought it was you."

Ron's shot down?

CHAPTER II

SPOOKY ONE IS DOW

"He's on fire," someone blurted out. Chills ran down my spine. I dashed back to the window, looked out, and saw a blazing mass on the south side of the compound. It looked like a dark shapeless mess, like a dead animal by the side of the road, run over by a hundred cars. I couldn't see well enough to tell if it was an airplane or anything other than a burning pile. Fear gripped my throat. I held my breath. A cold sweat covered my body. *What if Ron's hit?*

"Crew, get your shit together. Spooky One is shot down. Pay attention!" Ace yelled.

"We have to protect the compound and keep the Cong off our airplane. Sparks, contact Da Nang, tell them what happened and to send us another gunship—get me some guns on the line!"

My mind was numb. I went through the motions of arming the gun. *Ron and his crew were shot down.* I had the strangest feelings; pins and needles in my hands, a floating sensation, the aircraft was spinning around and I was outside my body looking down on the ground like a brother eagle. Then I went into my escapist's denial, *He's not hit, they're all okay. Ron'll save the crew and get a Medal.*

I felt lightheaded, drunk, and disoriented. I had the sensation of being on the ceiling of the airplane looking down, watching myself work on the guns. Through a dizzy haze, I could see Joe going through the motions of fixing and loading the guns. I felt sick, scared, frightened for the first time in Vietnam; hell for the first time in my life.

•   •   •

We began firing hundreds of copper killers encircling the perimeter of Spooky One. Then we returned to fire on the east of Tricky Misfit. We circled both the burning hulk and the compound for the next two hours. At midnight Ace said, "There's another airplane coming up from Pleiku. Da Nang's last airplane blew an engine on takeoff. We'll fire our remaining ammo, then RTB, get more ammo and come back for our friends."

There was no question: no matter how tired or scared, I was coming back to get Ron.

Sparks called for an update. "Tricky Misfit, has anyone seen the crew of One? We heard their emergency beacon, but no radio traffic. They should be trying to get to your outpost."

Great, they're alive and fighting to get to the outpost.

"Negative, Spooky, but our Commander is going to send out a rescue party when the firing slows down," Tricky Misfit answered.

My mind came back to the present when the other aircraft called us. "Spooky Three, this is spooky Two-Three from Pleiku. We're fifteen minutes out. What's the situation?"

While Sparks briefed the approaching aircraft, we loaded the remaining ammo into the two functioning weapons and prepared to fire our last salvoes.

One-half hour later, we landed and taxied into the gunship ramp where everyone was waiting. The fire truck was there, so we could load ammo and av-gas at the same time. The big olive-green, ten-thousand-gallon fuel truck was ready and waiting. Next to our parking spot, there were bomb dump troops to load the ammo, weapons mechanics to help us fix the guns and crew chiefs to repair any problems with the airplane.

Ace said, "We'll leave off one hundred gallons of fuel and take four extra cans of ammo so we'll have twenty-seven thousand rounds on board that will last all night. Gunner Joe, get extra gun parts."

I gathered the weapons men around the guns. We changed out every part that looked even slightly worn. *We are not going to stop firing under any circumstances.*

In record time, the aircraft was refueled, rearmed, repaired, restarted and taxiing out to the ten-thousand-foot runway. After take-off, Sparks called for an update.

"Spooky Two-Three, this is Spooky Three, fifteen minutes out from your location, fully armed and ready to assume our position on the target. What's your location?"

"Ahhh, Spooky Three we're at six thousand feet, dropping flares." a hesitating answer.

Ace got on the radio, "What do you mean six thousand feet, why aren't you at two thousand feet shooting?"

The slow cautious reply was "Ahhh, One-Three, there is a lot of bullets flying up at us at two thousand feet and one aircraft has already been shot down. We're staying up here and dropping flares, over."

Ace was livid and showed it over the intercom, "That chicken shit won't go down there and shoot the Gooks off our airplane. He's firing from such a high altitude he can't hit the broad side of a barn. We have to protect our crew. Gunner, give me hot guns."

Approaching the target from the north, I could just make out hundreds of camouflaged Gooks crawling out of the jungle towards the convoy climbing on the trucks, grabbing the 50-caliber guns ready to fire into the compound and shoot at us. The Gooks looked like stinking dirty worms, roaches and ants and I hated them.

I could see that we were way below our safe altitude, for the first time, I could see actual individual enemy soldiers climbing over the trucks. Ace was making a statement for the other gunship—'We're not afraid of a little Anti-Aircraft Artillery.'

The enemy didn't hear us coming, as we turned and began firing. Every fifth round was a tracer and it looked like a walkway of red carpet for a Hollywood premiere. The guns were on target and we lit the night with tracers.

GROOOOOOWLLLLLL!

My heart filled, *Puff the Magic Dragon screamed and breathed fire, the sword of Damocles was raised and the enemy was vanquished. Fire, steel, lead, vindication, and hate rained from the sky.* Gooks fell off the trucks, a gas tank exploded and burning Commies ran back into the jungle. The smell of cordite made my nostrils flare and they felt good. The red and orange fires hurt my eyes, but I barely blinked. After twenty seconds, reloaded a gun, and Tex got another while Ace peppered the remaining trucks. Tricky Misfit screamed, "You got 'em, you got 'em, you got 'em!"

Someone shouted, "Cong's going after the downed plane."

We turned our minds, hearts and guns to the smoldering wreck of One. I could see Gooks crawling towards the aircraft.

"*You are not going to get Ron*," I vowed. We fired a circle around the pile of airplane. The enemy either died in place or ran, screaming back into the jungle. We kept going between the compound and the downed airplane, killing Gooks anywhere they showed themselves. In the meantime, Spooky Two-Three quietly turned tail and crawled back to Pleiku like the cowardly sheep he was.

We climbed up to two thousand feet and fired for a long time. It was almost daylight when Tricky Misfit called and said, "Spooky, Spooky, it looks like The Cong has had enough for tonight. I think they have broken off."

Ace answered, "We got more ammo, we'll hang around and do some Harassment and Interdiction firing. Has anyone ever gotten to look over the gunship for the survivors?"

"Spooky, we have a team on their way, but we haven't seen any motion there for some time," Tricky Misfit answered. I was shaking and a lump caught in my throat and my heart seemed to stop.

I tried to carry on, turned my head so Tex couldn't see the damp under my eyes.

I know they are alive. Nothing can kill Ron. I sniffled to myself.

"Okay, crew, let's concentrate on the enemy."

Then the navigator piped up. "Ace, the sun is coming over the horizon and the aircraft is in daylight and an easy target. You know what the old man said; it's a court martial to fly in daylight since we had an airplane shot down last month flying after dawn."

Ace replied, "I know Nav, but they shot down One and we have to make them pay. We'll fire off the last of the ammo and RTB. Gunner Joe, get ready."

He fired a two second burst, then went one hundred yards further into the jungle and fired another two second burst. For the next fifteen minutes, we kept the weapons loaded and running.

"Pilot, Sparks. I can't receive any radio signals and nobody seems to hear us."

Ace replied, "Run your malfunction checklist and figure out what's wrong."

"They're running out of the jungle and down the road at five o'-clock," the loadmaster screamed.

Ace banked the plane to the left, and sure enough, the frightened enemy was running out of the jungle and down a dirt road. I turned on all three guns and we blazed away, slaughtering the hated enemy. I had never seen so many black pajamas running at the same time.

We fired until we were out of ammo and it looked like they were all dead. Finally, I had the guilty thought that it wasn't right to feel good about killing a human being. But deep inside my heart was warmed seeing so many enemies dead. For killing Ron, I believed the gooks deserved to die, and that retribution belonged to the mighty Puff the Magic Dragon.

It was daylight and we were out of ammo. Someone said over the intercom, "Can we fly over Tricky Misfit and check on Spooky One-One?"

"Sure thing," Ace replied. "Any luck getting the radios fixed, Sparks?"

"No, sir."

"There's Tricky Misfit, twelve o'clock and five miles ahead," screamed the Nav.

． ． ．

We flew ahead in silence, my eyes strained forward; contemplating for the first time what might really be in store for us. I thought about Ron, a father himself, with a wee bairn, as the Irish said. He was also a straight arrow husband, outstanding Airman, and perfect role model for a man. I had spent hundreds of hours learning from him. He had a baby daughter, just as I did and he had married an Irish girl. I asked myself the same question time after time; *how could she make it without him?*

Ron and I were like brothers and spent all our off duty time discussing what we would do after Vietnam. He was taking college courses and took me to the education office to do the same. "I'm not going to be a gunner forever. I'm going back to Colorado, to college, so I can be a veterinarian. What the hell do you want to do when you get out?" Ron asked me. After joking that I would be 'A Gunner on a Budweiser truck in Hialeah' I answered, I *wanted to be a scientist.*

I had promised him, "If anything ever happens to you, I will be there for your little girl. I will do everything I can for her." In truth, I never believed either one of us could be killed, I had this Superman complex. Naivety and stupidity were my constant companions, and until that very moment death was inconceivable. Reality crashed in on me and deep inside my heart, I started to wonder how I would make good on my promise if anything happened to Ron.

Even now, my Superman complex and my youthful optimism would not allow me to think for a nanosecond that the crew of Spooky One was wounded or dead.

"There's the airplane," someone shouted, "still smoking."

What a heart stopping sight. In the grey dawn light, clearly the outline of the C-47 on the ground; nothing much left but moldering aluminum in the shape of the fuselage and wings. It looked like one of those police outlines in white chalk that indicate where a body had been found, except this was in black fire residue. Only the clearly definable shape of that rounded tail stood erect among the littered crash site. I saw shattered and burned; they were all gone; my airplane, my friends and my dreams.

My eyes were damp and my voice choked up, as though I had swallowed an apple whole; sadness was my friend now. I kept thinking, *what a strange sight we must make, an AC-47 flying in the bright dawn light of sunrise, looking over the semi-dark battle scene of a gray, wispy smoked crashed sister airplane.*

I only hoped that my Squadron mates had gotten out and were safely inside Tricky Misfit. A cold chill and a sudden sorrow came over me as I pondered the possible death of so many friends and brothers. I silently prayed, *"God let Ron be alive and I will never curse, smoke, lie or do anything bad again in my life."*

CHAPTER III

FLASHBACK

With head spinning and hands shaking, my foolish pride was gone. Most of my boyish bravado had been taken aback with the murder of President Kennedy, the rest died with Ron that night. Bravado and naivety were gone, all gone.

I was shaking and confused, light headed as if I had been drinking, wondering what had happened. Sadness burdened my heart and moisture a constant resident in my eyes. I was disoriented, out of body, having seen the smoking outline of the airplane and been through the night of death.

Questions streamed through my mind; *What the hell was I doing here. How would my wife survive? How would Ron's wife and daughter survive without him? Why did I volunteer for this? Who would take care of Cindy? What had possessed me to do this insane thing? How did I get here?*

Then I remembered my father telling this story.

•   •   •

"Coward!" Pop was startled by the shouting Lieutenant. "If you step behind that line, you are a coward. If you stand tall and become a gunner, you're a hero." The Lieutenant glared at them through his avi-

15

ator sunglasses, then ordered," Cowards, step back," Pop stared him right in the eye as he stepped back over the line drawn in the sand. He glanced over at the other Soldier and winked. His buddy, New York, also stepped back and gave a mock salute.

"New York and I went to the bar on Miami Beach and laughed at those dummies for hours. They volunteered to die. They were the cowards," he laughed, "too afraid to stand up to some self-important Lieutenant so they all died as gunners." Pop sipped his beer. I hung my head, turned bright red and walked outside to the truck to read my comic book.

At seven years old the story was already familiar to my ears. Pop always portrayed himself as the street-smart soldier who never volunteered for gunner duty. He laughed at escaping certain death that befell most WWII gunners. He pretended to be street smart. I pretended to believe him. Deep down, in my secret heart, I thought he was a coward.

It was terrible for a boy to think his father a coward. When I looked at him I had a slight doubt in the hidden place in my mind. It made me question him and be fearful that Pop would show his cowardice at the most embarrassing time. I always wondered if Pop would abandon us when he should be brave. In my heart of hearts I never trusted that my father wouldn't run at the first sign of danger.

My deeply guarded secret was hidden in my soul. It was my great shame, my father was a coward. Other friends had pictures of their fathers getting medals, plaques on their walls and one friend even displayed a samurai sword captured from the enemy. I was fearful that the coward's streak in my family would be discovered and worse yet, come out in me when I needed to be brave.

Because of that, I shuddered to think that I had inherited the gene so I lived on the edge. At every opportunity, I tested my mettle; I was the first kid to dive off the highest train trestle in Miami, I rode the roller coaster alone at eight, I was a daredevil dancing in the crash prone busy streets of Miami. I would show him I was not a coward like him, I was Sir Galahad, Audie Murphy and all the bravest men in history.

I lived in that secret world with my hat pulled down over my eyes until one day, ten years later when my world changed forever.

• • •

The hopeful January sunlight shot through the living room window onto the floor. It warmed my feet and they drummed up and down at the speed of a typewriter hammering out thousand year words of encouragement. I couldn't stop grinning, bouncing or wringing my hands. The air tingled with excitement; electricity surrounded me like a cloud of pure energy and optimism filled my heart. Perched on the edge of the couch, my eyes were as wide as I could make them, straining to see all the important people on the black and white tube. My chest was tight and my heart beat like a Civil War snare drum marching to battle. Mom said, "Stop bouncing…There's Ike! The greatest General, I would follow him anywhere," her high pitched giggle was full of eagerness. "I can't wait to see Jackie," she said with a nervous laugh.

Sitting was impossible. I jumped up and walked around behind the couch, eyes locked on the tube the whole time; I didn't want to miss a single second of the most important occasion of my seventeen years. "This is historic, momentous, and extraordinary,…Most anticipated since Lincoln's…Youngest President,…Hope of a nation," the announcer said. At the same time, the phone rang.

"Don't answer it," Mom yelled, "Take it off the hook and lay it down," she pointed.

I leaned across Mom, "Don't block the T.V.," she said. "Where are you going?"

"To the bath…"

"Hold it, and don't talk. Sit down, Joe…"

"Mom, please, shhh I can't hear." She glared at me.

Then a hush surrounded the audience. The handsome young president, in top hat, spoke. His voice was clear, resonant, and proud. I didn't hear every word just snippets of heart pounding expressions of encouragement. The burning words leaving his tongue turned the freezing air to steam and echoed down the mall, across the nation and around the world. "Let the word go forth from this place...the torch has been passed, to a new generation," I held my breath; *he was talking about me, my generation.* "We shall pay any price, bear any burden, meet any hardship, support any friend, oppose any foe to assure the survival of liberty." *I know we can defeat Russia, I can beat them.* I looked over and saw a tear in my mother's eye as she mouthed, 'What a man.'

I closed my eyes, raised my chin to heaven, and felt the words surround me. They filled my heart with love, encouragement and boundless hope. I dreamt of marching over Russian tanks, freeing the Jews in Europe, opening schools in Africa. My chest filled with pride, I knew I could do anything; I could live the dream of my young President. Moreover, when he said, "Ask not what your country can do for you—ask what you can do for your country." I heard the drums again. My fate was sealed. I knew I had to become part of the greatest challenge of my generation, the new generation.

• • •

That speech buzzed in my ears until I could hardly concentrate on anything else. I didn't sleep that night and drowsily dreamt of joining the military and marching with President Kennedy at the head of an army of energetic and excited Americans, marching to build a better world. The next morning, I grabbed the *Herald* and read every single one of the thirteen hundred rousing and inspiring words. Those everlasting words, burned in my heart. They were meant for me, just for me a motivation, encouragement, and prod, a call to action to my generation to come out from under our nuclear-threatened children's desks and face the challenge of a new generation. *We will never cower again. We will face the Soviet threat that our fathers left when they defeated Germany. We won't stop short of Moscow.*

Monday morning I skipped school and hitched a ride to the Air Force recruiter's station. "We are assembling seventy five

American heroes to start basic training before February. Are you ready?" he asked.

"Give me the test, I can pass anything," I said, hopefully.

.   .   .

My father heard a different drummer, "Joe, don't listen to those war mongers. They got us into WWII and they're trying to suck you into WWIII. Those politicians are willing to spill the blood of all you naive children to reach their dreams. Don't listen, don't be gullible. Joe you can't go!" he screamed.

My face turned as red as the Russian flag, but, for once, I held my tongue against my father and said, "Mom, you heard the President, the torch is passed to my generation, I can go, but you have to sign."

"I'll never sign to give my son to the dogs of war," my father said.

I heard them fighting and yelling at each other late into the night. I pulled the pillow over my ears but couldn't keep out his wounding words. "Warmongers" he screamed, "hawks and military expansionists" he called our politicians. "Remember Eisenhower's last warning," he shouted with a shuddering fearful voice. He accused Mom of sending his oldest son off to die for some politicians dream.

.   .   .

The next night when I came home from the recruiter's office, I met them in our living room.

"Joe you have to do what it takes to be a man," Mom said, signing the enlistment contract.

Pop shook his head, cast down his eyes and looked heartbroken, he went to the bar.

.   .   .

I floated to the Miami Airport Monday humming. I almost danced into the entrance where I was surrounded by eighty or ninety fuzzy bearded boys. We thought of ourselves as men. We were the heroic Army of our young president, we felt the electricity in the air and the magnetic draw on our hearts to 'Do for your Country.' We all heard those drums and we sang as we climbed up the stairs to the plane.

"Off we go into the wild blue yonder…"

• • •

"We'll live in fame or go down in flames. Hey! Nothing can stop the US Air Force," I screamed along with eighty teenagers, inside the cramped, noisy passenger compartment of an airliner on the way to a new life. I kept hearing my mother's voice telling me it was time to become a man. I daydreamed of gallant deeds wearing my crisp blue uniform adorned with rows of bright heroic ribbons and chromed medallions. Evoking the memory of my young President made me feel like a Kennedy Ranger; capable of taking on any challenge and defending the mothers and daughters of America from the Russian hordes. Hope and optimism sizzled in the air and buzzed like a power line around me. Inside, inside my heart sang with joy.

A warrior, at least in my mind, I was filled with piss and vinegar, wild oats and excitement, testosterone and dreams; great dreams and hopes, vast hopes. I could take on the red army, deranged instructors, and even Marines if necessary.

We landed at 3:00 A.M. It was still dark as a guard waved our blue bus through the gates of Lackland Air Force Base, but anticipation rode with me and pumped through my veins at one hundred twenty beats a minute. We pulled up in front of a two story wooden barracks, the lights turned on inside and the Sergeant started yelling to get out and assemble in ranks. Of course we didn't know assemble in ranks from a Russian Fighter airplane. "Line up, new troops," a two-striped assistant said.

We ran through the double screen doors, into the barracks. The only thing I saw was a picture of President Kennedy facing the door. I felt like he was greeting me: his newest, '*ask what you can do for your country.*' He looked refreshed, unwavering, and confident; giving those same feelings to me. His presence gave me purpose.

"All the way with JFK," I shouted.

Two weeks later, a friend asked me to go AWOl with him to the Mardi Gras. I hung my head, frowned and the new man in me said "Can't go with you, buddy. I promised my family I would finish basic training." In my heart, I couldn't let my mother down, I couldn't let my president down and I definitely couldn't let my country down.

At reveille the next morning, I heard shouting, "Cajun's gone! I looked over to his bunk and it was empty. Further telling, his blanket was ridged down the bunk, made to look like a sleeping man. *Shit, Cajun did it. He went to the Mardi Gras!*

After Cajun, Basic Training was a long series of classes about the Soviet menace, the Chinese threat and the North Korean hordes, all just around the corner ready to pounce on an unprepared and unsuspecting America. In between we had classes on Air Force history, customs and courtesies and how to wear our uniforms. Sprinkled among our threat lessons were marches, exercise periods, latrine scrubbing, bed making, letter writing and buffing barracks floors. The time flew by and I was sustained by the picture of my young President. I graduated in April.

My thirty day home leave was a whirlwind of fun and dates wearing my omnipresent one stripe and crisp blue uniform. For the first time in my life, I was the hit in all the circles, especially with my mother who showed me off to all her friends. She couldn't wait to have me go to her restaurant. Every night when she finished her shift, she had me don my dress blues and come in and pick her up. She was chuffed with pride.

With a new anticipation I saw the apathy of my friends left behind and knew it was time for me to go on to a new life. My boyhood days were behind me. But I clearly did not understand the amazing world that awaited me in England.

. . .

In four of the shortest weeks in recorded history, I woke up startled; crash, boom, the airplane fell, my stomach was in my mouth and sweat covered my arms and back. I seized the armrest as if I were riding a death-defying roller coaster. The cabin lights brightened and a reassuring voice blared over the speaker, "We're encountering a little Atlantic storm. There is nothing to worry about. Fasten your seat belts. We should be out of it in a few minutes and landing in England in one hour."

My eyes felt as big as hula hoops and my heart beat fast like after a three mile run. Glancing around, I saw forty or fifty young airmen in their crisp uniforms looking about as well. We were awake now, barely able to contain our excitement. I pulled out the book my mother gave me *The Power of Positive Thinking* and read that man can overcome great obstacles to life with an affirmative attitude. My mind was so full of anticipation, expectation and possibilities that I could hardly contain myself and got up to use the latrine four or five times.

The sun flashed awake and I lifted the window shade to see out. Bright light flashed through the cabin and warmed me. I glued my face to the cold Plexiglas for a glimpse of my new home and saw the coast of a sparkling green wonderland. I could see the white cliffs of Dover and the gentle rolling hills of Merlin, Lancelot, and King Arthur.

In a van heading for Essex and my new base, I was mesmerized by the emerald green fields and fascinated watching the drivers on the wrong side of the road. When we arrived, Wethersfield was a cluster of Quonset huts, reminiscent of black and white WWII movies.

Very early the next morning reveille blared from the loud speaker and a youthful Airman came to get me. He showed me where to check in, I was assigned to a barracks, I threw down my duffle and walked back to my squadron. Before noon, I was up to my elbows in a freezing solvent bath, brushing dirt and grime from M-39 aircraft guns. I was whistling Oklahoma. After an hour, an old wrinkled Master Sergeant came in and wordlessly handed me a pair of rubber gloves to cover my carbon-doused hands and arms. Man, I was cold but still smiling. Was this how President Kennedy meant for me to fight communism? *I'll do it.*

As a junior Airman, I was naively happy but assigned all the worst duty: marching down the flight line picking up cigarette butts, grueling KP, frequent twenty four hour fire guard and the interminably cold night shift. But, I normally whistled and smiled through the entire work knowing I was doing my President's bidding. Every effort I made was to compensate for some ineffective, apathetic, or lazy Sergeant who couldn't pull his share of the load. All the Officers and Senior NCOs were on day shift where they could drink coffee, smoke cigarettes and bull shit with each other. The real workers, the young Airmen, were on night shift. A two striper I met said, "Bull shit makes the green grass grow, bull shit makes the NCO." I lost respect.

A month later, an Airman roused me and told me to go to the base theater. There I found all my night shift buddies, pale of skin, mingling among the people with all the stripes. We went in and sat down then someone screamed, "Squadron Attention!" My Pavlovian response was to jump up and stand rigid. A fat Major marched down the aisle followed by seven Captains and Lieutenants. "Who's that?" I whispered to my neighbor.

"That's our Commander."

The fat Major was up on the stage berating us for not knowing what was happening and enlightening us that we were screwing up all the aircraft. He warned us to straighten up and fly right or he would convene a Court Martial. I turned to my neighbor and said, "If he would ask, I would tell him what's wrong. The NCOs aren't teaching us anything. Someday, I'll take his place and I will run my Squadron better: I will ask the Airmen what's wrong."

President Kennedy and his bride visited Europe uplifting my spirits. He spoke in Paris and said, "I do not think it wholly inappropriate to introduce myself...I am the man accompanying Jacqueline Kennedy on her trip to Europe." He was a hit with the French people for his elegance and humility and even gave the British people a great charge

I learned we could volunteer for temporary duty in Libya where it was warm. I was smiling on an airplane within a week. The tropical blast smacked me in the face like a soft kiss from my mother. I played in the Libyan sunshine, but after thirty days returned to England.

Six months later, I passed my promotion test. My southern roommate Jerry and I celebrated with a night on the town. We went to the pub in Braintree, where we knocked back bitters, threw darts and had a grand time conversing with the old blokes. At eight o'clock, Jerry said, "I got a date with a cool girl. She has a girlfriend with her. Let's rock and roll."

He showed me to an underground coffee bar that was romantically lighted and played all the best music. "Over there in the corner is my squeeze Linda and her friend." I looked over and saw two dazzling girls with the most flawless pure white skin. "Hay Linda, this is my roomy Joe."

"Ello, Jooooe, please meet my dearest friend Tonia," she lilted out.

My gaze turned to her friend perched in the corner in a most elegant, upright posture. She wore a white dress and blue blazer and was my image of regal grace and dignity. A huge grin crossed my lips and I bent down and introduced myself. "Hi, I, I, I'm JJ Joe."

I felt my heart soar, I couldn't look away from her; it was like my eyes were glued to an elegant porcelain doll. Jerry played a Beach Boys song on the jukebox and he and Linda got up to dance. I couldn't speak but managed to eke out a weak "Wo-wo-would you like to dance?"

Thank God she thrust up her hand, and we danced to a couple of fast songs, eliminating my need to speak. Afterwards, we drank coffee and talked away until closing time at eleven o'clock where I walked her to the bus station for her trip home. I asked her for her number. A little embarrassed, I patted her hand good bye and waved as her bus left the terminal.

My heart was ready to burst and I floated back to see Jerry. I finally understood the word smitten. He drove us home and I was determined to see the beautiful English rose again soon.

But world events interceded in the October 1962 Cuban Missile Crisis. When it started, I was in Libya enjoying the Florida warmth and dreaming of my English Rose. At midnight, the Charge of Quarters had us assemble in the Day Room. Our Commander said we were close to war with Russia and we had to fly back to England the following day. We worked all night securing our equipment and loading it on cargo planes and as daylight rose over the Mediterranean, we broke ground and flew west.

After landing, we reported to work and were told to load all aircraft for war. The aircraft were parked side by side on the taxiway leading to the runway, each one loaded with a terrifying H-Bomb. It was midnight before I was finished and all personnel were restricted to base. I called Tonia and told her I was back in England but couldn't come to see her for a while. Bleak days followed cold and rainy nights as we waited for a solution to the crisis. We were one hundred percent behind our president, yet war seemed imminent.

Finally, on a cold and brisk November morning, the sun broke through the clouds and we were told to unload the planes and go back to our regular schedule.

I saw Tonia that Saturday and my heart thumped loudly in my chest. Over the next year I fell deeply in love with her. Despite the harsh objections of my anti-British, bigoted Irish mother and Air Force friends, we were married in June 1963.

The wedding raised my spirits, settled me down, and focused me on my family. I was progressing well, earning my third stripe in two years

Just after my wedding that summer, Kennedy did it again with a visit to Germany and his "Ich Bin Ein Berliner," stirring speech. My

British friends in the pub loved 'Johnny Boy' as they called him. He was a son of Ireland and his brother died flying bombers against Germany. The Kennedy ties were strong to England and stirred the people like no one since Churchill.

In September, the sky turned grey and our daughter Cindy was born in Chelmsford Hospital. The day after her birth the doctors were alarmed that something was wrong. They kept talking about a hole in her heart. I was stunned. I walked around in a trance for days. The pink baby girl was lovely and smelled like Ivory soap, but they said she had an imperfection. We settled down to loving her after realizing, like us she was human and not perfect.

Then all the excitement left the world. The universe turned dark, the clouds covered everything, and life was punched out of my heart. I held my breath for the reports from Dallas.

I kept seeing reruns of the happy hopeful couple, coming off Air Force One and laughing and dreaming for the entire world. I saw their smiles, the applause of America, the buoyancy of the world. I cried that day and I cried all that night. When I looked in the mirror, I saw hurt, tears, a rip in the universe and all the dreams spilling out. The soul of America and the joy of the world died that miserable, wretched, and hated day in November.

I walked outside to cover my tears and cold raindrops streamed down my neck. I remember my thoughts: *It's not raining, Mother Earth is crying for her murdered son.*

· · ·

The direction of my life change when I was reassigned to Cannon Air Force Base in New Mexico. A base newspaper article caused the profound effect. The article said: "VOLUNTEERS NEEDED FOR GUNSHIP DUTY." The story explained that there was a shortage of gunners in the Air Force and any weapons mechanic volunteering would find a career of excitement, a chance to be one of the very few enlisted Airmen flying in combat and receive a number of financial bonuses.

I hopped around and laughed in excitement. I explained to my friend, Skinny, "You get flying pay, combat pay, overseas pay, hazardous duty pay—and it's all tax free! What could be better?"

"Anything that good is a trap," Skinny twanged and reminded me of my father. "They don't give you all of those goodies for nothing. You could get killed?"

"Nobody gets killed. Listen, Skinny," I insisted, puffing out my chest "my father had a chance to be a gunner in WWII, but he chickened out. I have always wanted to be a gunner and do what he couldn't."

When I read that newspaper article, it was as if a light went off in my brain; all the forces of nature had come together for me to recover the family's honor. I felt excited, elated, and my chin was raised up and my chest filled with pride. I was a man and I would do the hero's walk and not the coward's.

But after reading the article and working all day loading bombs on jets, I drove home to our little cozy nest in the windy desert. On the fifteen-minute drive, through the orange land, I thought about the results of my decision. I rationalized, Tonia and Cindy would be fine; we had family, GI insurance (not that I would need it) and everything she could want for.

I focused on how I was going to tell her I was going to Vietnam as a gunner. She had too much common sense to think as I did. She would be hurt, threatened and divorce minded. She would plead with me, yet again, to get out of the Air Force and go into civilian life.

I pulled into our driveway; Tonia and Cindy were outside playing in the grass. My heart skipped a beat and I had butterflies in my stomach watching them; a beautiful picture they made, mother, and baby, with pure white angelic skin, rolling on a blanket playing in the emerald jade carpet just before dusk. The red desert behind our little house gave a color background to the vivid picture that was our life. The world was dry and deserted outside, but warm, moist and loving inside.

When she saw me, she scooped up the baby, ran to our little red beetle, and reached her head in to kiss me. *What a lucky man I am.*

We strolled into the house arm in arm, and I sat down to a table set for dinner. We ate and chatted. She always cooked dinner and we sat down and discussed the day's events, what the baby learned and what class I was taking that night. As often happened our talk turned to Vietnam and the fear of her friends that the men would be deployed to that far off hellhole, the constant man-eater and widow maker.

Tonia had a clutch, a coven, a clan of other British war bride friends married to base airmen, and very little escaped their scuttle-butt. Vietnam was always on their minds. They obsessed over their husbands going over there.

Is it fair to leave her and the sick baby while I go off to play war? How will she cope with Cindy being a special needs child? How will they find the correct assistance to overcome her learning disabilities? How will she make out for the long tour I will be gone? What if something happens? What if she has a car accident and gets hurt? Who will take care of the baby?

Then a great plan came to me.

I will bring her to my family in Florida while I'm gone. What woman wouldn't love a long vacation in Miami while her husband is slaving away in the steamy jungle of Southeast Asia? She'll be the envy of all the British wives and her family back in England. She'll be in heaven and won't miss me for a second.

I rationalized away our safety and security. Before long, it was time to go to class so I decided to leave it until tomorrow to tell her.

I sweated, tossed and rolled all night, worrying about the future of the baby and my crazy ideas about volunteering for gunner duty.

The next morning, I raced to the weapons hangar where we had reveille. I fell into formation, the bugle sounded, they raised the flag, and we were dismissed. I strutted into the office for the morning's work assignments.

I grabbed a corner and signaled my crew to join me. There was Mickey, my number two man, a bright kid from Seattle, and Skinny, number three, a blond southerner. As we assembled, the Sergeant in charge brought over a new man, as our previous number four man had rotated to Vietnam.

I shook hands with him and introduced him to Mickey and Skinny. He already knew Mickey, as they had been high school friends and joined the Air Force together.

Because I was the junior crew chief in rank, my crew usually took most of the work orders to load the munitions on the airplanes scheduled to fly that day. Sending the new guy with Mickey and Skinny to the truck, I went to get the morning's work orders. There were a couple of hours before the first take-off, so I grabbed the top five for the first flights of the day and read them more carefully. The first work order said ACFT 286-Dart Target.

As my crew walked away, I heard Mickey tell the new guy, "We're the youngest load crew and we're the best. We take on all the toughest assignments, work faster than anyone else and do a better job. On top of that, we all compete for the biggest awards and go to college at night. You are lucky to be on this crew. I'm competing for Airman of the Quarter Friday. We have an expression, HOYA! Meaning Hold On To Your Ass, you're in for a hell of a ride. When did you get here?"

"I transferred from the other wing, as you needed personnel, and I knew Mickey was here," replied the new guy.

"Okay, just stay close to me."

I walked out of the shop to the waiting truck with our work orders. New to this base myself; I asked Skinny, "What's a dart target? I've never loaded one before."

He replied, "Joe, it looks like a giant lawn dart, twenty feet long with four, triangular aluminum wings, and it has a reel and two thousand feet of cable on it. During flight, over the gunnery range, the first airplane releases the dart on the cable and the other airplanes practice shooting their guns at it. It's easy to load and I've done it hundreds of times. Since it's not a weapon, we don't have to be certified to load it."

I answered, "Okay, Skinny. If you're sure, we'll take the work order."

We left the weapons shop in a five-ton steel bed truck and started loading the aircraft. The dart target went on easily, as Skinny said it would, and when we torque it down I noticed the torque wrench was out of calibration. That meant we couldn't be sure we were putting the correct pressure on the stabilizers, so it would not be safe to fly on the airplane. I waved down the flight line supervisor truck and when the driver stopped, I walked over.

"What's the problem, Airman?" he asked, looking at my few stripes with a frown on his mouth.

"Sarge," I said, "the torque wrench is out of calibration. We need a new one."

"We don't have time for that. Just torque it as good as you think it needs. I have a calibrated elbow; I'll show you how it's done, kid."

"No way, Sarge. It's right or it doesn't go!" I answered.

"Don't make a big deal of it, Airman. I have sent out many airplanes that weren't torqued."

"I'm not signing off on an airplane that isn't right. We'll go to the calibration shop and get a new torque wrench," I said.

He spat back, "No need to make a federal case about it. I'll go over to Aircraft 549 and borrow theirs for you."

"Thanks, Sarge." I said in my most humble voice.

After torquing down the giant shiny aluminum 'lawn dart,' we went on to load the 20MM ammo into the guns and practice dummy bombs on the four remaining aircraft.

Skinny explained to the FNG, "That's how we do it—if it ain't right, it don't go. Got it?"

"Yeah, most crews don't worry about torque wrenches," he answered.

My chest swelled up when I heard him. I looked over and thought that he was quite handsome; a red-faced, blond-haired, freckled, young southerner who was accomplishing great things. A calm and quiet married man with a strong dedication to both his wife and succeeding in life, he had a great future ahead of him. I knew he was good, but the other load crews were amazed when he got a perfect score on his promotion test. Lee and I expected Skinny to do well, as we had spent countless hours with him in the weapons truck, practicing his answers every idle moment. But a perfect score was a rarity indeed.

My mind was not on loading the aircraft. Instead, I was thinking about my decision to become a gunner. *Here is a chance to do
something exciting. I can't imagine spending the next sixteen years loading dummy bombs on training aircraft in the desert sun. It will drive
me crazy. I have got to get out of here—this is a great opportunity to
better myself.*

I had the base newspaper in my pocket and I opened it and reread
the article. Skinny saw me, and as a newlywed himself, he was much
more cautious than I.

"Joe put that craziness down and forget that nutty idea," he
drawled. "You're not a boy, you got a wife, and daughter to think
about and running off to Vietnam is crazy. Besides, we need you here.
Lee, can you talk some sense into him?"

Lee answered, "Joe, you have to help me with the Airman of the
Quarter board and on our upgrade tests. Your crew and your family
need you," a long speech for a sullen man. Since Lee was running for
the base Airman of the Quarter, he had to prepare for the questions
a panel of non-commissioned officers would ask him about the Air
Force, his chain of command and his career field.

During the day, I had prepared flash cards with all of the possible
questions we could think of, and we continually quizzed each other.
Who is the Secretary of Defense? What's the speed of the AIM 9
Sidewinder missile? What's the rate of fire of the M-39 guns? So went
the questions hour after hour as we rode around accomplishing our
work. We were young, brash and expected to be the best at everything
we tried.

But my mind kept returning to the newspaper article. So when
we took a chow break, I went to the base personnel office to see what
they knew about the chance to be a gunner. At the office, I met a
young NCO who explained the program to me. He took out a manual
that outlined the process: Fill out a 'dream sheet,' get your Commander to sign it, submit it to personnel and an answer would be returned in about six weeks. So I took a copy of the dream sheet and
went to my Squadron Orderly Room.

As I walked in, I saw the First Sergeant, a seasoned veteran in charge of enlisted discipline, and asked to see the Commander. The F/Sgt asked what it was about and I told him. After speaking to the commander's secretary, he said, "Go right in."

I marched to the center of the room, stood at attention and saluted. "Airman Joe reporting as directed sir!"

He looked at me and said, "What can I do for you, Joe?"

"Sir, I want to volunteer to be a gunner and the paperwork requires your signature."

The bright young Captain looked at me and said, "At ease, Airman. Have a seat."

"Thank you, sir."

I sat down.

"Joe what's going on?" he asked. "Aren't you happy here? You are a crew chief and have every opportunity known to man. Why would you want to leave?"

"Sir, it's a once-in-a-lifetime opportunity to do what I have always wanted to do: fly an airplane in combat and be a gunner!" The excitement in my voice made my desires apparent.

He shook his head, "Geeze, we have given you every chance to make something of yourself. You could even become an Officer, and you want to volunteer to go to Vietnam. Are you nuts? Have you asked your wife about this?"

"Yes, sir, my wife agrees," I lied. "We could use the extra money."

He looked at me and said, "I'll sign it, but I think you're making a terrible mistake and throwing away many opportunities," he had a skeptical frown on his face.

I replied, "Thank you, sir. I'll make you proud." I saluted, did an about-face and left the room. I waited in the F/Sgt's office for the dream sheet to be signed, got it and returned to personnel with the completed form.

It normally takes the personnel bureaucracy six weeks to reply, but in this case I got a response in less than a week. We were sitting in the weapons shop, after loading all the morning's missions while the older crews sat on their asses drinking coffee. I was questioning Lee in preparation for his Airman-of-the-Quarter board.

"What's the difference between an MK 81 and an MK 82 bomb? How many rounds of 20MM ammunition does an F-100 hold? Who is the Base Commander?"

Skinny and the new guy were listening intently.

I further instructed Lee, "Let's look at your uniform and make sure it's perfect. The slightest flaw and they will throw out your nomination and select someone else. They think we're stupid weapons mechanics and don't know anything. You'll show them," I said confidently.

I reflected on my crew for a minute. Lee from Washington was the salt of the earth—hard working, moral and full of great dreams. Skinny was a southern gentleman, with a heart of gold, a soft voice and a country wisdom that far exceeded his twenty years of life. The new guy was sharp as a tack, quick-witted and a little brazen. But hey, they called me a smart ass so I guessed I could tolerate another one. My heart skipped a beat and my chest rose a little higher every time I thought about them.

Breaking my thoughts, the NCO in charge called over. "Joe, they want to see you in the orderly room. Report to the First Sergeant."

The whole crew got into the weapons truck and Skinny drove as I continued to question Lee. "What is the Birthday of the Air Force? What is the payload of the B-52? What is Article 32 of the Uniform Code of Military Justice?"

Because a load crew only operates as a team and cannot load any weapons without a full team, we traveled everywhere together. Skinny pulled up in front of the orderly room and I went in to the F/Sgt's office.

"Top, you wanted to see me?" I asked.

He looked up from his desk and said, "Airman, you're going to be a gunner!"

"Oh, man, what a great hit! I can't wait," I grinned so wide my mouth hurt.

"Go in and see the old man. He wants to explain it to you."

"Thanks, Top!" I bounced towards the Commander's office.

I knocked on the door, entered, saluted, and reported in. The Old Man returned my salute and said, "Have a seat, Joe. I have the answer back from personnel. You have been selected to become a gunner!"

"Thank you, sir. What do I do now?"

He said, "Personnel are cutting your orders as we speak. You will first go through the altitude chamber here on base while you out-process, and in three weeks you report to Hurlburt Field, Florida for Gunners school. After that, you go to survival school in Washington, Jungle survival in the Philippines, and finally to Nha Trang, Vietnam in October."

I jumped up and shouted, "Wait until I tell the guys! Oh, man, I can't wait!"

The Commander dismissed me and I returned outside to the truck. "I'm gonna be a gunner," I told the guys. "I'm gonna be a fly boy. I've wanted this for my entire life and I'm gonna do it!" I jumped for joy.

"What's your wife going to say?" Skinny asked with that skeptical look on his face.

Good question!

I snapped back, "Don't you say a word to your wife or mine about my volunteering, okay? I'm telling her I just got orders and don't have any choice in the matter. That's why they call them orders, right? Because we don't have any choice. Ours is not to reason why, ours is but to do or die."

Nevertheless, I felt bad about lying to my wife. I had never done that before, yet I wanted this chance to be a combat hero. I had these mental pictures of me, Sir Galahad on a white steed, riding to the rescue of the damsel U.S. in distress; I was following my young president's words, the drums sounded for me.

I felt like a kid walking on air, full of exhilaration. I was going to fight communism, enhance America's containment policy, and defeat the Chinese threat. I was getting out of New Mexico, taking my family back to the warm beaches and sunshine of Florida, going overseas. Here was the chance to do something no one had ever done in my family.

Despite my five uncles and my father having served in WWII, none of them had ever been in combat. They had all been support personnel, and in my childish mind this was my chance to gain their respect and admiration.

After work, I drove home. My wife knew something was up. She greeted me with the scuttlebutt from the British wives club. "Orders for Vietnam came in today. Do we know anyone who got them?" she asked.

"I got orders. I'm the one going," I blurted, trying to sound sad.

She looked stunned. Her face turned bright red and her eyes seemed to cloud over. She rushed over and put her arms around me, I could hear her sobs.

"Get out! Get out of the Air Force and you can go to college full time," she pleaded. "You don't need this; you can do better. The baby needs you, she needs her father. You can't leave her now! What are we going to do? Where will we stay? Who will look after us, Joe? You just can't leave me now!"

As I held onto her, my eyes began to mist over as doubts filled my head. *What the hell have I done? How can I leave her and the baby? Am I being crazy?* All the questions went around in my mind, making me feel dizzy. I grabbed on to her tighter.

"Sweetheart, we have gotten over more difficult things, and we will get over this one. It will be a short tour and I'll be home before you know what happened. This is a chance to get out of this God-forsaken desert and return to Florida. Everything will be fine, trust me," but now my heart felt heavy and I had read doubts in my mind.

Once again, I had a sleepless night filled with a combination of exhilaration for me and fear for my wife and daughter. My mind vacillated between unrestricted glee and stark terror. I would be the happiest ever, but what would happen to them? I finally resolved to make their circumstances the best possible, so I could put all my concentration on my tour as a gunner. Even though it was the middle of the night, I called my brother in Florida and told him about the orders and the chance to be a gunner. He was excited for me and asked, "Is it dangerous?"

"No," I answered, "I can handle it. But can my wife and daughter stay with you?"

"Sure. You know my wife and kids love them, and will be happy they're back in Florida instead of being in that shit hole in the desert."

I thanked him, hung up and went back to bed.

The next two weeks were full of activity as we arranged to sell the house, pack up, store the furniture, and move the family thousands of miles across the country. My wife was a trooper and worked late into the night packing and cleaning. She made the best of impossible circumstances.

At the weapons shop, I began the tedious task of training my replacement. An older staff Sergeant had just arrived and selected to be the new crew chief. I hated to leave the crew, my boys, as I felt like I was deserting them, but duty called. The training of the new crew chief went well. He was fine, but the crew looked depressed. We had established a record of excellence never equaled, and we were filled with excitement when Lee won the Base Airman-of-the-Quarter competition. By winning the competition, he had an opportunity to fly in an F-100 at faster than the speed of sound, received a savings bond and got a three-day pass away from base. We were very proud of him and immediately began the arduous task of training Skinny for the next board. The flash cards were worn down with constant fingering, but Skinny was studying as hard as possible.

During the second week, I started my long class in the altitude chamber. It was seven days of intense training about all of the things that can go wrong in an airplane. From loss of oxygen to rapid decompression, we practiced what to do in the event of every potential malfunction. I passed with excellence, even though I had a vacuum-induced toothache that had to be attended to. I graduated on Friday, was relieved of duty and as I left the weapons shop for the last time, I saw Skinny in the truck answering questions from Lee. I smiled at that, I had prepared them well and that they would succeed in anything they ever chose in life.

I drove to our little house for the last time and arrived just in time to see the moving truck departing around the corner with our worldly possessions. I picked up my wife and daughter and started out across the desert in a steaming hot Volkswagen beetle. In those days, they didn't have air conditioning.

We arrived at my brother's house in old Miami. I settled my family in and drove with a fire of passion to Hurlburt Field, Florida, for Gunner training.

This would turn out to be the most exciting and dangerous time of life.

CHAPTER IV

GUNNER'S SCHOOL

I sang along with the radio and laughed as I drove closer to Hurlburt, the home of the Air Commandos. Driving by the old C-47 Gooney Birds brought the widest grin to my mouth. I had read about these reliable old WWII airplanes that the Brits called Dakotas, the civilians called DC-3's and I called saviors. With noses high in the air and tail wheels on the ground, the Gooneys were angels ready to leap into the sky to save a soldier on the ground or their own aircrew. Even when they were shot full of holes, they never failed to bring home the crew.

Lonnie, my old buddy Lonnie met me at the NCO club. He introduced me to four student gunners who would be my classmates. Three were Staff Sergeants listening in rapt attention to one Master Sergeant called Big Don. When he walked into a room, everyone turned to see why he blocked out the light. He leaned against the bar with his flying suit zipped down to his navel and his hearty laughter could drowned out the roar of an aircraft engine. He was wearing cowboy boots rather than the regulation brogans; a fifty mission hat rolled up in his side pocket and mirrored sun glasses hanging from his t-shirt. He looked the image of a slightly overweight Chuck Yeager. When I walked up he was finishing a joke and everyone laughed uproariously.

After introductions all around I said I was going to get a Coors Light and Big Don said, "Get me a Courvoisier."

"What the hell is that, Sarge?" I asked.

"You have a lot to learn young Airman—it's the best cognac—that's all."

I went over to the bar tender and ordered the drinks and was floored when he told me it was six bucks; a buck for the Coors and five for the Courvoisier. I figured Don would pay his.

I handed it to Don. He took the snifter, swirled it, held it up to his nose, made an elaborate deal of tasting the drink and turned his back. My face got red, and I felt dizzy and rejected. I tried to join the conversation.

"That old Gooney Bird is just good enough to take off and get me get a medal so that I can get promoted," he crooned.

Still miffed, I answered, "The airplane is one of the coolest flying machines from WWII. I can't wait...' he interrupted me.

"Who gives a shit about WWII? There is going to be a new AC-130 in a few years and I will be the highest ranking and the first gunner to fly it. That's an airplane; this Gooney is just a ride."

"Than fine old airchine has saved hundre..."

"It's an old bucket of bolts, not aerodynamic, ugly wings, no armor and barely able to limp to the battle area," Don said puffing out his chest.

"Well, I think she's a great angel of the skies," I said to put a final word on it.

"Airman, you don't know shit. They call it the Widow Maker. So keep your mouth shut before you have even flown your first mission in that shitbird."

I dragged my tail out the Club and walked back to the barracks where I wrote a letter to Tiny and sent little XXX kisses to Cindy until lights out.

Next morning a screaming training NCO woke up the whole barracks playing reveille. 'Dah Dah tad a dah, Dah Dah tad a dah, dah dah to dad dah, daaadh daaadh daaadh.' "Hit the deck! You're Air

Commandos now! Be sharp, the Commander will be here on your first day to lead the exercise."

I jumped up, hit the latrine and was outside in five minutes. In no time a big black sedan drove up with an Air Force blue eagle flag flying from the left front fender. A full colonel got out and everyone jumped to attention. Someone behind me whispered, "Big watch, small dick, always in a hurry. Must be a Fighter Pilot," and we all laughed.

"Shut up and fall in, Commandos!" the training NCO shouted.

We got into a loose formation and exercised for about thirty minutes. The sun came up over the horizon and flooded the exercise ground in pale orange optimism. I felt young, happy, and full of piss and vinegar. When the exercises were over, I breathed a sigh of relief, ready to go to chow. The training NCO broke the serenity of the hot Florida morning.

"Line up, two abreast, for our run for your life. Stay behind the Commander for the first two miles. After that you can pass him and are on your own for the rest of the five mile run."

Five miles! Were these guys sadists or nut cases who thought we were in the Army?

I started to run next to Big Don from Detroit. Because of his rank, Big Don was the class leader. This gave him no privileges, just the right to tell the rest of us what to do, a task he seemed to live for.

"What a pain these guys are," I said to him. "Do they do this every day?"

"Yeah, and the Commander tries to kick everyone's ass the first day. But after two miles, I know a place we can break off, cut across and skip the last half," he gave me a knowing leer.

"No, thanks, Sarge. I need to work out and get some of this fat off." My smart ass acted up so I added, "You could lose a few pounds, too."

"Screw you sucker. Take the hard way," he scowled.

We ran along together for the next twenty to twenty-five minutes, breathing heavily and with sweat pouring off our bodies. After a couple of miles the training NCO yelled out, "Okay, you rabbits, go ahead and make a dash for the finish line."

I kept jogging at my normal long-distance pace; despite being out of shape I passed the training NCO and the Commander. The Commander was a short lean Colonel with sweat on his forehead, panting on his breath, fire in his eyes and determination on his face. We continued our route around a corner, away from the main buildings and toward an uninhabited part of the base where there were dense pine trees. I noticed Big Don cut through the woods.

I kept running with the crowd and after forty-five minutes, finished in the parking lot beside the squadron operations building. We fell into a loose formation and the training NCO dismissed us. Sweaty and tired, I headed back to the barracks. Don was leaning on a car in the parking lot along the route. He walked over and joined me.

"Have a good run, sucker?"

"Yeah," I answered breathlessly. "Where the fuck did you go.."

"Keep your mouth shut Airman," crossing his arms over his chest, he stared into my eyes. "Now, hit the showers, gag down chow and get to class by 0800," he sneered.

"Okay, Sarge, see you in the mess hall," I answered.

At chow, Don acknowledged me and said to the others, "This is Joe, a new Airman Gunner student in his first day." He growled out Airman like he was sneering at my meager rank, Air—man!

Don seemed to have made some friends already. He was the kind of guy who fit in anywhere. He had a comfortable attitude, relaxed manner but a little too slick for me. He was tall, over six feet, beefy like a football player, with jet-black kinky hair. He had charisma; he had flair and definitely a line of shit as long as a bandoleer of ammo. So, he attracted followers like sheep, or I should say who were sheep. I recognized him immediately, his type always had a trick up their sleeves, always knew a guy who knew a guy who could get anything, or get you out of any detail for a couple of bucks. I ate and listened to him and his buddies banter about how cool Motown, was and by inference how cool they were. They had a smart ass, sarcastic answer for everything.

I finished and as I walked away, I heard Don say, "He's just a low ranking Air—man. I'm going to be the chief gunner in the whole United States Air Force."

Entering the classroom, I saw a sharp Technical Sergeant arranging chairs and putting textbooks and workbooks at all the places. I introduced myself and helped him arrange the classroom. I had read about the infamous 'mini-gun.' It was a fearsome and fatal weapon, called the GAU 2A. It had six barrels, was air-cooled, and fired six thousand rounds a minute.

There was also a dash one (-1) operating manual on the AC-47 Gunship. This book described the entire aircraft, had diagrams of all the safety equipment, and included checklists for flight. There was even a section on gunner systems and responsibilities. I started studying early because I wanted to get a head start on my classmates. I intended to be the number one graduate, thereby getting my choice of assignments.

Soon the other students filed in and class started. Thus began a long series of lectures and practical exercises of taking guns apart and reassembling them; first in broad daylight, then in partial lighting and finally in complete darkness. After a couple of weeks, even Big Don could disassemble and reassemble the gun.

In the afternoon, a new NCO, Tech Sergeant Ryan, entered the classroom wearing a green flying suit. He was the head instructor gunner in charge of our flying schedule and he was here to brief us about our first orientation mission later that night. At 1900 all six of us student gunners reported to the flight operations building and sat in a classroom. Sergeant Ryan entered and began briefing us.

"Tonight is your orientation flight. Enter the airplane, put on a parachute and ear protection, have a seat and buckle the belt. For the entire flight, remain in the seat unless I instruct you otherwise. You are here to observe myself and airman Van. We will fly for an hour and a half to practice emergency procedures and fire off nine thousand rounds of ammunition. It will be dark, cold and noisy, so sit in your seats and learn as much as possible. When we land we will come back to this room and Van and I will debrief you about everything that happened during the mission. Any questions? No? Okay, see you at the airplane in fifteen minutes."

Just after dark, the pilots fired up the giant radial engines with a mighty roar and a puff of smoke, which almost made me gag. The smoke smelled like burning oil, stifled my lungs and brought tears to my eyes. It was noisy despite the rubber earplugs inside the helmets. We taxied out to the runway and began a takeoff roll; the tail wheel lifted off the runway and the sweetest airplane ever built rose into the air.

We climbed out to three thousand feet and Ryan and Van began to prepare their guns. As we were on a training mission, the guns were not loaded on the ground, so they began the arduous task of loading each weapon. They turned on the high intensity lights, situated by each gun, and cranked the loader handles rather lazily. We flew over the coast and over the waters of the Gulf of Mexico. I couldn't see much because of Ryan's admonishment to stay seated.

Soon—too soon—Sergeant Ryan, using hand signals, made a circular motion, indicating that the aircraft would enter the famous firing circle to fire the guns. I watched intently as he armed the weapons, turned off the lights and backed up to the right bulkhead by the gun switches.

The aircraft entered a thirty-degree bank and I could see the ground.

VROOOOOOOOMMMMMM.

I had not known the gun was going to fire and was startled by the frightening noise. The ear splitting sound lasted for five seconds and the cargo compartment filled with smoke. My eyes started to burn and I tasted the acrid gunpowder on my tongue. Now I stared intently as we entered a bank again and number one gun fired again.

VROOOOOOOOOMMM.

I noticed the spent brass ejecting from the bottom of the spinning gun and filling an ammo can.

I was enthralled by the sight of the tracers as the gun fired. The tracers were every fifth round and had burning red powder in them to show the bullet's path as it cut a graceful red arc toward destruction on the ground. It was beautiful and awesome.

The firing continued for some time. The ride was smooth except for the infrequent occasion when we flew through our own prop wash, which caused the airplane to bounce.

After a while, Big Don unfastened his seat belt and ran toward the back of the airplane. In the half-light I saw Ryan was red faced and grabbed don's shoulders and point him back to the seats. Don pulled back Ryan's earpiece and shouted. Ryan pointed to the seats again and Don went down to his knees. He doubled over and puked on the floor of the airplane.

Ryan walked around Don, went forward and brought back an empty ammo can and gave it to him. He put his head inside for a minute or two. Shortly he returned to his seat with the smelly ammo can in his hands. The stench almost made me puke as well. I stared away so I could hold my stomach. They say real men don't puke, but I was real close. Not soon enough, the firing ended and Sergeant Ryan turned on the lights, safed the guns and we returned to base.

After landing and engine shut down, Sergeant Ryan told us six students to unstrap, take off the parachutes and deplane. We climbed down the short ladder and assembled on the flight line near the aircraft door.

He said, "You students get some rags from the mechanics and clean up the puke, then meet me inside in the training room."

The other guys were grousing, "Don puked, so he should clean it up."

I told them, "We're all in this together. Let's get the rags and clean up the airplane."

Later, in the training room, Sergeant Ryan explained the entire mission.

"When we're ready to fire, the aircraft enters a thirty-degree left bank and we arm the guns. If the pilot can keep the bank true, we can theoretically fly a complete circle, called the 'cone of death,' and all the rounds will impact in the same area on the ground. While we're firing, the gunners watch all the guns and repair them as required and reload them when needed. Your jobs as gunners are to make sure the guns are never armed unless they are pointed at the target and they are always repaired, full of ammo and ready to fire. Got that?'

"Yeah Sarge," I answered.

Ryan went on, "Don, you're the class leader and the senior NCO, so when I say stay in your seat I mean **stay in your seat**! If you have to puke, take off your helmet and puke in that, but if you ever get up and interfere with the crew again, you're out of here. You'll be thrown out of the gunner's program immediately. You got that?"

"Yeah Sarge, I got it," Don said. Then he added sullenly, "But I couldn't help it."

"Don't give me that shit. Just don't get up when I tell you to stay in your seat."

"Okay, Sarge, I got it."

"See you in the morning—and get ready for your first written test Friday. Study the handouts you were given and go over the flight in your mind. Class dismissed."

I started walking to the door and Big Don said, "My new buddies invited us to the NCO club for a couple of drinks. Want to go?"

"No, thanks, Don. I gotta hit the books for a while."

As we walked outside Don added, "I have a homie who works in base supply and can get us some of the brand new Nomex flying suits reserved for pilots and race car drivers. With those and a cool set of flying sunglasses the girls will fall all over us."

"Thanks, Sarge, but I have my regular-issue airman flying suits and they're fine for me." I walked back to the barracks for a quick shower and a couple of hours of studying.

I had to do a lot of studying because this gunner's career field information was significantly different from any of my other weapons training. It required the same detailed attention to safety, but the personal and individual requirements were different. In most weapons handling, a team of men worked together and they all watched each other and looked for the slightest irregularity. If anyone missed a step or made an error, the other team members immediately brought it to his attention. Everyone double-checked every step of every checklist.

As a gunner, however, I was on my own. I worked on my gun without lights and there was no one to check my work. If I made a mistake, I could damage a weapon, at the minimum, or jeopardize the entire crew, at the maximum. This job would take the ultimate in individual performance and self-reliance—and an utter dedication to perfection. I knew I was in for a long two months of study to ensure that my performance was flawless.

I hit the sack around 2000 and slept like a baby until midnight when I heard Don and his pals come in. They were noisy and started playing music and talking loud. I rolled over; put the pillow over my head and slept until the training NCO woke us. I kicked Don's bunk and told him to get up and hit the deck running. He dragged his sorry ass into the latrine and shaved.

Later we entered the classroom for aircraft systems training. Don got a seat next to me, and kept distracting me all morning with questions. It was obvious he had not read his assignment and it irritated me that he expected me to answer the questions for him.

"What's the APU? Where's the hydraulic pump? Where's the landing gear manual extension handle located?" he asked.

I pretended to not hear him, but I did answer his questions during our hourly breaks. As there were only six students, it was obvious Don wasn't properly prepared. However, the airman instructor didn't say anything to him because of his rank. So Don skated and relied on me for the answers.

We spent that first week learning about the aircraft and our guns. Because I had always loved aircraft, I relished the lessons, reading the Aircraft Handbook every night before lights out. Don, on the other hand, spent most evenings in the NCO club with his new friends. They were not gunners, just guys from Detroit. If they'd been gunners, he might have at least picked up a couple of hints from them.

We flew a second time that week with a full student crew in the operating positions and an instructor crew beside each of us. I had Sergeant Ryan as my instructor and he was one heck of an NCO—sharp as a tack, always prepared and early to every flight. I stayed on my toes, as I wanted to learn everything he could teach me. He was a hell of a taskmaster on that flight.

He made me turn off the lights shortly after takeoff and operate in the dark. I was slow and clumsy and he jumped in to get the guns armed on the first and second pass. On the third pass I got it right, seconds before we fired the guns.

While flying in a circle, we flew into our own prop wash and the aircraft bounced up and down around fifteen times, making me hot and flushed. I had butterflies in my stomach and felt a little scared. All of a sudden, my stomach rose up and I felt like gagging. I grabbed my stomach and signaled to Ryan, with a hand covering my mouth, that I was about to lose it. He pointed to the empty ammo cans and I sat down on the floor next to a can and hung my head inside it. I heard the guns fire but had absolutely no interest in what was happening. I spewed ingloriously all over the ammo can while I was outside of my body watching the scene.

I worried that they would ground me because I couldn't fly. In the air force, they call it MOA-manifestation of apprehension—meaning scared as a rabbit. For some long, bad moments, my whole universe was inside the vomity ammo can.

But miraculously, as soon as I barfed I felt much better. I jumped up to help Ryan; he put a hand on my shoulder and pressed me down towards the floor. He pointed to the seats in the front of the cargo compartment and signaled for me to sit down and put on a seat belt. He worked the rest on the mission while I sat in the passenger's seat.

This was a humbling experience: feeling like a vomit pig, sitting idly by like a passenger while the gunner did my duties. I swore I would never vomit again; that I would never eat before flight again. After we landed, Ryan made me carry the vomit-filled ammo can around to the briefing room.

"These things happen," he told me, privately. "Flying in a left hand circle for hours causes many of us to get sick. Just handle it professionally, don't make a big deal about it and you'll be okay. We fly together Monday night, and you'll be fine then," he said. "You picked up the gun action very fast and were excellent on arming the weapons. You'll make a fine gunner," he said.

"Thanks, Sarge," I answered and cast my eyes down and left.

The next week was much the same, with more PT in the mornings, classes all-day and flying every night. Our first phase test was that Friday and all six of us studied hard every night. All of us studied except Don, who seemed to have met a girlfriend in the NCO club.

I had the test pretty much wired, I told myself, after the rest of us had a long study session without Don. By the time I went to sleep Thursday night, I knew I was ready.

We got to class on time and Don drove up just as we entered. He had obviously stayed out that night and looked a little ragged. We went in and sat at our desks and the instructor airman began handing out test booklets.

"This is your phase one test and you all know the rules and how to fill out the answer sheets. I will sit in the back of the room and answer any questions you have. You have one hour. Begin," he said.

Don immediately subtly shifted his chair closer to mine and I leaned down and put my arms in a cradle around the answer sheet. The test rules stated clearly that if anyone cheated and anyone else helped them or even knew they cheated, both were automatically failed and subject to punishment. I intended to do my own work and help no one, especially that skater, Don.

When we heard the airman leave the room for a coffee refill, Don leaned over and said, "Move your hand; I just want to check a couple of answers."

I didn't say anything but slid my desk away at a different angle so he couldn't see my paper. After the test was over, he cornered me outside and asked, "What's going on? I just wanted to check a couple of answers. You don't have to be an asshole about it!"

"Listen Sarge, we're going to be flying together and the whole crew depends on you to know what you're doing. Do your own work and don't expect me to take your test for you. I'll take my tests and you take yours," I said.

He huffed off and I was glad to see him go.

The rest of the month went by like a blur, with classes every day and flying very often at night. I had been able to avoid cheating with Big Don and was in position to be the distinguished graduate. The flying was more comfortable. I had come to the point where I understood what was going on in the airplane at all times. After fifty flying hours, Sgt. Ryan passed me on to take my check ride with the standardization evaluation, or check gunner.

The old war-dog check gunner was Master Sergeant Rockney, known to all as 'The Rock.' He was reputed to be the most demanding, straight laced, by-the-book NCO who ever lived. Students and instructors feared flying with him, as he would ground anyone at any time for the slightest infraction. The training standard required that every gunner had to memorize the emergency procedure checklists and repeating it by rote on request. A story made the rounds that The Rock had grounded an instructor for stuttering when spouting off his emergency procedures. The errant instructor lost flying pay for three months and had to work in the gun room, up to his elbows in cleaning fluid. The Rock was definitely the man most respected and feared by instructors and students.

I had been preparing for weeks, practicing disassembling the gun in the dark, studying the airplane and gun manuals and reciting my emergency procedures checklists hour after hour until I fell asleep at night.

The night finally came when I was required to take my check ride. I arrived at the operations building two hours early with the plan of pre-flighting and checking out the airplane before anyone else arrived, so I would know the status of everything and have less to do when the flight began. I was out in the airplane checking the three guns when I saw Don drive up to the ops building. I thought that was odd but returned to my duties.

An hour before takeoff, I returned to the ops building and sat in the briefing room next to Don. I noticed that his flying suit looked pristine. He must have had it dry cleaned for the flight. Mine, on the other hand, was soaking wet and smelled of perspiration from my hour in the hot airplane. He looked cool and collected and I looked like I had been in a fight with a jungle cat and lost. I felt hot and smelly and thought about trying to go back to the barracks and change, but then The Rock walked in.

The Rock was five feet, eight inches tall, with a football lineman's chest about five feet around. He was reputed to have over three hundred combat missions and shot down twice, saving his entire crew on the last shoot down. Someone said they had downgraded his Congressional Medal of Honor submission to an Air Force Cross, the second highest medal for bravery in combat. A no-nonsense Sergeant's Sergeant, with his back straight as a board he marched to the front of the room.

His deep voice resonated, "The gunner is the most important man on this airplane. Without you, the airplane is just a taxicab without a fare, but with you at your best it is an awesome weapon that can save the lives of soldiers and Marines on the ground. Your primary responsibility is to the success of your mission, the safety of your crew and the protection of the Americans on the ground. You have been recommended by your instructors because they think you're ready to fly on your own, so just show me what they have taught you and you'll do fine. My job is to check your training, determine if you're good enough to protect your crew and if the training is the same for all the gunners. We take off at 2030, fly south to Range 44, arrive on target at 2250 and fire twelve thousand rounds on target. We will RTB around 2400. During the entire mission be as safe as possible and obey my every instruction. If you perform an unsafe action, I will tell you to have a seat; at that time, put on your lap belt and remain in the passenger seat for the remainder of the mission. Don, you are the lead gunner and Joe, you're number 2. Any questions?"

We had no questions so he said, "Okay, go pre-flight your airplane."

I walked out of the door toward the airplane where all my gear was already stowed. I pulled my checklist from my thigh pocket and went over the emergency requirements for 'MAIN GEAR MALFUNC- TION,' 'CARGO COMPARTMENT FIRE,' and 'WEAPON MAL- FUNCTION' and walked and read until I arrived at the airplane. I pulled out my preflight checklist and checked every item yet again, wondering where Don was.

I saw Don and The Rock walking across the ramp together with Don chatting away. I thought, *what a kiss ass that son of a bitch is, a real brown noser, and Rock is falling for it.* They climbed into the airplane and Don put his tool bag and helmet bag down and immediately turned to me. "Airman, what are your Weapons Malfunction emer- gency procedures?"

The son of a bitch was show boating for Rock. He did not know his checklist but by asking me, he avoided answering it himself.

I answered, "Master arm switch, off, gun switch off, disconnect drive motor, disconnect safety sector, alert the crew, analyze the mal- function." I glared at him and repeated the other steps I had just reread before pocketing my checklist.

"What are your procedures for fire in the flare locker?" He went on.

I answered correctly.

Then Rock said, "I'll ask the questions, Don. You finish the pre-flight."

While Don was looking over the guns, Rock pulled out my stu- dent folder from his clipboard and wrote something down. I looked down at my flying boots. I looked like a rag doll, shoes dirty, soiled flying suit unzipped and sweating like a pig. Great.

Rock said, "Don, Joe and I are going to step out of the airplane while you finish the pre-flight."

When we got on the ground he said, "Walk over there so I can have a cigarette." I followed him fifty feet away.

"How's your training going, airman?"

"I'm doing fine, Sarge. Sergeant Ryan is a fine gunner and has taught me a hell of a lot. I'm ready to graduate!"

He said, "I'll be the judge of that. What are your procedures for protecting the crew after crash landing?"

I knew this was not a checklist in training, but is always practiced by crews in actual combat. I had read about how The Rock had done it when he was shot down, so I recited what I had read about him.

I answered, "Get the entire crew out of the airplane, bring your personal weapons and the classified cipher book, put a pyrite grenade on the body of each of the guns, and destroy them. Then assemble at the nose of the aircraft, find a suitable defensive position and protect the crew until rescue arrives."

He looked at me and said "What about calling rescue on the survival radio?"

"I guess I never thought about that," I answered.

"That's okay— it's really the radio operator's responsibility, but you have to do anything you can to back up the other crew members. You did fine, airman, and your instructors say you're doing great. Just be safe and this will be a piece of cake."

"Thanks, Sarge," I said.

We returned to the airplane, finished pre-flighting, and strapped in for takeoff. For the first hour over the training area, everything went fine. I had one gun malfunction and fixed it in a reasonable amount of time while Don ran the gunner's control panel. I loaded number one and two when they were empty and felt reasonably confident that unless we had a major malfunction everything would be all right.

After about an hour, the crew took a break while the pilot and copilot changed positions. During a check ride, the entire aircrew is evaluated at the same time. So there comes a point where crew members must change positions. Rock called me and Don over to where he was standing and shouted over the noise of the engines and air rushing by the open doors and windows, "Airman, you're now number one gunner on the control panel, and Don, you're on the guns."

Don's glare said this was beneath him. As a Master Sergeant, it would be very unusual for him to fly missions, let alone act as a lowly ammo loader and gun fixer. But he reluctantly assumed his position behind number one gun.

After a few minutes, we began firing again, and when number one ran out of ammo, Don began trying to load it. He had a time disconnecting the feeder, but got it done. In the darkness, I could just make out him trying to connect the loader and struggling with it. I made a move to help him when Rock put his arm in my way and pointed to the control panel. Number two was firing and soon ran out of ammo, so I turned on number three. Don finally finished number one and started loading two while three was firing. When Rock wasn't looking, I went over and armed number one to be ready when we needed it, but thought Don was getting behind the power curve; maybe I could load three when it was empty.

Three fired its last rounds and I turned it off, then went over and safed it by disconnecting the cannon plug and feeder. I went to get a can of ammo and Rock glared at me so I left it alone and returned to the gunner's panel. Don was slowly loading number two. Number one was firing when all of a sudden it jammed to a halt.

The pilot called out, "Gun malfunction! Give me a gun."

"We're working on it sir; have one in a minute," I answered.

I leaned towards number one when Rock put out his arm and stopped me. He pointed at Don and at number one as if to say, 'Go get it and fix it.' I turned off the master arm switch and the number one gun switch and Don went to the gun. He jumped to the right side of the gun to look into the feeder to see what had happened, without disconnecting the electrical drive motor, as the emergency checklist required. He'd reached in to disconnect the feeder when Rock jerked Don's hands away. I could see them shouting at each other, then Rock pointed to the passenger seats and pushed Don in that direction. I went over and disconnected the drive motor cannon plug and then the feeder and saw a round jammed. I cleared it out, put the feeder back on and went around connecting the drive motor. Rock was standing by the gunner's panel and turned on number one gun.

He came over and shouted, "You're number one gunner, I'll be two, but help me by loading number three gun while I get two."

I did as instructed for the rest of the mission. When we were out of ammo, The Rock turned on the lights and I began cleaning up the airplane. Rock sat beside Don and waved his arms and hands around. Don hung his head down. It didn't look like they were having any fun, so I just concentrated on my weapons clean up. After landing, I secured the aircraft and went into the ops building.

I heard Don speaking in a loud voice. "Listen, Rock, I'm going to be the non-commissioned officer in charge. I'm a master sergeant and I'm not going to be flying daily missions. It doesn't matter if I know every step of every checklist; I will be running the shop. There is no point in you showing me up and reporting I had a bad mission. One little mistake and you want to make a federal case out of it! Honor between senior NCOs demands that you give me another check."

I heard Rock answer, "Sergeant, you may have gotten away with that shit at your last base, but it won't fly here. You flunked your check ride. *I* didn't flunk you, *you* flunked you. It wasn't a simple mistake; you were slow and clumsy on the guns, and failed to safe a weapon before working on it, jeopardizing yourself and your entire crew. If you did that in combat and hurt yourself, the entire mission would have failed. You' re lucky I am only washing you back a week and not requesting elimination by a flight evaluation board, because your poor attitude has been observed by the other instructors and you think you can get by on your rank. Now, get out of here and report to the Commander at 0600 tomorrow morning!"

I heard the door slam and a car start in the parking lot.

"Airman, get in here!" The words startled me back to the present.

"Yeah, Sarge!"

"Here's your debriefing. You were fine on the guns, a little slow on loading, perfect on your emergency procedures and good at repairing the malfunction. I didn't like that you tried to do Don's work for him, but I understand trying to help a crewmate. However, if I ever think you are trying to cover up for his inadequacies, I will fail you on the spot. There is no room in this program for a marginal gunner and we remove the week mercilessly, at once. The entire crew relies on your professionalism. You had better never let them down. You passed FQ, fully qualified. Report to the orderly room tomorrow at 0900 for graduation."

"Yes, sir!" I said with obvious glee in my voice.

I left for the NCO club and found the rest of my classmates. As courses were over and graduation was tomorrow, we had a fine night of drinking and singing. One of the instructors had flown the gunship in Vietnam and began singing.

"Puff the tragic dragon died by the sea and took with him the sons and men from the land of Hanalei—OHHHH, puff the tragic dragon…"

We had a short graduation ceremony in the morning and I immediately got in my Beetle and raced for Miami. I was happy to see Tonia and Cindy. They had a party for me, and we went to the beach and had a great time resting and relaxing.

All too soon, I had to board a plane for the most feared destination in the flying world, AIR FORCE SURVIVAL SCHOOL. A place of legends, stories of agony and the end of many careers, the name sent shivers down the spine of every aspiring flyer.

CHAPTER V

SURVIVING SURVIVAL SCHOOL

Bang! He must have slammed the heavy baseball bat against the side of my three foot cubed box. "Fifty-nine, I vill coming for you, you America pig. You tell interrogator everything or I vill beat you," the guard spoke in a gravel voiced Russian accent. "I catch you sleep, I kick you ass."

Screw you dip. I curled into the fetal position and shivered.

His footsteps retreated into the distance. I heard him hitting other capture boxes to torment my brother airmen, locked in their own small world.

BAM, "Wake 67. No sleep."

I swiveled my head around the dark box and saw five air holes in the front door now crushed against my head. The place felt cold and smelled like mildewed snow so I squeezedd my arms around my legs and fetaled into a ball to keep in the body heat.

"Let me out of here you son of a bitch, I can't stand it," a high-pitched voice screamed and kicked at his box to break it open. "Get me out before I kill someone." I heard heavy thumping of his boots against the door of the box, footsteps running from three separate directions toward the box kicker.

There were whispers, the door opened and I heard sobbing. "This is an academic situation; you're fine do you need a doctor?" Gravelly voice asked in perfect English.

"I, I, I can't go back into that box," high pitch whimpered. "I'm clust…"

Weak dick. The sound of their footsteps receding made me feel strong. I decided to sleep, even though getting caught meant more punishment.

The next thing I knew the door jerked open and the bright lights pierced my eyes. "Sleeping, 59? Get out, you vill get it now," gravel voice had a full beard, a Russian uniform and was bigger that a pile of elephant shit. He pointed to a door as I climbed out. I stretched my legs, "Go there immediate pig!" he spat.

He pushed me from behind as I looked around and shuffled toward the door that had a sign: *Interrogation Room.* The place was an aircraft hangar bathed in bright florescent lights. Behind were sixty or so the internment boxers stacked three high with two guards goose stepping back and forth carrying Kalashnikov's. He pushed me into the door and I tripped and went down to the floor inside a small room. I looked up and saw a guy sitting behind a small desk, dressed in a grey uniform with red stars on the lapels. "Get up, imperialist pig!" he shouted.

I stood and was flooded with a single intense light suspended from the ceiling.

"Stand at attention, Yankee murderer," he said.

I stood directly under the bright light, feeling like a murder suspect in an investigation in a T.V. movie.

"Why you fly over Vietnam and kill innocent children?" he shouted.

"Airman Joe, 123-45-6789, 3 March 1943," I answered.

"Smart Alek. Why you kill our women and children?"

"123-45-6789."

"Get in the stress position!"

I squatted down into a deep knee bend and stretched out my arms, palm up. The instructors said this was to simulate the stress of capture. *I am not going to be fooled by some phony stress position.*

"Are your arms tired?" he asked.

"123-45-6789," I answered.

He jumped up knocking his chair to the floor and came around behind me. "I will jump on your shoulders and destroy your knees," he shouted.

I spun around like a trapped panther, looked him in the eyes and said, "I'll knock your nuts through the roof of your mouth," taking a fighting crouch.

"Red armband, red armband," he threw down the training rag to signal that the exercise was over like a referee's whistle. His accomplice turned on the rest of the lights.

"Exercise over. You can never threaten the interrogators or else you will be killed by your captors," he said.

I still refused to talk even though I was taught I could open up after a training exercise was stopped. *He is still my enemy, He won't stop me from flying.*

On the way back to the barracks, I reflected on what I had heard about survival school since first volunteering to be a gunner. The school trained downed flyers to evade capture escape enemy prisons and fight to the death. The reputation was that it was one of the hardest schools, but one I had to pass to fly in combat.

When I first arrived at Seattle airport, a motor pool van was waiting to take us to Fairchild AFB. We were issued bunks and lockers and settled down in a long, two-story barracks. I saw Don and another gunner I knew and we went to chow together. Don had to spend an extra week at school and miss out on leave in order to graduate. He covered his failure by saying he had to attend a special orientation course exclusively for senior NCOs that had all of the secret techniques, too advanced for us airmen. He was full of it, as always.

Three weeks of Survival School began with a week of classes about capture and interrogation procedures used by the enemy. The staff spent countless hours going over the techniques: from the Germans and Japanese in WWII to the Chicoms in Korea and the VC in Vietnam.

On the eighth night of training, we went to a mile-long obstacle course. We crawled through simulated minefields, under barbed wire, over gullies and around armed guards. The rocks tore at elbows and knees. I was miserable the entire hour, and a half it took me to complete. At the end of the crawl from hell was the capture zone, where I was funneled into a stockade and captured.

The guards folded me into a 3x3 foot box, locked the door, and made me wait for the interrogators. This lasted for three days and then I was marched in a large POW compound that was cold and wet.

There were about two hundred of us, 'Prisoners of War', milling around a cold, and wet wire enclosed area that looked like Stalag 19. There was one big watery soup pot that we dipped our canteens into, at least it was warm. This cold sobering experience, caused me to reflect on the conditions of the real POWs in Vietnam, and that thought brought me back to reality and made me stop whimpering about my training environment. In the camp two people were permitted to attempt to escape. I went up to the class leader and quietly asked, "I want to escape, I found a way out behind the HQ building where the guards can't see me."

He looked at me with a funny wry grin and refused. Later I learned that he gave the escape chit to two AF Academy graduates. The favoritism continued.

After three days, we were 'repatriated' and sent back to the barracks. It felt like three days before I warmed up.

A week of concentrated classes about escape and evasion began. We learned what we could and could not eat. We had the joy of tasting spiders and beetles in class—licorice and dirt were my thoughts. We also learned how to navigate and how to use the emergency radio to get help. The day before we began our five-day trek in the forest, an NCO came to class and ordered that all the gunship personnel report to the school commandant's office.

There were eight or nine of us, including officers. We assembled in the commander's outer office when the adjutant told us to go in.

We filed in rank order and stood at attention in front of the Lieutenant Colonel.

He said, "At ease. Gunship crews have been lost," I knew he meant killed, "at an unsustainable rate, they need you in Vietnam immediately. There is an emergency requisition for you to leave school early and report directly to your squadron ASAP. Continue in class and we will try to get you through the entire Escape and Evasion trek before you depart. However, your jungle survival class has been cancelled. After you're done here, it's straight to Vietnam. Questions? Dismissed."

As we filed out, Big Don looked worried not knowing what to make of the recent revelations. One of the officers spoke up. "Let's make the most of our time here. They wouldn't try to cancel our class if it wasn't an emergency. If you need any help, here is my name and number, call. But be prepared to leave at a moment's notice."

As we started in our separate directions, I asked him, "Captain, what can I do?"

"I'm going to the command post to try to call the squadron. You can come with me, and if necessary, notify the enlisted men of what we learn," he said.

At the command post, he got through to the duty officer in Vietnam. I heard him say, "We'll go through the Escape & Evasion trek and then get on the first thing smoking. We should be there in seven days. Roger, sir, all leaves are cancelled as of now and we're on our way."

I returned to the barracks and told the others.

The next morning, at zero dark thirty, we boarded a bus for the mountains in the high sierras. It was cold as hell, but we were dressed nearly warm enough in parkas, gloves and boots. Once out of the buses, we met with our survival instructor, who would teach us for two days before starting our trek.

My instructor, "Quarter mile more or less," showed us how to make a rough shelter and showed us what we could eat in the forest. We practiced navigation, fishing, first aid, and escape-and-evasion techniques. On the second night, we navigated a specified route. We had to go over hills, through streams, and bypass roads in order to locate hard-to-find checkpoints.

This course was designed so we could practice what we were expected to do, behind enemy lines, if shot down in Vietnam. I was in a two-man team, buddy system, with a young pilot recently graduated from the Air Force Academy. We had both studied our lessons well, so navigation was a breeze and we found our way to the three checkpoints easily.

On the second night, I heard the aggressors close behind. The aggressors were instructors sent to look for us. If they caught me, they brought me back to the starting point and we had to do the whole thing over. Aggressors acted like enemy soldiers tracking us in Vietnam.

When I heard the aggressors, I grabbed the lieutenant's shoulder, put my index finger over my mouth, and pulled him down behind a log. We squatted there in silence and he soon heard what I had heard. In just ten minutes they passed by, and we returned to locating our final checkpoint for the night. We finished and succeeded again the next night. Hungry and cold, we were bussed back to Fairchild, dreaming of a big steak dinner, hot shower, and soft bunk.

The story circulated that one of our class mates, a pilot, had a devastating accident. He stabbed himself in the eye with a branch while navigating at night and was blinded. He was hospitalized and taken off flying status. I thought it was worse to lose flying status than to lose an eye.

We Gunship students assembled before reveille the next morning, carried our duffle bags to the orderly room and got on an airliner to Nha Trang, Vietnam. As I walked down the aisle, I noticed Big Don sitting by the window and I sat down beside him. I broke out my records folder and got out my writing pad, intent on communicating with my wife and daughter. I had promised a letter a day and I would keep that promise.

I wrote for a while, rested, and napped. After a couple of hours, Don banged my shoulder; he needed to use the latrine. I looked around and noticed there were no civilians on the airplane except for the pretty stewardesses whom Don was chatting up at the rear of the airplane. I pulled out my folder and started to read *Catch 22*, a book about someone else's experiences in war. I thought it was a book about flying in combat and that I would enjoy it.

Now the pretend terror of training was over and I was about to learn the real terror of combat.

CHAPTER VI

WELCOME TO VIETNAM

After a thirteen hour flight chewing gum, walking to the back and generally just being a pain to the other passengers I finally landed in Vietnam. Climbing down the staircase at Nha Trang Air Force Base, the oppressive heat made my time in Africa seem like living in an air-conditioned iceberg. The intense sunlight blinded me as I went to a pile of green duffle bags to retrieve mine. The blue dress uniform coat stuck to my sweaty neck and like a beacon signaled to all the old warriors that I was a new troop, just landed in country.

I hoofed it to a Quonset hut labeled Transit Airman Billeting. I found a bunk, tossed down my duffel, changed into a cooler flying suit and strutted outside to find some chow. I saw a camouflage arrow pointing to the NCO club and remembered that Don would be there.

I rolled into the club as if I owned it and saw banks of nickel slot machines all shiny and chromed along the curved sides of the corrugated tin roofed Quonset hut. One of the slots was ringing; somebody yelled 'jackpot' and the lights brightly flashed on and off. People were running around excitedly. *I don't have time or money for this phony bull shit.* There was a cashier's cage, on the left, to change bills in for rolls of coins, and to the right a long teak bar. I saw Don and three other NCOs huddled together at the bar, so I walked over and joined them.

Don was leaning back against the teak wearing his pickle green flying suit zippered down to his navel for the breeze, a pair of alligator cowboy boots to look cool, and aviator mirrored sun glasses to look like a flying hero. He appeared big in his six foot five frame and had a knowing grin. The other NCOs were obviously ground pounders and Don was the center of attention telling war stories. I heard him say his Congressional Medal of Honor was downgraded to an Air Force Cross, so I recognized the story about Sergeant Rock, but now it was about Don. He was buying drinks so I listened and he promised to show them his Air Force Cross tomorrow. He was talking about the gunship detachments, as if he had done it all before.

"Da Nang is up north next to the DMZ and closest to North Vietnam and fights for the Marines every night. I'm going to volunteer for Da Nang because they get the most combat!" He said winking his left eye. He had a big nasty cigar in his mouth and blew the smoke in my face. It smelled like burned cabbage and hurt my eyes so I looked for a way to escape.

I saw a Sergeant come in the door wearing the 4th Air Commando Patch and I went up and introduced myself as a new troop. We sat down at a corner table and he told the bar tender, "Give me a Commando seven course dinner."

The bartender grinned and answered, "A hot dog and six Budweisers?"

We sat around shooting the shit until Don dismissed his adoring fans and joined us. The Sergeant was telling me about the trouble in the Squadron. "Da Nang is the worst hell hole in the world and I been to Korea and even North Dakota" he said.

"What's wrong with Da Nang?" Don asked.

"They fly against the toughest armed enemy. They lost two airplanes this year."

"What about the crews?" I asked.

"No crew member ever lives from getting shot down. All seven brothers—dead."

I held my breath, Don's eyes opened wide as a silver dollar and his skin turned ashen color he looked like he had been hit in the gut with a baseball bat.

I was thinking, in my normal denial—a one in five chance of going there—no sweat.

I returned to the barracks early enough to read more of *Catch 22*. I felt like Yosarrian, the war was happening around me and I was just an abandoned cog in the military/industrial complex and the reality of where I was sinking in. I decided to write a letter so I pulled out my writing tablet with a picture of my wife and Cindy. I placed it on the foot locker and stared at it for a while. My heart yearned for them and I couldn't help thinking that I was one hell of a long way away. I was restless and sleep-deprived all night.

In the morning, I couldn't wait to finally get to the Air Commando compound. It was behind a ten-foot high brick fence with barbed wire on top. Inside the compound walls were a white washed building with its own flag, two three bladed propellers out front, captured enemy Anti-Aircraft guns and a white rock driveway with the shiniest army Jeep I had ever seen. The orderly room stood out with 4th Air Commando and American flags. I went in and told the chief clerk who I was, and turned my records over to him. I heard two old guys talking about the loss of a gunship at Da Nang the week before.

Don came in a few minutes later and glad-handed the clerk and spoke loudly asking for the First Sergeant. Reeking of day old alcohol and stale cigar smoke, he was a remarkable sight—same flying suit as the night before—with toilet paper on his chin where he had gouged himself shaving. He glared when I laughed at him. The chief clerk said the commander was ready to see us. We marched in to the office with Don leading, he was large and in charge, I trailed. We stood at attention, saluted and then Don reported for both of us. "New gunners reporting for duty, sir!" he puffed out his chest and kind of smirked.

"At ease, take a seat," the commander ordered, pointing at a couch. "We have a difficult mission here. Combat every night, fighting the fiercest battles the soldiers and marines have. We fight any time American troops are in contact with the enemy. We never leave a battlefield until every American is accounted for. The Air Commandos are some of the finest warriors America has, and I expect you to do your duty every single night. Any questions? See the First Sergeant, as he has your assignments, dismissed. "

We came to attention, saluted, about-faced, and marched out.

The First Sergeant was waiting for us. He stood up, shook hands with Don and nodded my way. "We have been short of gunners for months. We had two aircraft shot down at Da Nang, and have sent all our spare crewmen there. They haven't had a break in weeks and will be happy to see you. Airman, you're going to Bien Hoa." *Wow, close to Saigon.*

What he said next changed the entire attitude of the room.

"Don, you're going to be the chief gunner at Da Nang."

Don's face turned white. His eyes got large and glassy and he looked like he was punched in the mouth. Ashen and strange, his jaw shivered. I secretly had a little sneer in my heart knowing this was the last thing Don wanted.

"Wait a minute, Sarge. I'm the highest ranking gunner here; I get to choose which assignment I want. Why should this airman get the choice assignment? I have family stationed at Bien Hoa and have always wanted to go there," Dons voice stammered.

Talk about knocking me for a loop. Now he had family in Vietnam? This was the first I'd heard of it, despite being with him for the last six months. I wondered what breed of chickens his family was. I had heard of Long Island Red pullets, but his family had to be Detroit Yellows backs. For all his faults, I would never have believed that Don would chicken out in front of the first sergeant. I felt like asking to see his Air Force Cross.

"Have a seat and I'll see if I can work it out for you to go to Bien Hoa," the First Sergeant answered. He made a phone call and spoke in hushed tones for just a minute. "Okay, Sarge, you're going to Bien Hoa and the airman is going to Da Nang."

We left the orderly room and walked toward the NCO club for lunch and I asked Don, "What the hell is going on? Are you afraid of Da Nang? I thought you were the hero of the NCO club?"

"Just shut up airman. This is above your rank. Go to Da Nang, sucker."

I actually felt empathy for him. The situation reminded me of the story my father told about stepping back over the line. Would he regret his coward's stance, or laugh at his great luck at being the highest rank when assignments were handed out? But, there was no time to worry about these esoteric thoughts—I had an airplane to catch.

CHAPTER VII

ROCKET CITY

I ran to the flight line and the same Commander cranked up a C-47. The sound of the finely tuned radial engine reminded me of a dragster shooting off the racing line in a cacophony of firing cylinders. A cloud of grey blue smoke blasted out of the exhaust and it smelled like a combination of sweet onions and gasoline. It made my eyes water.

The plane was a slick; it had no guns or offensive weapons. He taxied us out and after the take-off, we turned north, and I stared out the square windows at the country below.

As we flew along, the coast looked tranquil, I saw peaceful San Pans fishing in the South China Sea. The landscape looked much like sleepy Florida where I grew up. After flying along the coast, we turned inland and the ground was emerald-green and beautiful, reminding me of England. Then the panorama suddenly changed. The ground became dark and chaotic; I saw the remnants of the war: an endless battlefield reminiscent of black and white pictures of WWI with thousands of yards pockmarked with hideous bomb craters. The craters were like ugly small pox scars on older people's faces. They were deep black scars, half filled with stagnant pus water, pockmarks all over the beautiful face of Mother Nature. Any other time this would be a tropical paradise, but now it was a diseased war zone.

I was startled out of my nightmare thoughts by the loadmaster, who indicated that we were getting ready to land. I went forward, put on my seat belt. After landing at Da Nang, I went to the aft door and looked out. The sweltering heat and bright sun felt like Miami.

We taxied to where I saw three gunships with newly painted black undersides, all parked in a row. I recalled the controversy about flying white-bottomed airplanes at night. After two were shot down, the crews disobeyed orders and spray painted the bottoms black. The airplanes looked beautiful to me, with their guns sticking out of their left sides.

A square-shaped panel truck, called a bread truck, waited for us. We got in and rode to the Orderly room to sign in. I met the First sergeant, who told me to get a ride to the barracks, check in with the chief gunner and then bunk down for the night. The orderly room clerk drove me to a hooch: my new home.

Hooches were fifty-yard long, single story, wooden buildings, constructed with plywood sides up to three feet high. Screening above the plywood kept out the mosquitoes. Sharply pitched corrugated tin served as a roof.

We parked behind a hooch with the air commando patch on it. I pulled open the screened door and walked into a dark room. I stood in front of a long aisle, down the center, between two rows of double-decked bunks against each wall. Tall metal lockers formed partitions between each set of double bunks. Every neatly made bunk had a mosquito net draped across a metal frame. I saw a break area in the center that held a card table, eight to ten chairs and a ping-pong table. Four or five men wearing flying suits sat in the break area. In the background beautiful music was playing—I recognized it as the Mama's and the Papa's *Monday Monday*.

I walked to the recreation area and announced myself. "Airman Joe, a new gunner to your tropical paradise. Is the Chief Gunner around?"

I was sent to a bunk area where a kindly looking, slightly balding, older man was sitting and reading some Air Force publication. He was wearing a flying suit and black rimmed plastic glasses nicknamed 'Birth Control,' because even Adonis couldn't get laid wearing those glasses. "Hi, I'm a new airman gunner. Are you Sergeant Jerry?"

"Sure am, son, they call me Commando. I'm glad to see you. Grab your duffle bag and settle in the bunk next to mine. It's empty and there's a good locker for you."

"Thanks, Sarge." I did as instructed, came back and sat down next to him while he explained the current situation.

"Joe, we are short of gunners. We have even been using orderly room clerks and aircraft mechanic volunteers to fly some missions. We lost two aircraft last month, and there aren't sufficient replacements to enable us to fly with full crews. But this is Da Nang, and we hack the mission. We fly our sorties and defend our brothers, come hell or high water." I was impressed with his 'can do" attitude, which displayed rare spirit for an NCO of his rank and age.

"For the first few missions we will have you fly with a more experienced combat gunner, but I want you to learn everything you can, because I will give you a new Airman as your second gunner very shortly. We have four new replacements coming in a couple of weeks and you must be a lead gunner by then. The gunners haven't had a day off in a month and they have exceeded their allowable flying time. You've got to get up to speed ASAP, so I can put together two new crews and get back to a normal rotation."

I heard the hooch door slam closed and Commando Jerry said, "Here's Ron. He will be your lead gunner."

A tall, slim, blond-haired young man ambled up to us. He looked at me with intense blue eyes that caught me as intelligent. He appeared to be more like a bright eyed, California surfer, than a gunner. His hair seemed a little long, his smile a little knowing and his deportment a lot laid back. His gaunt, angular face made him look like a young Beach Boy. "Ron, this is your new second gunner, Joe. Give him the briefing."

"Roger, Commando. Glad to meet you, Joe. I can sure use your help," he reached out his hand and we shook.

"I'm ready when you are."

"Jerry, is he flying with me tonight?" Ron's speech was slow, melodic and California-like. He had an aura of calm leadership.

"Yes, so take the crew van and get to Personnel Equipment. He needs to be ready."

Ron walked over, turned off his reel-to-reel tape recorder, and led me out of the back door of the hooch where he had parked a bread van by the latrine. We got in and he started driving. "We're going to the survival equipment section to get your first aid kit and radio; the personnel equipment section to get your flying helmet and checklists; and the tool room to get your repair kit. Then you're ready to fly tonight. Did you eat yet? We're going right by the chow hall."

"No, I haven't eaten yet, but I'm glad to get back to flying."

He said, "You won't get bored flying here. We call Da Nang 'Rocket City' because of the fast life-style and because Charley likes to shoot rockets at us."

We went through the chow line and had a seat. Ron briefed me about flying at Rocket City. "The normal sequence is: we fly the early mission on the first day, Spooky One, which takes off at 1600 and lands at 2400. Next night we fly Spooky Two, which takes off at midnight and flies until daybreak. These two aircraft fly base Combat Air Patrol or CAP over Da Nang and if they get called away for a fight, the ground alert bird, Spooky Three, takes off and flies over the base unless needed at another fight. We fly Spooky Three on the third night and it lasts from 1600-till dawn the next day. Any questions?"

"No, it's pretty much what they told us at Hurlburt, but how do the missions go? What do you want me to do when we're flying?"

"I'll be by the gunner's control panel and you start out behind number one gun. I'll talk on the intercom, don't you talk unless it's an emergency. Bring the cans of ammo to the back of the guns and as soon as one is empty, safe it, load it, rearm it and go on to the next gun. This is not Hurlburt; never turn on any light. The light helps you see, but it helps the enemy see you. At all times keep every gun loaded and ready to fire. If a gun malfunctions while you're in training, I'll fix it and you take over the control panel and the intercom. When we land, I will duplicate every malfunction and show you how I corrected it, but in combat, I will fix every problem. If I'm working on a malfunction, you reload the empty guns and return to the control panel and answer the pilot's questions. He won't ask many questions, as he is busy as we are. You got it, Joe?"

"Got it, buddy."

He drove us to the survival equipment shop, where a sharp staff sergeant met us. He issued me the required survival equipment and Ron explained it.

"These chaps fasten around your waist and have pockets for all your equipment. The two survival first-aid kits contain everything you need to fix an injured buddy, and they also contain medicines like No Doze pills if you have to stay awake to escape and evade the enemy. There is the K-Bar knife and whetstone, as well as the switchblade in the pecker pocket in your crotch, in case you have to cut yourself down from a tree after bailing out. There is the survival radio tuned to the dedicated emergency channel, Guard. The last pocket has a spare battery and a collapsible splint."

Ron had this unusual signal he made with his right hand. I had seen Hawaiian surfers use it before, as a greeting or salutation: a closed fist with thumb and pinky stuck out. They wagged it back and forth and said, 'Hang in there man.' Ron made the signal. We left.

A young NCO met us at the door and led us into a MacDonald's sized supply room with bins along the wall and a counter that he went behind. "New gunner, we will issue you a helmet, flying suits and a parka for cold nights at altitude. In addition I have a set of checklists for you."

"Thanks," I said.

At the tool room I was issued a cloth tool bag and a standard issue of gun-repair equipment that included a hammer, pliers, needle nose pliers, water pump and a socket-and-wrench set. The only unusual item was a fifteen-inch, common screwdriver that Ron said was the best pry bar in the airplane. After hitting the tool room, we returned to the hooch.

At 1430 Ron and I went out to the crew van. "We're going to pick up the officers, then go to Intel, the mess hall and the airplane."

The intelligence building was along the flight line near our orderly room. We went in, me like a puppy following Ron, and sat down in plush theater seats. A captain went to the front of the room and stood before a projected map of Vietnam.

"Here's the action in I Corps today: there is an attack at two Marine outposts in the west and some rocket activity along the coast. It appears that there are heavy enemy resupply convoys along the Ho Chi Minh trail. There has been a great deal of Intel that there is a pending attack at Dong Ha, a marine firebase in the demilitarized zone. Your mission is to fly to Dong Ha and sit ground alert. When the enemy attacks, take off and defend the base. If no attacks occur, depart the base at 0400, fly along the trail and interdict any enemy trucks you see. The trail is a free-fire zone and no prior permission is required. After expending your ammunition, return to base by daylight. Questions?"

There were no questions, so we got back in the van and drove to the chow hall, where Ron and I went in and got a case of C-rations for the flight, then drove to the flight line. We parked and carried the C's over to the airplane and began our pre-flight. Ron showed me how he thoroughly went over each gun, insuring that every single piece and part was in operating condition. The ground weapons mechanic came over, and Ron introduced me to him.

"Hi, Joe. If there is anything I can do, let me know. How do the guns look, Ron?"

"The guns look great, Jeff, but do you have an extra feeder for us to take?"

"No, sorry, no extra feeders left; I gave the spare to Spooky One."

"The feeder is the weak link on the entire gun," Ron explained. "The feeder takes the round from facing inward in the drum, cycles it around and forward, transports it to the bolts and feeds it into the chamber. At the rate of speed they are going, the smallest flaw in the ammunition makes the feeder jam, so half of the malfunctions are feeder problems. But it's okay. I'm good at fixing feeders."

At dusk, the airplane next to us started up and began taxiing. Our pilot fired up our airplane and we followed down the taxiway towards the end of the runway. After takeoff, I immediately unstrapped and walked to the door to look at the green jungle, blue sky and white beaches. It reminded me again of Florida, with lush tropical palm trees on the beaches and small boats all along the shore. We turned north. Ron came over and shouted next to my ear, "Dong Ha is a twenty minute flight away. We will land and rest in a tent until needed. We won't arm the guns now, as we are in no danger and aren't expecting to use them any time soon."

We flew on to Dong Ha and I could see the runway in the distance. Ron said, "It has a two thousand feet PSP, temporary runway. That's a steel erector that can be put down in a hurry and make a runway. The new copilot is making his first short landing on this runway, so let's strap in."

We took our seats. It was a beautiful balmy dusk and I saw the side of the PSP runway pass by the open door. We hit the runway kind of hard and bounced way up into the air, about twenty feet. I could see the control tower underneath us as we bunny-hopped down the runway. I grabbed on for dear life and thought, my God, I have never bounced this high in an airplane. When we were about to bounce down for the third time I heard the engines speed up and the pilot on the intercom. "Let's go around. I have the airplane!" He took over and climbed and circled around. My heart was beating like a drum. He landed the airplane as smooth as a feather. I was sure glad he took over and made the final landing.

"The Lieutenant copilot has a new nick name—Kangaroo!" Ron said.

"Maybe Peter Rabbit is better," I answered as we climbed down the three-rung ladder in the aft door of the gunship.

I looked around to assess where we were. We parked very close to the runway at the downwind end so we could affect an immediate take-off if necessary. There was a fifty-man tent set up next to the parking spot. Inside there were lights, bunks and a break room with a card table and some couches. The seven-man crew came in and sat around the break area.

I sat next to Ron and asked, "What happens now?"

"We sit ground alert, meaning the airplane is fully armed and loaded but the guns are still safe. There is a base warning horn and the phone by the pilots is to the command post. If they need us they know we are here and ready to go. We have to take off with the slightest warning and be ready to shoot anyone attacking this base. When the horn sounds, run to the airplane, go around and pull the chocks from the right main landing gear, get into the airplane and arm number three gun during takeoff. I'll go directly into the airplane after pulling the left chock and arm number one and two guns. We take off in less than two minutes and begin firing almost immediately. In the meantime, just relax, practice your emergency checklists, and read the flight manual."

I replied, "Thanks, buddy. Where's the latrine?"

"Follow me. When we go out of the tent, make sure no light escapes to show the VC where we are. We stand in the doorway and pull the inner flap around ourselves before we open the outer flap, so that way they can't see the lights of the tent."

We went to the entrance, did as Ron explained and then we were outside the tent. He walked around the side to the back, ten yards off the aircraft-parking ramp.

"See those old rocket tubes half buried in the ground? Just pee in there." He pointed. "There's a benjo ditch further back if you need it." Then he pointed further behind the tent. "There are the Marines' big guns. They have five-inch howitzers that they use for artillery."

I could just make out the silhouettes of a line of gigantic guns in the dark distance, hulking down, and standing by to lurch up and kill someone.

I walked over to the buried rocket tube, unzipped my flying suit, and started to relieve myself. The night was very peaceful; and without lights from the base to dim my vision; the heavens were a delight of bright sparkling diamonds. A lifelong student of astronomy, I could easily pick out the Big Dipper, Orion's belt, and Seven Sisters.

BAROOOOMMMM!

A gun thundered and a hell of a flash almost knocked me over. I squatted as a natural reaction and lowered myself to the ground. I felt warm piss all over my stomach and hand, and saw Ron running toward the airplane as the alert siren went off. I jumped up and ran toward the airplane, hoping the Marines guards wouldn't shoot me. They could have mistaken me for a VC trying to blow up the airplane.

The rest of the crew climbed the ladder to the airplane. I ran around to the right side, removed the chock, and jumped into the airplane as the left engine was starting. The engines raced and we started to taxi as I armed the gun.

Number three gun sat in the open door of the airplane, so I had a good sight of the camp as we took off. I held onto the safety strap the loadmaster had put on the door after we had all gotten in. I could see the dark camp with Marines running everywhere, and behind the tent I saw the big, five-inch gun that had scared me half to death and made me piss all over myself, firing gigantic salvoes.

"Joe, get your head in the airplane," Ron shouted in my ear.

I stood up and we walked to the gunner's arming panel and I began listening to the crew.

The pilot briefed us about the situation he had just gotten over the radio.

"The base mortar detector saw a round shot at them and rang the alert horn. The round came from two clicks south by the river, and we have permission to fire at anything we see. We have to watch out for Cobra Helicopters, as they will be working the same target and looking for whatever shot at us. Give me a gun on the line."

"Number one on the line," Ron answered. He turned on the arming switch and opened the tie-downs remaining on the line of ammo cans. I dragged a can along the floor to number three gun. Ron had a can positioned behind each of the other two guns. We flew back into firing routine, into a thirty-degree left bank, shot a short burst and leveled off. Forty-five seconds later, we headed into another thirty-degree left bank and another short burst. Number one was empty and I loaded it while Ron watched the gunner's panel. We were firing only occasionally now, not hot and heavy.

Ron said, "Joe, when you're loading the gun, operate the loader handle as fast as possible. Don't slow leak it—we may need the gun immediately, and you were too slow the last time."

I took his admonition seriously, so when number two was empty I cranked the handle like a Tasmanian devil on fire, loading the whole fifteen hundred rounds in a minute or two.

After a couple of minutes the pilot said, "False alarm, we're going back to Dong Ha."

We landed, prepared our guns, and retreated into the tent where Ron pulled me to the side for some philosophy.

"Joe, don't ever slow-leak your crew again. Every second a gun is unable to operate puts your crew at a risk. When a gun is empty or broken, load it and fix it as fast as humanly possible. Of the hundreds of thousands of airmen in the Air Force, and the thousands of weapons mechanics loading bombs, we are the few who are privileged to be flying in combat and we represent the best of the best. Everyone knows exactly what you are doing every second you're in the airplane; you must be the absolute best you can. We do not get into an airplane to be average or mediocre; we get into the airplane to be the best. Every time you go up, you must try to be better than the last time and be as perfect as possible. If you can't live up to those standards, then you can't call yourself a gunner."

I felt embarrassed, and my face flushed. "Ron, you're absolutely right. I apologize for my below-average performance. I treated this mission like a training flight and didn't take it seriously enough. I will do better."

"I'll definitely help you. Now let's go over your emergency checklist again. And next time we come on ground alert I want you to bring your gunner's text books with you so we can study and test each other."

"Roger."

We continued studying for the next five to six hours, until about 4:00 A.M. when the pilot announced, "It's time to saddle up and go back to Da Nang by way of the Ho Chi Minh trail."

I asked Ron, "What does he mean?"

"We're going down the trail to look for any action and fire all of our remaining ammo. We'll land at daylight."

When we arrived at the trail, Ron explained that this was the main route from North Vietnam to South Vietnam for the NVA to infiltrate troops and supplies to their forces in the south. The trail wasn't just one trail, but a series or network of roads.

The trail was reputed to be one of the most heavily defended targets in country. The enemy felt safe and had emplaced AAA guns and even missiles. The allies had never ventured into the territory of the trail, as part of it was in Laos and diplomacy didn't allow us access to that country. The gunship crews had lots of war stories about shooting along the trail, and they usually ended with some harrowing event involving green tracers.

Ron explained, "Green tracers come from a 100MM Anti-Aircraft Artillery guns. The gun has copper in the tracer material and is usually positioned high up in the mountains. I have only seen it once, and they were shooting at a fast-mover above us. Fast-movers are fighter jets that attack the trail all the time."

We expended our ammo and returned to Da Nang. Back at home base we cleaned up the airplane and went to chow at the big chow hall. The officers went to their area and Ron and I sat down with the loadmaster and engineer. They laughed about me pissing myself when the five-inch fired.

"Joe, you're a pisser," one of them said, reminding me that I needed a shower.

We went back to our hooch and Ron showed me where the latrine was. It was still 6:00 A.M. so I took a cold shower. *How could it be this cold in a tropical paradise*, I thought, and hit the sack.

All too soon, Ron shook my rack bringing me out of one of the sweetest sleeps I had ever had. After hitting the latrine, we got the van and left to pick up the rest of the crew and repeat the daily routine of chow, Intel, preflight and combat.

CHAPTER VIII

SAN PAN CITY

This mission was Spooky One, the first sortie of the night. We took off and flew base CAP waiting for a call to action. After loading the guns, Ron called me over between number one and two and turned on the high intensity light.

"Grab your aircraft flight manual, so we can work on our job knowledge."

I got my books from my helmet bag, sat on the floor and read about the airplane.

The beloved C-47, called Skymaster to those who built her and Gooney Bird to those who flew her, was a workhorse airplane. Developed before WWII to carry cargo and troops in all kinds of conditions, over ten thousand were built. They were still in service around the world twenty-five years later. The C-47's history spanned from D-Day in Europe to resupply duty in Burma, and now they were being used as attack gunships, as a weapons platform to defend American Soldiers and Marines. The plane was adored by all airmen and there were countless stories of damaged airplanes bringing their crews home safely, despite all odds.

"We totally trust, love and admire our airplane," Ron said, "and we must learn everything we can about her. Let's go over the safety equipment. There are fire axes, first aid kits, fire extinguishers, walk-around oxygen bottles, a rescue rope and flashlights. The Gunner must know where each and every piece of equipment is, so he can find it in the dark after getting shot down if it comes to that." My full orientation of this combat airplane was different from the orientation in school of the training airplanes. This combat C-47 was stripped down to essentials so it could carry additional ammunition, fuel and flares. Further, it had a flak curtain along the left side of the fuselage to stop small arms ammunition from penetrating.

"The flak curtain is here to protect the plane, not the gunners. If the airplane gets hurt all seven of us die, so it's more important than any single one of us is," Ron said.

He went on to explain the flare rack in the back of the airplane. There was a large rectangular aluminum box on the floor about a foot high. There were twenty-four slots in the box for aircraft flares, plus sixteen additional flares strapped down in the front of the cargo compartment to be used after the first twenty-four were gone.

Another crewmember, his loadmaster, explained, "These are awesome flares. They are three feet long, five inches in diameter and weigh thirty pounds. They have a timing device on the top and when I throw it out of the airplane, the attached lanyard strap it is activated. Once it falls five hundred feet the can blows off, the parachute deploys and the candle lights. It has two million candle power, burns at four thousand degrees and lights up the night so we can see the enemy. The flares are the most dangerous items in the airplane. If they are ever hit by enemy fire, they will light and burn through the floor of the airplane, where the control cables are. If I get shot and drop the flare, to save all of us, pick it up and throw it out of the door before starting my first aid."

I felt more afraid of the flares in the airplane than of the Viet Cong. I would have to pay careful attention to what was going on behind me in the airplane.

"If you drop a flare," Ron said to the loadmaster, "I'm throwing you out with it. So keep your head up and take care of your flares."

He turned to me. "Let's go forward and I'll introduce you to the rest of the crew."

We went into the cockpit compartment, where an Asian man sat in a little room to the left.

"Joe this is Sergeant Tran, our Vietnamese interpreter. He is in the Vietnamese Air Force (VNAF) and acts as our radio operator. When we get to a place where there are no Americans, Sgt Tran speaks to the Vietnamese Army (ARVN) on the ground or to the village chieftain we are defending. He tells us where to shoot and explains what is going on. Sgt Tran has over a thousand missions and he's not on a one year tour, he's in this for life. He is dedicated to defending his country from foreign invaders, from China and North Vietnam."

"Thank you, Ron," said Sgt Tran, "and welcome to our country, Joe. We are overjoyed that you are here to help."

I stood there, feeling very small, going over Ron's sobering words: "He's in this for life." I had never thought of it as a life or death struggle. It was only a whim for me, a test of my bravery and a chance to win some medals, not a lifetime struggle for freedom for my family. I cast my eyes to the floor and thought; *Over one thousand missions was an awesome number. In* Catch 22, *all the characters were preoccupied with completing thirty-five missions to survive. Sergeant Tran's one thousand missions were astonishing.*

We shook hands. I saw a determined, hard look in his eyes, one that I had never seen before. He looked thankful and I probably looked dumbfounded and awestruck.

I was pulled out of my thoughts by the sound of the engines speeding up and the pilot speaking over the intercom. "We have a target, crew. I'll brief you when I know more."

Ron and I walked to the back of the airplane, unstrapped the ammo cans and pulled one behind each gun. I put my books away and pulled out my checklist, reflecting on my emergency procedures and what Sergeant Tran had said.

I thought about the noble struggle of an invaded people who only desired safety for their families and freedom to live in peace and harmony.

Are these not the same ideals that our forefathers wanted for America? Life, liberty and the pursuit of happiness? Having achieved them ourselves— rather, having been given them by our forefathers— is it not our obligation to bring those noble ideals to other humans? Who could fault us for wanting to lead the world out of darkness, communism, and subjugation?

The screaming engines of reality called me back to the gunship. Ron and I began connecting the guns and getting the ammo cans ready.

The pilot came on the intercom. "Crew, we have a small compound south of here that is taking sporadic mortar and rocket fire, and they want us to support them. They think the VC may be getting ready for an all-out attack and want us to knock them back. Nav, give me a course and get the weather."

The navigator came back, "Pilot, Nav. It looks like the sky is overcast down to 1,500 feet. There are mountains higher than that in the surrounding area, so I don't know how we'll get in there to fire."

"If it comes to it," the pilot said, "we can safely let down over the ocean and fly in between the mountains, so I'll begin to do that. Everyone, keep your eyes out for anything you can see under the clouds."

Ron went to the left side of the fuselage and looked through the open door. He called me over, "Low Ceiling, tall mountains. Can't see through the clouds. We let down over the water until we can see, then fly between mountains to the target." He pointed to the small window on the right side of the aircraft, "Look for mountains."

Finally Ron said, "Pilot, I have a light at eight o'clock. Looks like it's on the water."

"Tally ho," the pilot replied. "I got it also. I will let down here, under the clouds and we'll drive inland when we can see better." I could feel the airplane descending. I kept looking for the deadly mountains.

After a while the copilot said, "There's a break in the shore line. We can cut inland from there. Nav, can you find our destination?"

"Can do," came the reply. "Pilot altitude!"

The pilot replied, "I know the altitude, just find our route to the target."

Ron came over to me and got next to my helmeted ear and yelled, "We're not supposed to be below two thousand feet because it's too dangerous from ground fire. Anything can hit us at this height, and we are silhouetted against the white cloud cover. We just lost an airplane and crew because they were too low and got shot down."

I nodded understanding and glued my eyes to the window as we proceeded inland. After a few minutes of vectors from the navigator, the pilot, satisfied we were over the target, lowered the left wing and entered the firing circle. He fired a short burst and the radio operator said, "The target is one hundred meters north of where you are firing." The aircraft went a little north, fired, and then the radio operator came on and said, "Two hundred yards north of that last burst."

The copilot asked, "Can we drop a flare to see what's firing?"

"Can't do it with this cloud cover. The flare would light up our airplane against the clouds like a spotlight. We just have to follow directions from the compound. They are finding a firing solution from their incoming trajectory indicator."

That, it was explained to me later, was a system that detected incoming rockets or mortars, and calculated from where they had been fired. When the detector determined the location, the compound relayed the information to us and we fired there.

"The rocket is coming from four hundred yards south of where we just fired," the radio operator said.

We rolled in and fired a short burst. This had gone on for about a half an hour when the frustrated radio operator said, "This is crazy. North then south, then north then south—and we haven't seen a thing. What the hell gives with this target?"

The pilot said, "Ask the compound if they can fire a low flare over the target and we will back away a mile to see what we can see."

"Roger, pilot, they're preparing to fire an artillery flare."

I saw a very small arc of light leave the compound. It reminded me of those roman candles on the fourth of July, shooting up into the air before the firework explodes in a shower of light. I saw the flare light a couple of miles ahead of us, close to the ground.

The pilot started to laugh. "Do you see what I see? The gooks have a rocket launcher on that san pan in the river, and are going up and down before we can adjust for their previous location. They're pretty smart, but peek-a-boo, I see you."

With those words, we returned to the river and in short order sank the san pan and ended activities for the night.

I learned more about Ron's philosophy about why we were fighting, the next day.

CHAPTER IX

MORAL AND ETHICAL COMBAT

I got up early to organize my bunk area. Three feet to the left, and facing the beds, were a couple of double-wide wall lockers. The left one had everything I owned. My uniforms were hung on the bar on top, I turned on an electric light bulb to keep the clothes from molding and I put my shorts and T-shirts in the drawer at the bottom.

I taped pictures of my wife and daughter to the open door, along with a short-timers calendar. The calendar was a line drawing of a vivacious, nude 'round eye' (western) girl with 365 numbered squares that were colored in, each day, until the tour was over. The last three squares were in strategic places only a horny man could picture. Ron had the Mama's and Papa's tape on and *California Dreaming* was playing in the background.

A teen-aged Vietnamese girl was in our barracks sweeping the floor. Ron said her name was Baby San. She was Mama San's niece and worked to keep the clothes and barracks clean. Once a week they polished our boots, washed, and ironed our clothes. They gave the cold masculine hooch a warm and lived in atmosphere and caused us to keep up our appearances, dress and act more cultured, not like a college frat house. In addition, they constantly swept the dusty floor and wiped down everything. Ron said we each were to give Mama San five dollars on the first of the month, for her to feed her family.

After a while, Baby San sat down on one of the bunks with a staff sergeant gunner. He had a Sears' catalogue open and was paging through it, with her.

Ron came over to my bunk and spat, "Look at that son of a bitch Slick," he sneered. "trying to entice Baby San with trinkets from the U.S. He's married and trying to get in her pants, the scum bag! He bought her a little refrigerator last month, and Mama San and I were very mad. We know what he's up to and it's morally reprehensible and bad for Baby San. She's a good girl who needs to finish school and not get pregnant."

He went on about war being the moral and ethical combat between different social cultures. He said we had to be better than the communists to win this war, and we had to conduct ourselves as the noble and honorable defenders of the people.

He leaned in close to me and said, "We're not here to conquer the Vietnamese, but to liberate them from the immoral invaders from China and North Vietnam." Ron looked me straight in the eye, "We have to earn the respect of these people. They already respect America for her defense of the oppressed, but when they meet Americans like Slick, they have serious doubts about our honor and motives. We must act in the finest tradition of American liberators. We can only win this war in the hearts and minds of the people, not on the battlefields with the blood of our enemies." His eyes were dark and serious.

"Wow, Ron, is it really that big a deal?"

"Yes, it is, Joe, and until we all learn that we will lose this entire effort. Now get some rest. We have to fly later."

I lay awake that night thinking about all that Ron had to say, and all that he taught me. He was cut from a different cloth and wise beyond his years. Ron wasn't focused just on himself. He was aware of the world and on an ethical mission to do what was right; to live a good and meaningful life.

My last conscious thought before falling asleep was that I needed to become like Ron.

CHAPTER X

SPOOKY THE COMBAT ACE

I walked outside into the bright sunlight and was almost blinded, sweat beading on my forehead. Looking like a drunk stumbling and swaying toward the truck, I approached the right side door while trying to look over my emergency checklist. Helmet bag and tool bag in hand, I was in my own little world, thinking about the mission tonight and what emergencies I might have to face.

MASTER ARM SWITCH OFF, GUN SWITCH OFF, GUN SAFE.

GRRRROWWWWL, RUFF-RUFF!

Now that was definitely not on the checklist.

A set of gigantic teeth snapped at my shins from under the truck. I jumped back, dropping my tool and helmet bags.

A snarling canine snout menaced me. I backed up slowly about twenty feet, so I could better protect myself and assess the danger. I squatted down and put my left hand over my eyes to shield them while I got my K-bar knife out with my right.

I slunk low to see under the truck, but all I could glimpse in the dark shadow was two rows of gleaming white teeth through retracted gums. Rising to a crouch, I backed my way to the hooch door, keeping a wary eye peeled. I grabbed a mop handle from the drying rack and decided to go around and sneak up on the back of the truck and get in through the rear door. Armed with the six-foot bludgeon and on tiptoes, I silently crept to the back of the truck. I gently placed the end of the mop handle on the bumper while I inched my hand to the door.

RUFF, RUFF, RUFF!

I jumped back, but the mop handle slipped down through the bumper and was stuck tight. I tripped over it and fell on my ass. I got up as fast as possible and jumped into the defensive, judo, hands-forward position to defend myself. I looked cooler than lying on the ground like an idiot. I dusted my rump off and slowly retreated toward the hooch. Ron was just coming out.

"One of the MP's K-9 attack dogs must have escaped and it's under our truck. It tried to kill me," I blurted out.

Ron looked around and laughed. "Did you just meet Spooky the Wonder Dog?"

I said, "What the hell are you talking about? I've really been attacked."

He shouted, "Spooky, Spooky! Here, boy!"

With that, the horrible beast crawled out from under the truck and came toward Ron with his tail high in the air and wagging like a high-speed windshield wiper.

"Good boy," Ron said, as he petted his head.

He was the nastiest-looking mutt I had ever seen. He looked like some sort of diabolical mixed-breed with German Police dog the dominant gene, and Pit Bull the recessive. He was a lot thicker and more muscular than either breed. He was dirty, dark and dank and had a coat of matted brown fur that was filthy with dust and truck oil. He had a jagged triangular scar from his right eye to his ear. A big tuft of long hair had pulled out of his neck, leaving a mangy bare spot with an open sore, and he had a large grease-spot on his back. He was gaunt and lean, as if he had not eaten in a couple of weeks. Flies were buzzing all around him. The only part of him that looked healthy was his glistening teeth.

The teeth were wolf-like, long, sharp fangs that could rip through flesh and crack leg bones. Spittle dripped from his face, reminiscent of the vicious mongrel in the Hound of the Baskervilles. He had a stumpy tail that must have been broken because it was tilted to the left, at a thirty-degree list, from two inches past his rump to the end. To make matters worse he smelled like a pus-filled open wound, mixed with burnt oil and rotting flesh. He was the most sickening and frightening cur I had ever seen.

He stayed on the other side of Ron, away from me. He didn't like me—and the feeling was mutual. I would rather face the VC any day than meet him in a dark alley.

"Spooky is our Squadron mascot and has been here for years. He has over five hundred combat missions and loves to fly," Ron said.

I thought he was kidding me. But he and the mangy cur walked around the back of the truck and they got in. I picked up my tools, helmet, and climbed in the passenger seat. We headed to the mess hall to pick up a case of C rations to have on the airplane. I went in, signed for the C rations, and tossed them into the back of the truck, not thinking about the mongrel. The heavy box landed on his outstretched leg. He growled at me and showed me his enormous teeth as if to warn me that my time was coming.

We picked up the rest of the crew, pre-flighted the plane, and prepared for take-off. While taxiing out, I got ready to sit down in my seat along the right front of the fuselage and the damn mutt was lying there. Ron was reading his checklist and didn't notice my predicament. As I neared the seat, the hound from hell showed me his teeth and growled, his lips folded back. I decided discretion was the better part of valor and sat on the floor between the guns. *Let the damn dog have the seat.*

We took off and flew base CAP over Da Nang, with Ron asking me questions about the airplane from the manual.

"Where are the fire extinguishers? How many first aid kits are there? Where is the fire ax?" he droned on.

After a couple of hours I was hungry and opened the C ration. These Cs were left over from WWII but were not bad. Each case had twelve boxes of one meal each. The meals were an assortment of large cans of beans and franks, ham and lima beans, ham and eggs, pork slices, chicken and dumplings and a couple of other entrees.

Each box had crackers, bread, peaches in heavy syrup, an accessory pack with utensils and a P-38 can opener. I liked the ham and lima bean meal best, so I opened that case to make sure I got my favorite. I sat down on the floor with the ham and lima bean can and had just opened it when the damn dog jumped in front of me, baring his teeth, and barking over the roar of the engines. Even though I shrank back, I could smell his diabolical breath: eau de dead, rotten rat. Ron ran over, pulled back my ear piece and said, "Give Spooky the ham and lima beans, they're his favorite."

The last thing I would ever do of my own volition was give that hideous creature anything to sustain his life, let alone my delicious ham and lima beans. I stood up and backed away, with him still challenging me with his bare teeth.

Ron appeared with a disposable aluminum bowl, like the ones from a chicken pot-pie, poured my ham and lima beans into it and put it on the floor for Spooky. The cur lapped it up, always keeping a wary eye on me. He didn't trust me and he must have thought I didn't know my place in this pack. He was the alpha dog and I was his bitch. He was not about to let a challenge go unanswered.

I crawled back between my guns and ate the closest C ration I could find. I did not want to go near Spooky and incur his wrath again. For now, I would give him a wide berth. I warily watched him out of the corner of my eye and kept my K-Bar close at hand.

Immediately, I heard the engines race and we started to clean up the cargo compartment. We armed the guns and untied the ammo cans, getting ready for the fight.

The pilot called out, "Rest is over crew! We're going to a large free-fire zone and do some H & I firing to keep the VC up all night."

After Ron and I got the guns ready, he went to the gunners' control panel and I stood in the doorway behind number three. There were two straps across the doorway as a safety restraint and I held on to them and looked out, as the calm and peaceful cool night was a delight to view.

Ron said, "Number one is on the line."

Predictably, the left wing went down and the aircraft entered the firing circle. BBBRRRRRRRRRROOOOOUR!

I heard an unfamiliar sound along with the gun, like chaos, between and behind number one and two guns. I looked back and the damn dog was running in circles as fast as he could, a left hand circle, barking his head off as long as the gun fired. When the gun stopped, he stopped.

I gingerly stepped around Spooky and went to number one gun to load it. While I loaded it, number two fired and I watched him do the same routine. He ran in circles, as if chasing his tail, and barked his head off. I knew for sure, now, that I was looking at a violently mangy animal.

For the next hour or so, the same act continued. We kept firing short bursts, with the dog going crazy behind the firing gun. At one point, it actually looked like he was foaming at the mouth. I knew he must have at least mange and probably rabies, so I kept my pistol close and I loosened the leather strap that kept the hammer down. I was ready if the insane animal ever attacked me.

Soon we ran out of ammo and headed back to Da Nang. I cleaned up the cargo compartment. I picked up the spent brass and links, replaced the empty ammo cans in their tie-down and safed the guns. After about fifteen minutes, I had the back cleaned up and moved forward in the dark to take a seat next to Ron.

As I sat down I felt a sharp pain in my right ass cheek. Spooky had struck again, and he was very vocal about it, but not nearly as vocal as I wanted to be. I jumped back and reached for my .45.

Ron jumped in front of me, he looked stern, "You scared Spooky. He was tired and sleeping and you sat on his injured head. Leave him alone. You're picking on him! He's just a defenseless animal. Don't pick on him!"

Pick on him? The son of a bitch is picking on *me*. He's taking my place in the heart of the crew. He's even eating my chow. The damn dog has to go!

I sat between the guns eyeing the dog and thought about ways to assassinate him. Poison came to mind. I would find another can of ham and lima beans and put arsenic in it. I hated to waste the ham and lima beans on this mangy mutt, but I couldn't tolerate this for one more night.

After landing on a beautiful dawn morning, the orange sky east of Da Nang was clear and cool. We got back into the bread truck to drop everyone off at their quarters. We were driving along the perimeter road by the Marine helicopters at about thirty miles an hour, when all of a sudden the damn dog began barking his head off. I picked up my feet and saw a flash as he dived past me out of the open door. He hit the dirt road tumbling forward in a cloud of dust, rolling over and over. I didn't have a clue what was happening, but Ron slammed on the brakes as I looked out.

The entire crew came forward and everyone crowded around the open sliding door as we watched Spooky jump at this ugly, bow-legged bulldog. Spooky was bigger, but the bull-dog hunkered down and faced him growling. They bared their teeth and circled each other like human boxers watching for an opening. Around and around they went, while a group of Marines gathered to watch the dogs facing off. We all climbed out of the truck and in a second Spooky jumped in, grabbed the other ugly dog by the scruff of the neck and shook him. The bull-dog yelped but Spooky held on.

One of the Marines kicked at Spooky.

Our Captain pilot said, "Stay out of it Sailor. Let them fight it out." Calling him 'sailor' was a left-handed insult to a marine.

After a couple of seconds, the bulldog got loose and ran into the Marine compound with Spooky in close pursuit.

Ron shouted, "Get him, Spooky."

One of the Marines gave him a look that would freeze hell but stopped short when he saw our three officers. They would not get to fight the Airmen today.

After a minute, Spooky walked back and jumped into the truck to the pats and pets of the entire crew, minus me. They were very proud that he had finally beaten the Marines' mascot. I heard later that the Marine mascot, "Chesty," named for the Korean War hero Chesty Puller, hung his head in shame and never went near the perimeter road again.

CHAPTER XI

AIRMEN GUNNERS

The next night I was to fly Spooky Three, the alert aircraft. That meant, we sat on the ground ready to go, while the other aircraft flew overhead on Combat Air Patrol, a form of airborne alert. In preparing for the night, we pre-flighted the airplane and then stood-by in an air-conditioned trailer until needed. We said we were spring-loaded to the combat condition, cocked and ready to fight.

With us on alert, there was always an airplane flying over the important base at Da Nang and ready to fight or to go to the biggest battle in I Corps. If the airborne airplane went to a fight, we took off and assumed the base defense role. When we were assigned to Spooky Three, we never knew when we would have to fly. Sometimes we had no mission and practiced our procedures the entire evening.

During ground alert, our pilot waited next to the red telephone, a direct line to the command post. When the phone rang we launched immediately.

In the communications chain, the command post was in constant contact with the higher echelon, corps command post, which was in contact with all troops in theater. For onsite coverage, an airplane aloft with command of all the flying assets in the corps area, and was able to direct their fire. That aircraft was always airborne and flew over the biggest and most important battle at all times. 'Cricket,' was the eyes and ears of the battlefield commander.

On this, my first ground alert, I had a long personal talk with Ron. Rather, Ron had long personal lessons for me. He and I were the only low-ranking airmen who were gunners. All the other gunners were older and more senior NCOs or sergeants. It was noteworthy that Ron was a lead gunner and selected to be my instructor at such a young age and minimum rank. There were certainly more senior and experienced instructors, but the chief gunner wanted Ron to teach because of his expertise and capability.

"Joe, let's talk about what it means to be a gunner. I don't mean the technical school part of being a gunner. This job needs much more than technical competence."

With a serious look on his face, Ron continued, "First of all, there are thousands of Airmen on this base who perform all the tough duties, and they don't get to fly."

He was right, because the airmen always performed the dirtiest and hardest work. They were the people who cooked the chow, cleaned the airplanes, fixed the trucks, humped the ammo, refueled the airplanes, cleaned the latrines and performed every other menial task. Airmen were the ones who worked all night on the graveyard shift and every weekend. Rank definitely had its privileges, and the airmen had no rank and no privileges.

"Every airman sees you in your flying suit," Ron said, "and envies your position, your flying pay and your special status. They hold you in high esteem, and they expect you to be an example. In particular, the weapons mechanics expect you to be harder working, smarter and better than they are. In everything you do, you must set the highest standards for them."

I knew he was right about that, as I had seen the envy in the other airmen's eyes. The cooks and M.P.s always watched me and the other flyboys with a wary eye. The supply troops and weapons mechanics treated me with more respect when I was wearing my flying suit than when I was wearing fatigues.

"Our Pilot, co-pilot and Navigator never get to fly with airmen. Heck, they hardly even meet airmen. Even the enlisted Loadmaster, Radio Operator and Engineer, rarely fly with airmen. You represent the entire enlisted corps to the officers, and the airmen to our NCOs. I expect your very best."

"Jeez, aren't you being a little dramatic?" I asked rubbing my chin.

"No, man. You and I are the Air Force test to see if airmen can cut the mustard. If one of us fails to live up to the highest standards, the Air Force will return to the requirement that all gunners be NCOs. There is a lot riding on your performance."

There had been a rumor that there were no other airmen gunners, but this was the first I heard of an official test program. I had seen that all the other flying enlisted members were at least Tech or Master sergeants. I knew the instructors watched me carefully, but they seemed to watch everyone carefully.

"We were selected because we were going to college at night and had advanced faster than most airmen. It took a special recommendation from our commanders and senior NCOs to go to gunners' school. That's an onus, an obligation we have to live up to."

"I'll try, Ron."

"It means more than just trying to be the best gunner you can, it means being the best airman and *man* you can be. I think we have to be the hardest working people on the airplane and willing to take on any task. We are the youngest and lowest ranking, so we have to be ready to help everyone on the crew and do everything we can to make the mission successful. When the loadmaster needs help, jump in. When the flight engineer is struggling, lend a hand. And do it cheerfully," he said with a broad smile.

"Okay," I said.

Ron's talk put me in a reflective mood. I wanted to be brave flying an airplane. I wanted look cool tooling around base in a flying suit, and get the respectful gazes of the other base people. But I had never thought of becoming every airman's role model.

"On the airplane," Ron continued, "you have to work hard, do your best, set the example and take on every task required. To the other troops and the Vietnamese, you have to be a man of great moral character. We must be honest, patriotic, honorable, and even chivalrous in our conduct in front of our allies. We have to work to learn, grow, and educate ourselves so we are setting the right example."

"Ron, that's a tall order. I expected to do my job and work to be the best gunner I can, not to run the entire effort in South Vietnam," I joked.

He had a look of distain on his face after my last smart-ass answer. "Joe this is a big job, I hope you're up to it."

"I'm up to it, Ron. I'll make you proud," I answered and walked outside to the airplane.

It was dark now and I climbed up the short ladder, into the cargo compartment of the Gooney Bird, to think about what Ron had said. It was very unusual to hear a young airman speak as he had. It was rare for one so young to speak of the morals and ethics of American fighting men. However, the more I thought about it the more I believed in what he had said.

He became a man in my eyes, no longer just my friend and playmate. He became my teacher, my leader, my mentor, I swore in my heart that I would do my part and live up to the high example he demanded.

I climbed out of the airplane and sat on the ramp under the wing. It was a bright, overcast night with low clouds. I watched for the lights of the lone gunship, circling overhead, assuring the safety of us all. I spent all night thinking about the onerous assignment Ron had given me.

Later, he came out and sat under the wing with me. No words passed between us, just a feeling of deep goodwill. We would be together throughout this ordeal.

I will do it, I thought. I will be the best I can be.

CHAPTER XII

CHARLEY ONE PLUNK

Since the base was still short of gunners, we had to fly every night. Tonight, I was flying Spooky One with a lead gunner; Country. Country was a thirty five year old lifer with a great deal of experience, who kept to himself. He quietly resided in a bunk near the door and secretly kept tabs on who came in and who left.

I went to Country's bunk, where he was lying down writing in his notebook everyone who came and left the hooch.

"Sarge, I'm Joe and am flying with you tonight."

"Okay, boy, grab yo' stuff and meet me at the bread truck in fifteen," he twanged back in a slow southern drawl. "Call me Country, boy, and welcome to the best damn aircrew at Da Nang!"

I walked back to my bunk, picked up my helmet and tools and went out back to the trucks. I saw Country coming out of the door dragging two enormous B-4 flight bags. B-4 bags were three feet square and one-foot high, olive drab rectangles for carrying ancillary aircraft parts and expendables. I helped Country heft one of the bags into the back of the truck and it felt like it weighed two hundred pounds.

"Damn, Sarge, what you got in these things?"

"Just extra ammo in case we need it, boy," he answered. I remembered hearing from the other gunners that he carried all kinds of things with him, lots of M16 ammo, and even hand-grenades he got from the Marines.

I had no fears about having extra ammo, hell extra ammo is the cure for every ailment in war. But hand-grenades? Hand-grenades were another thing. We rarely ever messed with them and I personally knew nothing about grenades.

Country started speaking slowly with a gleam in his eye. "They is a VC on the beach of Da Nang City that's a shooten' at us. It happen ev'ry day just after takeoff when we fly low over the water. We call him Charley One Plunk 'cause he takes a single shot at every airplane that takes off. I'm a gonna get him." He had a knowing smile on his lips and hate in his eyes.

"I thought that was a restricted fire zone, so how you going to get him?"

He unzipped the B-4 bag and pulled out a Mason jar, a normal glass jar. But it had a hand grenade in it.

"What's this?" I asked.

"It's a hand grenade with the pin removed, so when I throw it out of the airplane it smashes on the ground and the spoon flies off the grenade and it explodes, killing Charley One Plunk."

"Pretty cool," I replied.

We picked up the rest of the crew and they all spoke with southern drawls. I suspected they had gotten together to fly as a team because they were comfortable with each other.

I heard Country tell his pilot, "I'm a huntin' me a Cong 'coon' tonight."

"Don't do nothin' crazy. You know we can't fire at Da Nang beach," the pilot answered.

"I ain't firing; I'm a throwing this here delayed hand-grenade at him." He pulled out the bottled grenade from his bag.

"No, you ain't. You cain't throw the grenade or any of those little bombs out on Da Nang beach," his pilot ordered.

Now, I knew why the bags weighed so much. In them he had ten practice bombs, weighing twenty-six pounds each, that he had gotten from the bomb dump. He was planning to throw all those munitions at Charley One Plunk.

"Besides that, I don't want you killing Charley One Plunk. He's just shooting off his required quota of ammo. He ain't ever hit anything and if'n you kill him, they'll replace him with someone who can actually shoot and hit us. They could send in a real sharp shooter," his pilot replied.

"But, sir, he's the enemy and he's a trying to kill us," Country pleaded.

"Just leave him alone and he won't hurt us," was the final answer.

We took off and flew west about half way to the Ho Chi Minh trail to a free-fire area that Intel wanted us to hit. It was an H & I target and if we were successful, we'd disrupt the NVAs resupply efforts. We flew there and fired until we were out of ammo.

I noticed that Country kept separate empty ammo cans for the discarded steel links from the expended brass. When the gun was loaded, the individual rounds were stripped from their links, which provided a continuous belt, keeping the ammo flowing correctly. A second can under the gun caught the expended brass after the round was fired. Normally one can was used to catch both and then returned to the bomb dump for recycling. Tonight, Country carefully moved around the ammo cans to keep the links and brass separate.

After firing our ammo, we returned to Da Nang and I noticed that Country asked the pilot what landing pattern we were going to follow.

"We're landing on Runway 27 from over the water," the co-pilot replied.

Country smiled and signaled for me to bring over the four cans of empty links to where he squatted by the open door. I dragged the cans over. He had them open by the door and he kept putting his head out the door to look forward. As soon as we heard the landing gear come down he grabbed a can of links, dumped them out the door, then grabbed another and the third and the fourth and did the same, all with an eerie smile on his face. Before I knew what had happened, he had dumped the whole lot out the door. I had never seen anyone do this before and was somewhat befuddled, but said nothing.

"I got the son of a bitch," Country said, smiling, after we got back to the hooch.

"Who did you get?" I asked.

"I got Charley One Plunk. As we were coming in, I seen him fire from in front of us and directly in our path, so I dropped them links on his head. I got me a Cong Coon."

"Your pilot said not to get him."

Laughingly, he said, "No, boy, my pilot said I couldn't shoot him in the no-fire zone—and I didn't shoot."

I sat back and considered the answer but other issues pushed it out of my mind for the time being.

This was my first time to consider the accuracy of the enemy gunners. Charley One Plunk was merely firing to use up his quota of ammo, purposely never hitting anything. But on the next few missions, I faced the wrath of a true sharp-shooter, the dreaded nine level gunner.

CHAPTER XIII

THE NINE LEVEL GUNNER

We drove to a Quonset hut surrounded by a twelve-foot high fence and barbed wire. There was a Security Police Guard who checked our identification and then let us proceed into the building. We went into a small theater-like room that had comfortable looking seats. We sat and an officer entered and went to the stage.

The Captain from Intelligence began his briefing. "There is a report that the VC has opened an anti-aircraft gunnery school on the Ho Chi Minh trail. Here's the scenario: They have an instructor gunner who is an extremely accurate nine level. He launches up an artillery flare that burns very bright, when it opens he shoots at it with tracer ammo. You can tell it's him, because the rounds are dead-eye all over the flare.

After he instructs the students, he gets off the gun and one of them mounts. Another flare is shot up and the student practices firing at it. Now, we think you can watch for this pattern and when the student gets on the gun, his rounds will be erratic and miss the flare. Then you can zoom in and shoot up the whole camp. However, we do not recommend flying the low—and slow—gunship directly at the nine level, as you are too vulnerable a target."

The term nine level came from the Air Force system of upgrade training, whereby an airman began as a three level trainee, took tests to become a five level specialist, grew in experience to become a seven level technician, and finally qualified as an extremely capable nine level superintendent. The designation of nine level commanded the greatest respect for his experience.

In the truck on the way to the airplane, Ron's pilot briefed us on our course of action.

"If we don't have a TIC (Troops in Contact) mission, we will go over to the anti-aircraft gunnery school and take a shot. The crew from Spooky One-Three almost got hit last night, and asked us to take care of the problem for them. Nav, plot a course for the school and we will stay about ten miles back, with the engines as quiet as possible, and observe the firing pattern. When we see the nine level get off the gun we will put all three guns on the line and scream in at the highest possible speed. I'll kick the rudder over the camp, fire and leave as fast as possible."

We took off and proceeded as briefed, arriving about ten miles from the school just as night enveloped the jungle and eventually our airplane. We looked out of the aircraft door, straining our eyes to see the flare.

"There it is," said the co-pilot.

I watched as the tracers arced up from the dark jungle below toward the flare, which was about six or seven thousand feet above. Whoever was shooting was very accurate. This gunner was good. Things had changed.

There was a short pause in the firing, then another flare went up and the rounds arced up but were nowhere near the flare.

"Here we go, crew. Put the guns on the line: we're on our way." We dashed at the target, engines at full power, and the props straining. We armed all three guns and peered out the door to see the action. We were approaching at top speed, one hundred twenty knots, and just over the target, the pilot kicked the left rudder hard and I held on for dear life. This was the sharpest pylon turn I ever mad I heard our guns roar and I thought I saw a big gun in the clearing with lots of black pajamas running to and fro. In less than ten seconds, we were done and flying east away from the target.

"Nice shooting, Pilot," Ron said. "I saw them running for their lives. I think you got most of them."

"Thanks, crew, good job. We showed them!" The pilot boasted.

This, however, was not the last I would hear about the nine level gunner. A couple of weeks later, as I was flying with Country and his crew, I was at the Intel briefing and the captain Intel officer gave the same scenario. The school shot up a flare, the nine level shot at it, a student took over, and it was easy pickings from there.

So we repeated our efforts of a couple of weeks earlier, watching for the flare after sunset and getting ready. I heard Country and the pilot talking about a turkey shoot and Country's pilot said, "I been a-looking to get that turkey for a couple of weeks."

Guns armed to the teeth, engines to the max, Country and I stood in the door laughing. Going at full bore when the rounds were all over the sky, we flew in directly over the target. All of sudden something was wrong—I saw tracers coming directly at me, big red tracers.

I had been told that when the tracers stop moving across the sky in a tiny red arc, they are coming right at you. These looked like big red stoplights. I hit the floor and heard a crack in the tail behind me, just as our guns sputtered and then went silent. The pilot kicked an abbreviated pylon turn and dove the airplane for speed as we high-tailed it out of there, with tracers chasing us all the way for a few miles.

I looked straight down at the dark clearing in the jungle. I could barely make out the outline of a Bofors 40MM anti-aircraft pom pom gun. I thought I could see the old nine level gunner still on the gun, wearing a big shit-eating grin on his face, with all the students in a line feeding five round clips into the gun. I saw flashes from the dual barrels as tracers once again streamed straight for me. I ducked down and heard the wind screaming by the door as we raced away at top speed, escaping the fangs of a flak trap.

"I got the airplane. Is everyone okay back there?" the pilot asked. "I can't trim the damn thing, did we take any hits? You guys inspect the airplane for damage!"

I looked around to assess damage and noticed Country lying face down on the floor. The loadmaster was crumpled in the back corner. I didn't see any damage, though, and helped Country get up.

"What the hell was that?" he inquired over the intercom.

"That's a classic flak trap, where the gunner sucks you in and at the last moment lets loose on you. I don't think he got us though," the pilot answered.

"I can't trim the airplane; it wants to go to the left. Are you sure nothing got hit back there?"

Country checked the entire rear of the aircraft. After asking permission, he turned the lights on.

"I don't see any damage," he reported.

"Engineer, go back there and check the control surfaces. I'm having too much trouble keeping it flying straight," the pilot ordered.

The master sergeant flight engineer came back and looked all around the cargo compartment. He looked out of the windows at the flaps and ailerons but found no damage. He next leaned out of the cargo door and looked toward the rear of the airplane. After about thirty seconds, he came back inside and called the pilot.

"Pilot, Engineer. We were hit in the rudder, but it looks like it's still functioning."

"Engineer, watch the vertical stabilizer while I move it left and right."

"Roger, sir."

The Engineer leaned out the door a long way, teetering on the restraining strap, and watched the vertical stabilizer as the airplane yawed left and right.

"I see about a one foot chunk taken out of the upper half of the stabilizer."

"Okay, crew, we're on our way back to Da Nang. Put on your parachutes and be prepared for an emergency landing. I don't know what other damage we sustained," the pilot instructed.

"When we get to within gliding distance I will test the landing gear and hydraulics systems to insure everything is okay."

"Radio, call ahead and let the squadron operations officer know we are returning early with undetermined damage."

I pulled out my emergency checklist and began safing the guns. Country stood next to the gunner's arming panel, safing the weapons switches. He came over, shouting over the engine noise.

"Get your landing gear failure checklist out and go over it."

"Okay, Country," I yelled back and opened my checklist.

While the landing preparations were going on, I thought back to what had happened. How had we gotten into this predicament? Had the nine level known we were out there, ready to pounce on him? Had he seen us operate this scenario too often?

"Cricket, this is Spooky," the pilot radioed. "We were just jumped by a flak trap out by the trail. I think you need to send fast-movers in on it." Fast-movers were fighter bomber jets that scream over the trees so fast that the gunners don't have time to train their weapons on them.

"Roger, Spooky, we'll take it under advisement."

"Okay, crew, we're five minutes out. Make sure everything is tied down and get ready to observe the landing gear extension," the pilot said.

"Gear down, three green lights," the copilot said, with relief in his voice.

We landed on the long ten-thousand-foot runway 09 as fire trucks followed us with their lights flashing. We taxied back to our original parking slot at the gunship ramp, rather than shutting down on the runway, the procedures for an emergency landing. I think the crew was too embarrassed to shut down and bring further attention to our predicament. They instead wanted to crawl back to the safety of the gunship nest.

We got out and inspected the airplane. There was a one square foot section missing from the vertical stabilizer, shot off clean. It looked like a giant hand had grabbed the stabilizer and just broken off a section. It didn't look like a bullet hole or shrapnel hole.

We got into the crew truck and Country spoke first.

"What the hell happened?" he asked.

"I guess the nine level knew we were out there, and pretended that he was a student firing all over the sky. He must have known we were inbound and aimed his loaded gun where we came over the trees. The nine level just blasted away at point blank range. He had us dead to rights and thankfully only one round hit us before I got off a few rounds," the pilot said.

After the debriefing, the Intel officer told us that a flight of four F-4 Phantoms had gone in after we left and destroyed the enemy camp and weapons.

The only comment worth repeating was on the trip back to the hooch.

"We taught that stupid son of a bitch a lesson!" Country said.

Laughing to myself, I wondered who had taught whom a lesson.

CHAPTER XIV

LAST FLIGHT WITH COUNTRY

The next night, I was again scheduled to fly with Country and his crew. We followed our normal routine, takeoff for base CAP, and fly around for a couple of hours. I was getting a cool sleep on the floor of the airplane.

I was startled awake by a recurring dream, in which I could see my wife and daughter standing in the cold rain at my funeral. They looked so forlorn and alone, as if no one in the whole world cared about them. These thoughts made me sad, as I felt that I had not done enough for them. Sure, I had G.I. insurance, but I had not really done what a father and husband should do to make them safe and secure.

The engines of the airplane brought me back to the present, as the big radials revved up to full speed.

"We have a mission," the pilot said over the head set.

"We're going south, where a single tracked vehicle is bogged down and under attack. The weather is keeping the helicopters on the ground and we are to defend the vehicle until help arrives. Country, get the guns ready. We are fifteen minutes out. Prepare for combat!"

We armed the guns, turned off the light and stood in the open doorway looking for the target area. "There it is. It's a giant flame-thrower shooting in a circle."

I saw a tracked vehicle that looked like a tank, but it was shooting out a flame about fifty yards long. The turret rotated fifteen degrees and it shot out another flame, rotated, and shot another, time after time. We entered the firing circle and began shooting short bursts around the perimeter where the flame-thrower was shooting. I did not see any return fire and was just amazed by the sight of streams of burning napalm, lighting up the entire countryside.

Number one gun malfunctioned and I ran around to fix it. When I passed behind number two gun, I stepped on something big and round and my feet slipped out from under me. I fell down on my back, hard, on the floor of the cargo compartment. What was that? I felt around to see what I had tripped on. My hand hit something hard and sharp; it was the fin of one of the twenty-six-pound bombs that Country kept in his B-4 bag. I picked up the little bomb, went over to Country and said, "Keep these damn things out of the way; I nearly killed myself. I'm more scared of flying with you and your makeshift arsenal than I am of the enemy! Put this shit away and never bring it on an airplane again."

I brushed myself off and returned to fixing number one gun, angry at the ridiculous situation created by Country. After a couple of minutes, I calmed down and my thoughts returned to the situation below.

We stayed over the flame-thrower for a couple of hours, until the recovery team arrived and the enemy departed. Country and I cleaned up the cargo compartment and prepared for landing.

"Roger, left downwind for runway nine," the pilot radioed the tower.

We proceeded into our normal landing pattern over the beach and I watched out of the door as we approached Da Nang. The bright lights of the gigantic runway never failed to impress me as we approached.

"Gear down," the pilot ordered.

"Gear in transition. Three green lights. Gear down and locked," answered the co-pilot.

"What the hell was that flash below us on the beach?" the pilot asked.

"Tower, Spooky, what was that flash on the beach?"

Our crewmember interrupted, "Pilot, pilot, radio operator! A round just passed through the radio compartment. We're being shot at."

"Da Nang tower, Spooky is taking fire from the beach; we'll continue our landing, but alert the Marine helicopters," the pilot called out.

"Roger Spooky, Da Nang Tower. We have had reports that the VC replaced Charley One Plunk with someone who can shoot and he has hit three airplanes today."

The pilot yelled into the microphone "Country, I *told* you not to fuck with that old Charley One Plunk. Now they've replaced him with a back-woods sharpshooter who is causing havoc for all the airplanes. You had better listen to me in the future or you're never flying with me again."

"Yes, sir," Country whined back contritely.

The truth was that he was the real threat to our lives, with his dopey bombs rolling around the airplane, his failure to follow clear orders and the makeshift hand-grenades in jars he loved to carry.

I resolved to never fly with Country again and if told I had to fly with him I would tell the chief gunner about the danger he caused for the entire crew and airplane.

As the saying goes, it is better to fight with a crazed enemy in front of you than with an insane ally behind you.

CHAPTER XV

FLYING WITH SLICK

"We're critically short of gunners, so you're flying with Slick tonight," Commando Jerry said. He smiled and shrugged his shoulders, "Be ready to work hard, Slick believes in the second gunner doing everything."

I barely knew Slick, despite living in the same hooch. He bunked ten beds forward, close to the entrance and kept quiet and to himself. I had heard some remarks about him being married and cheating every chance, so I had doubts about his character. Ron called him a sleaze-ball.

I looked him over as I approached his bunk. He had longish, light brown hair that was Brylcreamed back in a smooth style. He had a round, cherubic, pretty face, a little pudgy. His blue eyes quickly darted from face to face, all over the room. His body was a little flaccid and weak, as if he didn't get to the gym often enough. His skin looked pasty white, so pale I was sure he never went out in the sunshine. I introduced myself.

"Hey, Sarge, I'm Joe, your second gunner tonight."

"Hi Joe. There's nothing big going on, so I expect a quiet night. I'll meet you by the crew vans at 2300. You drive," he answered.

"Thanks. I'll be there."

We picked up the equipment and the rest of his crew. They seemed a very quiet bunch, with no introductions and very little talk. We drove to the Intelligence building.

The captain began briefing us. "For the last two nights the VC have been attacking a small outpost along the coast, call sign Tactical Spider. They have fought off the VC, but may need your help so be prepared to go there when your base CAP mission is over."

We took off and began circling Da Nang for a long, boring night. I went over to talk to Slick but only received one word answers to my questions, so I quit after a couple of yes's and no's. He was either uncommunicative or just didn't like me. I pulled down a canvas gun-cover and laid it on the floor to make a bed for a little nap, and noticed that Slick had a big, civilian, down-filled sleeping bag in the back of the airplane, where he intended to camp out for the night.

I turned on the high-intensity light and wrote a ten-page letter home to my Tonia and Cindy. I filled them in on all of my first impressions of Da Nang and my friends, but did not mention the combat missions or anything that could scare them. After writing for a couple of hours, I turned off the light and put my head down to nap.

Hours later, I heard the engines speed up, signaling we were off to fight. I jumped up and turned up the volume of my headset to hear what they were saying.

"Pilot, Nav. heading of one eight zero, southbound for Tactical Spider, thirty minutes out."

"Roger, Nav. Look over your notes from Intel and brief the crew," the pilot answered.

"Crew, we're going to Tactical Spider, which is being attacked by the VC from all directions. The commander and first sergeant are on top of the water tower with a 50-caliber machine gun and M-16s with all tracers. They will mark the VC and direct our fire from the tower. The rest of their troops are in a thick, sand-bag bunker under the tower, guarding access to the entire fort. Any questions?" he asked.

Slick answered, "No questions. Number one is on the line."

I went to the door and looked forward. I could just see a thin stream of smoke wisp up in the air against the cloud backdrop. As we got closer, I saw the outline of TS with the tower in the middle and a ring of fires around the perimeter, about three hundred yards in diameter. I heard the Nav talking to the commander on the ground.

"Tactical Spider, Spooky Two approaching from the north, two minutes out. What's the situation?"

A deep southern voice answered, "Spooky, Tactical Spider. The VC are coming over the fence on the western side, and I need maximum fire. I will show you where to shoot with a burst of tracers."

The pilot ordered, "Slick, put two guns on the line. I want to surprise the enemy."

I went around to number two gun, doing my part while Slick stayed by the arming panel. I walked back to stare out the open door at the fight.

We were close now and I could see quite a bit, because of the bright fires on the perimeter. Twenty yards inside the razor wire fences, there were fighting trenches and there was a bare area about 250 yards square. Inside the perimeter of the trenches was a row of tents, with truck parking to the right and a water tower in the center with a large sandbag bunker under it. As I looked at the water tower, a long burst of tracers shot out like a finger pointing about one hundred yards away on the fence in the west. As soon as the tracers had fired, every gun in Vietnam started firing back at the water tower. It looked like D-Day all over again.

We rolled into the thirty-degree bank and fired both guns along the fence. The Cong, firing at the water tower, stopped immediately. I moved to the line of ammo cans and got one ready. I began loading the empty guns and thought: what a brave son of a bitch that Tactical Spider was. He had his troops protected in the bunker and he was on top of the wooden tower directing fire. Every time he fired, all the VC guns trained on him, trying to kill him. But he kept it up, despite the phenomenal danger. The tracers showed us where to shoot, but they also pointed back to where he was, showing the way to the Cong.

"They're coming over the east wall. Watch my fire," he yelled.

Again, I saw the stream of tracers from the tower. Then all hell broke loose as hundreds of guns fired back. I thought he was surely dead by now.

We rolled in and fired at the east side of the fort, later the north side and back to the west. After an hour were getting low on ammo and I heard the pilot tell him, "I called Da Nang and they're sending a replacement gunship in about an hour. We'll shoot more slowly to conserve our ammo until they get here."

He answered, "Roger Spooky, they have fallen back to regroup, so you can take it easy for the time being. Before you depart, though would you fire a big burst of all your remaining ammo into the jungle east of here where they are camping out?"

Just then he began again. "I spoke too soon—here they come from the east!"

He fired a burst of tracers and the VC were ready because all kinds of guns trained their return fire on the tower. It looked like they'd found a big, 50-caliber to shoot at him as I could see larger tracers than normal coming from the south. We rolled in on his red indicator and began firing. As soon as we fired, the enemy fire stopped. We moved over and trained the guns in the direction of the 50-caliber fire, and let them have a nice long burst.

"Good shooting, Spooky. You got the 50-caliber crew," Tactical Spider called.

"Thanks, we'll fire our remaining ammo into the jungle and depart."

After landing and cleaning up the airplane, we dropped off the rest of the crew and returned to our hooch. After showering, I hit the rack and had long dreams of my wife and daughter.

• • •

I felt someone shaking my bunk as I rolled out of a foggy sleep. I looked up and saw a huge, barrel-chested black man in pickle-colored jungle fatigues and a helmet. He looked to be about thirty five years old, medium height and built like a tank with a sixty-inch chest. He had a 50-caliber bandoleer over his shoulder. He had the subdued gold oak leaf of a major on his helmet.

"Were you on Spooky Two last night?" he asked.

"Yes, sir, I was," I rubbed sleep from my eyes.

"Then this is for you," he said as he pushed forward a fifth of liquor in a dark brown bottle.

"Sir, I don't understand."

"Son, I'm Tactical Spider." He had a bemused smile, "I wanted to thank your crew for helping us out last night. You did a fine job," he eyes were bright and laughing.

Flabbergasted, I answered, "Thanks, sir—we were just trying to hel—"

He continued, "The troops appreciate your support and you got most of the VC. Now, where are your officers? I want to bring them a little present too."

I got up from my bunk, pulled on my flying suit and answered, "I have a truck out back, I'll take you there."

"No need, I have a Jeep; just show me where it is."

I finished dressing and showed him where Slick was asleep and he gave me another bottle with instructions to give it to him when he woke up.

I walked outside with the major and saw an olive-drab WWII Jeep with a 50-caliber mounted on top and a long whip antenna bent down over the front. There was the first sergeant sitting in the open driver's seat with his right foot on the dash. He had a radio to his ear, giving instructions.

"You drove up here in that?" I asked incredulously. *He had driven one of the most dangerous roads in-country to bring us some booze and thought nothing of it.*

"Yeah, it's just an hour and a half. I needed extra ammo anyway," he answered.

"Follow me," I said as I got in our crew van and led him to the officer's compound. I introduced him to the Slick's pilot and left.

On the way back to my hooch I couldn't help reflecting on the remarkable heroism of Tactical Spider. I have never seen a more valorous or brave human being in my life. After assuring the safety of his troops in a fully protected bunker; he purposely and repeatedly exposed himself to enemy fire to enable us to destroy the VC. If he's not the definition of heroism, courage and valor, I don't know who is.

CHAPTER XVI

THE FAC (FORWARD AREA CONTROLLED)

That night I was assigned to fly with Slick and his crew again. We were ready early and drove to the chow hall to eat before picking up the rest of the crew. The normally silent Slick started a conversation when we sat down at the square four-man table.

"I met a friend of yours when I was on R & R. A guy named Big Don, a master sergeant running the gunners down south," he began.

"I'm not sure he's a friend of mine, but I know him from Hurlburt and survival school."

"They tell a story about him. On his first combat mission, he fell and cut his hand on a C ration can and went to the medics the next day and demanded a purple heart."

"Who ever heard of a purple heart for a cut from a C Ration can?" I asked.

"He told the medics it happened during a fire fight, and they wrote the medal out for him."

"Amazing," I said. "It sounds like Don: always trying to get something for nothing."

Slick went on, "I think it's pretty cool. If you get six purple hearts you get to go home early. I'll drop a can of ammo on my foot and see if they'll give me one," he joked.

"Yeah, and I have an ingrown toenail."

It bothered me that Don would tell someone he was my friend, and that he would take advantage of the system to get a medal he didn't deserve. I wondered what in his personality was so weak that it cried for the attention of a medal. I felt sorry for him, but in a strange way— as one feels sorry for a bear with his leg in a trap, sorry but wary. It all sounded pretty low-class and tasteless to me. Furthermore, it caused an ache in the pit of my stomach to think that most of the real heroes had *earned* their purple hearts and he was lessening the value of the medal by arranging to get one undeservedly. But it sure sounded like Don.

We finished chow, picked up the crew and went to Intel. The Intel officer introduced a captain in an Army flying suit. He called him a Forward Area Controller, or FAC.

"He's one of the FAC's responsible for a specific area. In his area he flies low and slow every day. As there are no fire fights going on tonight, I thought he would fly with you and show you his area of operations (AOR) and have you H & I any suspicious activity."

We all got into the van and drove to the flight line while the FAC explained himself. "I fly an O-1 bird dog, a single-engine, high-wing puddle jumper, made by Cessna. It lets me see the entire AOR where I know all of the villages and the chieftains. They tell me when anything bad is happening, and I call in friendly fire and use my smoke rockets to mark targets. I am concerned about one section where the chieftain is afraid to go, where he thinks the VC are building up their forces. I would like you to fly over that area and fire on anything suspicious. The Chieftain assures me there will be no villagers there tonight." The FAC spoke with great assurance.

We took off and followed the FAC's directions to an area fifty miles west of Da Nang. It was just turning dusk and we were at six thousand feet while the FAC spoke about the area over the interphone. "This is called Jinks Valley. The river runs west to east, and is swollen with water this time of year, during the rainy season. Most of the year it's just a trickle. The jungles and hills surrounding it are prime hiding places for the VC.

In the plains to the east are large rice paddies tended by friendly villagers, who only want to be left alone to raise their families and live in harmony with nature. Charley comes in and intimidates the villagers to act as scouts and spies for him, revealing all the locations of the Americans. Occasionally the VC steals the rice the villagers grow. The villagers help us find and eliminate the enemy."

I looked out the rear door and saw the beautiful area from a whole new perspective. The placid river meandered through a lush green jungle, surrounded by densely-covered low hills. This place was a lovely home to peaceful people who only wanted to be left alone.

To the east I could see orderly dikes separating square rice paddies. Often there was a placid bamboo hut beside the paddy. It looked like a nice peaceful area for simple, honest peasants to raise their families.

We flew over the area, just admiring the docile and serene sight for over an hour. After it became dark, the FAC pulled out his portable FM radio and spoke to another airborne FAC flying below.

"That FAC is a friend of mine. We can trust his guidance," he began. "And he sees VC camp fires in the jungle north of the bend in the river."

We descended to three thousand feet, entered the firing circle and fired a short burst where directed. I saw nothing but the stream of tracers pointing to the ground north of the river. We fired again and again, while Slick and I reloaded the guns as required.

We moved our firing circle north at the direction of the airborne FAC, and fired again.

"Spooky, you're taking ground fire," the radio blared as the FAC warned us. I stared out into the black night but saw nothing. Eventually, I thought I saw a single muzzle flash and reported, "Ground fire, eight o'clock by the river. A single shot."

"It's just the reflection of the moon off of ground water," Slick said over the intercom.

I was somewhat miffed. The tone of his voice indicated that he was questioning my integrity. But I let it go.

After landing, we were post-flighting the aircraft when a crew chief, the mechanic assigned to that particular aircraft, came up to Slick and said, "There's a bullet hole in the bottom of the aircraft, near the entrance door."

Slick walked over and looked. I followed and saw them examining the small hole under the curved bottom of the fuselage. They called over the rest of the aircrew and the FAC and showed off the bullet hole.

Our pilot said, "I guess your FAC buddy was right, we were taking ground fire."

CHAPTER XVII

CHECK RIDE PREPARATION

The next night I was back with Ron, preparing to pick up the crew and sit ground alert on mission Spooky Three. On the way Ron said, "This is our last night together. Commando Jerry is giving you a check ride tomorrow. If you pass, you become a lead gunner when we get the new airmen next week for our second gunners."

"Do you really think I'm ready?" I asked.

"You're ready and I recommended you. But before we're done tonight, I'll tell you exactly what to expect and we'll practice different scenarios. Okay?"

"Yeah, but I could sure use some work. Show me what to do. My only check ride was at Hurlburt and this will be much harder."

After the pre-flight Ron said, "It's like standing up on a surfboard. Once you do it you never forget how. Let's stay here and practice. First, remember that Commando Jerry is fair. He is incredibly cool and has been through hundreds of missions. There are two things he fails guys for. If you are ever the cause of a gun breaking, you're done. He can live with you not being able to fix everything that can possibly go wrong, but don't do something that damages a gun. And second, you better know your procedures for aircraft emergencies and protecting the crew. He will ask you every single bold face checklist item you have. That's why I had you practice them every time we flew."

Ron and I stayed at the airplane for hours. He had me run through every conceivable safety malfunction. He meticulously went over each and every checklist, many times, until I knew it cold. He made me practice procedures: crash-landing, fire in the cargo compartment, flare-fire, run-away-gun and the other five or six checklists the gunners have.

On that last night, Ron also had special guidance for my personal development. "Joe, you can do better than this. You don't have to be a gun-monkey for the rest of your life. I really think you can apply yourself and become an officer. At the very minimum, you can get a college education. I think your major weakness is a lack of confidence in your mental and educational ability."

"I don't know, Ron. Those guys in college are a lot smarter than me. This is all the opportunity I ever wanted."

"All of us think the people in college are smarter than we are. A hell of a lot of them *are* smarter than you, but you don't have to be smarter than all of them, you just have to be smart enough to pass. You don't have to be the smartest in the whole school, you just have to be willing to work hard, and I have seen you work hard. Your family deserves better. Hell, *you* deserve better. You can do a lot more than clean guns the rest of your life. As a matter of fact it is a patriotic duty to become as educated as possible, so you can do more for your country."

Ron continued. "I heard about a soldier who got a battle field commission and went on to become the Chief of Staff of the Army. There are opportunities out there and it is your responsibility to take advantage of them and do the best you can for your family and the country."

I mulled over what he'd said that night, during my preparations for my check ride. When I looked over from studying my emergency checklist, Ron was studying his text books. In fact, he was always studying when he wasn't flying. I thought over his advice and realized that he never went to the club and drank with the other gunners, he never played poker all night and he never just hung around and wasted his time. It struck me that he spent all of his time being the best gunner he could or studying his texts to become the best man he could.

"I will be just like him," I swore.

CHAPTER XVIII

CHECK RIDE

I was as ready as possible when Commando Jerry came to my rack the next night before my check ride. His eyes looked worn and grey and his shoulders were slouched. He immediately relaxed me by explaining, "This is just another mission. My job is to confirm what the other lead gunners have told me: that you're ready. So take it easy and recite your run-away gun procedures."

As we walked out of the hooch, Ron looked over at me and said, "Surf's up, hang ten." I didn't understand everything that meant, but took it as a comment wishing me good luck. With his right hand, he made the 'Hang in there' sign.

I mentally went through my emergency procedures during the truck ride until we picked up the remainder of the crew. At Intel we were told that there was not much action. We were to fly base CAP until just before daylight and after that they wanted us to hit an H & I target by Hue Phubi.

We went to the airplane and surprisingly, Commando Jerry helped me get the gunners' compartment prepared for the night's work. He set up the ammo and guns and didn't seem to pay much attention to me. I was relaxed as we took off and began flying circles over Da Nang. I recalled a comment of Jerry's that most missions

131

were, "Hours and hours of utter boredom, punctuated by seconds of stark terror!"

I thought it was a strange comment, but would learn later how prophetic and descriptive it really was. I settled down to a long night looking over my checklist. I also had *Catch 22* with me and kept reading it. Around 4:00 A.M. the pilot told the navigator, "Plot a course to the H & I target."

"Got it. A heading of 345 should get us there in twenty-five minutes," he answered.

We proceeded to the target and the pilot briefed us. "There is an H & I target fifteen to twenty miles west of Hue that we are going to spend a couple of hours shooting up. Keep your eyes open to see if we get any return fire, as the Marines believe there is a brigade-sized force there. If we can determine exactly where the brigade is located, it will greatly help. Now, arm the weapons and prepare for battle!"

Commando Jerry assumed the position of lead gunner by the control panel and I stationed myself by number one gun for the start of firing. Firing went well, with short bursts at the objective, as all of the crew watched for return fire. I went from gun to gun, loading them. After about thirty minutes, number two malfunctioned.

I disconnected the cannon plug from the drive motor and removed the safety sector from the top of the gun. The safety sector is the most important mechanical device on the gun. It is a three-inch wide, six-inch long part of the housing that contains the critical section of the cam path. The bolts follow this to push the round into the breach and lock it, then rotate to release the firing pin and shoot the round. When the safety sector is removed, the gun cannot fire. Disconnecting the cannon plug electrically isolates the gun, and the safety sector mechanically isolates the gun.

I went around to the right side of the gun and fixed the feeder jam, then put the gun together and went back around the left side to arm it. As I installed the pip-pin that holds the safety sector in place, it did not operate smoothly. It was a three-inch long pip-pin, with a button in the handle that released two ball bearings in order to re-move it from the gun.

To reinstall it, a gunner pushed the button, which retracted the ball bearings. The pin could then be installed in the gun to secure the safety sector. Releasing the pin allowed the ball bearings to extend, and locked the pin and safety sector in place. In this case, the pin did not operate smoothly and I put it in place anyway.

A couple of minutes later, Commando turned on the switch to activate number two gun and it began shooting at its full speed of six thousand rounds a minute. Suddenly it slammed to a halt and the cargo compartment filled with smoke.

I ran around, disconnected the cannon plug and immediately saw the problem. The pip-pin I had put in had fallen out during firing, so the safety sector flew off. The next bolt that came through at high speed hit the side of the housing, the roller was sheared off and the entire gun rotor seized up. This was a catastrophic failure.

Commando came over to look. He signaled me to safe the gun and go to the gunners' arming panel. I did and he came over and pulled back my earpiece so he could talk directly to me without the rest of the crew hearing.

"What the hell happened to the safing sector?" he asked.

"The pip-pin came out and sheared the roller off the bolt," I an-swered.

"How did the pip pin come out?"

"It was damaged and I didn't think anything about it until it fell out during firing."

"Okay, you run the control panel as number one gunner and I'll take care of the guns."

I went to the control panel and began operating the firing switches as normal. I knew I'd caused the problem. I should have noticed the pip pin was sticking and taken one off of another gun and kept them all operating, one at a time. Now number two was really messed up. We could not take it totally apart in the airplane, and besides we didn't have a spare bolt to fix it with. Man I'd dicked that one up.

I was sure I had flunked! Jesus, what was I going tell Ron and the other gunners? I mused as Commando worked on the remaining guns.

I felt like hell. I had committed the greatest mistake a gunner could make. I had caused the malfunction. I alone was at fault for damaging a perfectly good weapon, and probably should be grounded and never allowed to fly again. Perhaps they'd assign me to the gunroom where I'd clean dirty weapons for the duration of my tour.

I couldn't believe that I'd let my crew and the other gunners down. My moment of thoughtlessness had resulted in the loss of a gun and exposed my crew—and the Marines on the ground—to great danger.

Hating myself and feeling like crap, I continued operating the control panel as the sun gradually came up. It was a new day. I would just have to live with the consequences and swear to do better if I ever got another chance.

Commando signaled to me that we were out of ammunition and I informed the pilot.

"Okay, guys," the pilot said, "wrap it up. We're out of ammo and about to RTB to Da Nang. No more fun today. It's too light to fire anyway. Let's go home."

He turned the airplane south and I saw the beautiful green jungle in the dawn light with thin, white, wispy ground fog floating over the river. I thought about what would happen. Then the copilot broke the silence. "There's a single person standing in that rice paddy, pointing a gun at us."

"Give me the binoculars," the pilot answered. "He's not pointing a gun at us, he has his hands raised in surrender in the middle of the rice paddy!"

I grabbed my pair of binoculars, went to the back door, and stood next to Commando. As the pilot entered a thirty-degree left bank, I saw a figure barely discernable, standing up between rice paddies on a dike, with his hands in the air.

"He's watched us firing into the jungle and thinks we're about to shoot him. He wants to surrender. What the hell do we do now?" the copilot asked.

"Shoot him," someone remarked.

"Don't be ridiculous," the pilot answered. "We don't shoot unarmed people who are surrendering. Radio, call the control agency and have them send out someone to pick him up. He may have information for Intel."

"Roger, sir," the radio operator answered.

As he made the call, Spooky One-Three was returning back to Da Nang and apparently heard of our situation. I recognized Country's pilot's twang over the radio, "Spooky, this is Spooky One-Three, what you boys up to? I heard you got a captive?"

"Rog, Spooky. The Marines are sending a chopper."

Then a disembodied voice over the radio said, "Shoot the gook! Shoot the gook!"

My pilot answered, "We're warriors, not murderers. We'll wait for the chopper."

"Okay, Spooky. See you back at the ranch, One-Three out," came the only answer.

I wanted to get back to Da Nang, but was very proud of the pilot for his stance. I had heard stories of torture, rape and murder by insane Americans. However, this crew was going to do the right thing.

Within fifteen minutes, a chopper flew down to the dike and picked up the surrendering prisoner, and we returned to Da Nang.

After landing and cleaning up the airplane, we dropped off the crew and drove back to squadron operations for my check-ride debriefing. All the while Commando filled out the forms required to document a check ride, and wrote his remarks.

We sat down in the debriefing room on both sides of a table and the squadron operation officer came in. He was a major, wearing an old worn flying suit, and he said nothing.

Commando began, "Joe, nice job, you knew your emergency check lists cold and did a perfect pre-flight. Your interaction with the crew was fine and you took great care of the weapons. The only question I have is: what happened when number two malfunctioned?"

I took a second and then answered truthfully. "When I put the gun together, the pip-pin didn't feel right. It felt like there was grit or dirt in it, and it didn't operate smoothly. However, when I inserted it in the safety sector, I thought it was okay. It seemed to work, but obviously didn't. It fell out during firing and broke the gun."

"I'm impressed with your honesty, but not with your attention to detail. You have to make sure everything is perfect with the gun. That is the only thing you can control: the gun. Your crew and every Marine expect you to be perfect. Never let the smallest defect go undetected and immediately correct the slightest problem. Never let a gun fire if you are not positive it's in the best working order possible."

Ron had warned me that I must never be responsible for damaging the guns, and I had failed. I lowered my eyes to my boots, ready for the hammer to come down. I felt miserable. I had failed to protect my airplane and crew and had damaged a gun.

"However," Commando Jerry continued, "I am certifying that you are qualified to be a lead gunner. Sure, you made a mistake, but you corrected it immediately and went on to fly a nearly perfect mission. I will be watching you and will fly again with you in three months. Welcome to the ranks of lead gunners," he concluded.

I let out a sigh. A weight had been taken off my chest. I felt elation and joy, sprinkled with embarrassment. I returned to the hooch, where Ron was waiting up for me.

"How'd you do?" he asked.

"Not good. I broke a gun! The pip-pin in the safety sector fell out during firing and broke off a bolt roller," I explained.

"Jeeze, did you really? I'll bet Commando ripped your head off!" he remarked.

"No, he passed me, but gave me a come-to-Jesus ass-chewing session I will never forget," I answered.

"Wow, he passed you! Well done. Now get some rest. We have

three new gunners who just arrived and we're off tonight. We're going to the enlisted club to celebrate."

CHAPTER XIX

THE EYES OF TEXAS

After a month of preparation, I was finally ready to be a lead gunner. Ron woke me at 1700 and told me to shit, shower, shave and get ready to party on my first night off. I hit the showers and had started to dress when Ron brought over a tall, lanky guy.

"Texas, this is Gunner Joe. He's your lead gunner. Joe, here's Tex, your second gunner. Let's hit the club."

Tex looked like a kid. He must have been all of nineteen with a freshly scrubbed face, crew-cut hair and brand-spanking-new flying suit. He was six foot three, and as skinny as a rail. I reached out my hand to him. He was carrying a white cowboy hat, and shifted it to his left hand as he took my hand in his and returned a very strong shake.

"Take it easy cowboy, you're hurting me."

He replied, "I'm sorry sir. I'm just mighty pleased to make your acquaintance."

"Don't call me sir; I work for a living, just like you. Call me Gunner or just Joe. Welcome to Rocket City. We're glad to see you 'cause we need your help."

"Thank you, sir. I asked to come to Da Nang, where an airman can become a lead gunner in no time," He pronounced it Daaaaa naaanggg, with six syllables.

139

"Tex, join us—we're going to the club to have a couple of drinks," I said.

"Thank you, sir. I will, as soon as I write a quick letter to my momma telling her I arrived safely. She frets some, if I don't write."

"Okay, Tex, I'll give you an hour and then I want to see you in the club," I replied.

Ron and I went out the front door into blazing sunlight and walked the five hundred yards to the enlisted club compound.

I had never been to the club before, so it was new to me. It was a giant Quonset hut. Those semi circles of corrugated steel have been used since WWII to quickly erect buildings. There were four ancillary, smaller Quonset huts coming off the giant one, where the kitchen, game room and bars were located.

We entered the club and I could smell food, *real* food—steaks and baked potatoes, hamburgers, hot dogs and all kinds of goodies. Oh, man, what a delight. We sat down and I ordered a T-bone and a baked potato. Ron did the same and we decided to get right to the drinking.

An hour later, Tex walked in, wearing his white cowboy hat, and came over to our table, where he ordered something called Wild Turkey.

"What the hell is that?"

"It's fine Texas sippin' whiskey," he replied.

"I'll have a beer," I said to the waiter. There were only male waiters in the club; a woman among the hundreds of horny GIs would only lead to trouble.

All the rest of the men throughout the big open room were in fatigues, indicating that they were mostly ground support personnel and services people. We were the only guys in flying suits. There were a couple of tables of soldiers sitting across from us wearing their jungle fatigues. There was a big sign that said WEAPONS MUST BE CHECKED AT THE DOOR.

The drinks came and the waiter gave me a dark brown bottle with the numbers 33 on the front. He explained, "It's called ba muoi ba. It's the national beer of Vietnam. We're out of American beer."

I tried the Bomey Bah and it tasted like cold piss. "What the hell is this?" I asked.

"It's the local beer made with formaldehyde," Ron answered.

"What's formaldehyde?" I asked.

"It's embalming fluid, and it's supposed to preserve you." Ron laughed.

I called over the waiter and asked for a gin and tonic. Tex and Ron thought that was too 'pansy' a drink, so I changed to a scotch and water. I had never had a scotch and water and it tasted a lot like gasoline, but I kept my mouth shut, already feeling like a crybaby.

My steak arrived and I just stared at it. The first steak after a couple of weeks of C Rations is like perfume to the nose. The aroma made me salivate like a Pavlovian dog. I felt like a kid seeing an Oreo cookie, filled with anticipation. It was blood dripping juicy, warm, fresh and delicious. I relished every bite. I even picked up the bone and gnawed on it after the meat was done. Many years later, even when stimulated by epicurean delights, my mind always returns to that night and that T-bone steak.

We turned our attention to drinking and BS'ing. Ron told Tex all about flying the gunship, stressing the importance of doing everything correctly and by the book. He also shared war stories and dangerous missions he had flown.

"Do you know the difference between a fairy tale and a war story?" Ron asked.

"No," said Tex.

"A fairy tale begins 'Once upon a time…', and a war story begins; 'Now this ain't no shit.'" Ron laughed. "Some war stories are hymns; 'Like, hymn, hymn, *fuck* him!'"

We had a great laugh about that. After a while the soldiers came over and joined us. They had just come in from the field and a Spooky had shot up the VC for them so they thought we were their friends for life, the crew that saved them. We did not correct their belief, nor discourage their overzealous description of our bravery and heroism. They bought drinks for hours.

As the sergeant at arms got ready to close the club, Ron decided to teach Tex the official gunner's song. The song was based on a WWII custom: that mothers with sons in war displayed a blue star in their windows until the son returned. Mothers whose sons had died displayed a gold star.

Slurring his words a little he began.

"Oh, take down that blue flag mother,

And hang up one made of gold,

Your son is an aerial gunner,

He'll die 'fore he's twenty years old."

We all laughed at the morbid foxhole humor of the song.

We left the club, three happy gunners stumbling back to the hooch, arm-in-arm, singing.

"Ohhhhhhh, takkkke down that blue flag, motherrrr

And hangggg up one made of goooold,

Your son is an aerial gunnnnnner,

He'll die 'for he's twenty years old."

CHAPTER XX

SPOOKY ONE IS DOWN, RON IS DOWN

I kept staring at the smoking hulk of gunship on the ground. I fished around in my helmet bag until I found my binoculars. I brought them up to my eyes and strained to see if I could pick out my friends in front of the crashed airplane. I could not see any people. My skin felt like bugs were crawling over my back and I wrapped my field jacket tighter around me.

If only they are alive ...

The view was surreal: wispy smoke coming out of the fort to the north, green jungle to the west, the sun rising in the east and a smoldering gunship on the ground. The smoking convoy of ambushed trucks was scattered along the road to the west of the fort, it looked like giants had wrecked a toy truck scene and lit the entire set on fire. I stared and stared, looking for a sign that my brothers had survived and made their way to the safety of Tricky Misfit.

Tex came up beside me and yelled, aloud and not over the headset, "What do you see, gunner?"

"Nothing, absolutely nothing." I turned away so he wouldn.t see the tears streaking down my face.

"Let's RTB," Ace called out

We landed, pulled off the runway, and taxied back east toward our ramp. As we approached, I could see one gunship parked and the unarmed C-47 slick airplane with both engines running. We nosed into the parking space, Ace stepped on the left brake and gunned the right engine, and the airplane pivoted left with the tail wheel just on the edge of the concrete. The crew chief signaled to shut down the engines. Ace shut down. I ripped off my helmet and began working on the guns and straightening up the cargo compartment. I shuttered with cold thoughts of death, a chill ran down my spine.

I could see the slick airplane running next to us when the first sergeant climbed down the ladder and came over to our airplane. He climbed up the ladder, walked past us without a word and went into the cockpit. Tex and I focused on the guns as the ground weapons mechanics came up to begin repairing them for tonight's missions.

Ace and the first sergeant came out of the cockpit, walked right by us and went out the door over to the running aircraft. Zoomie came out of the cockpit and said, "The commander is pissed off because he hasn't heard from us. He was taking off in the slick to go and look for us. Ace told him the radios were out."

The first sergeant came back into the airplane and said, "The commander wants the whole crew over in the slick. He wants to talk to you."

I looked at Tex and he looked at me. I had no idea what was going on. We went over to the other airplane and climbed in. Ace was standing in the cargo compartment and he raised his voice over the idling engines to explain the situation. "The commander is pissed at us for flying below assigned altitudes, and flying during daylight. When he couldn't contact us, he thought we'd gotten shot down with the other gunship. We are flying to Nha Trang to meet with the wing commander and the Provost Marshall to see what he recommends. Sit down and put on your seat belts and I will try to explain while we fly."

Ace went forward and we sat down as the First Sergeant closed the back door. We taxied out and took off westward, but we soon turned south.

I noticed Tex had a headset cord connected to his helmet. As this aircraft wasn't a gunship, it had only a few interphone cords to listen and talk over. I took the cord away from Tex so I could listen in to the conversation.

I heard Ace explaining, "Listen, sir, we weren't unsafe. We went low so we could be sure of protecting Spooky One; we had to keep the gooks away from the airplane and our brothers. There was no real fire at us and we were safe."

"I warned you before, Ace. No cowboy antics. You could have killed your crew. And besides that, what the hell were you doing flying after daylight? How many crews do we have to lose before you get the word? No flying under any circumstances, after daylight! There is no target so important that you should kill your crew. We can send in jets or artillery, but you will not fly during daylight."

A contrite Ace answered, "Yes, sir, I understand. But the real problem wasn't us, it was Spooky Two-Three, who left a downed gunship crew undefended because he was scared of enemy ground fire. If anyone deserves to get court-martialed, it is the aircraft commander of Spooky Two-Three. He abandoned his squadron mates and climbed to six thousand feet rather than shoot at the gooks!"

"What do you mean he abandoned his squadron mates because of ground fire?"

"Yes, sir, we returned to Da Nang to get more fuel and ammo and left Spooky Two-Three on the target. When we got back to Tricky Misfit, Two-Three was at six thousand feet, dropping flares. He refused to come down and shoot because of ground fire. I think that's cowardice in the face of the enemy." He concluded in a quick staccato pattern — almost like a mini-gun.

"Ace, are you just covering your tracks here?" the commander asked.

"No, sir! That's what happened. Ask the crew."

"Navigator, plot a course to Tricky Misfit. I want to fly over it and personally see what the place looks like, and see Spooky One on the ground, and talk to them. Ace, show me the situation at Tricky Misfit."

As we approached Tricky Misfit I heard the Commander on the Radio. "Tricky Misfit, Spooky Command One. How do you read?"

"Five square, Spooky."

"Tricky, what's the situation with the spooky bird on the ground there? Have you been able to rescue the crew, yet?"

"Negative, Spooky. The crew didn't make it."

"Come again, Tricky. You have the crew?" The commander almost pleaded.

"Negative, Spooky. The crew never made it out. Repeat, the crew never made it out. My Commander is coming and wants to brief you. Over," he answered.

Oh, my God, they hadn't made it out.

They died in the airplane.

Burning and crashing to the ground.

Oh, my God!

I got an ache in the pit of my stomach.

I felt light headed. I was out of my body, hovering, looking down at the crashed, smoldering wreck on the ground.

Maybe he's wrong, and that's why their commander wants to brief us.

I jumped up and ran to the window on the left side of the airplane to look at the scene. *Oh, my God! They couldn't have gotten Ron, he's too good. He's alive in the jungle waiting for the VC to go away so he can lead the crew to the compound.* I felt cold and rested my head on my forearm.

It's not possible. They couldn't have gotten Ron. He can't be dead. He has too much to live for. He's not dead! He's hiding in the jungle. The Marines have to go out and find him in the jungle. I'm sure he's alive.

I searched the ground below for any signs of movement. The binoculars were shaky in my unsteady hands and it was hard to hold them still, so I propped them against my forearm for support. I stared even as we turned more into the rising sun and it blinded me.

I stared.

I stared, despite the pain in my eyes.

I knew he was out there. I couldn't accept the alternative.

The radio broke my concentration. "Spooky, Tricky Misfit command. Do you have a secure radio?"

"Roger, Tricky. Switching over."

My commander and Tricky Misfit's commander switched over to a radio frequency I couldn't hear. I just wanted to look at the wreck and find my missing friend.

He is definitely alive. He's just waiting for the Marines to come out. Hey, he's got his survival radio and he will see us flying above the airplane. He'll call us on the emergency radio.

I pulled the brick-like radio out of my flying suit and turned it on, awaiting the call.

He'll call. He can't be dead! He'll recognize the airplane and call us.

Our commander came back on the intercom. "Okay, crew, we're going back to Da Nang and drop you off. Tricky Misfit cleared up everything that happened last night. You did a fine job and should be proud of yourselves. Despite your valiant efforts, Spooky One-One is dead. They have recovered the bodies and no one survived."

CHAPTER XXI

HOW THE LOSS OF HIS MENTOR
FORCED A BOY TO FACE MANHOOD

We flew back to Da Nang in silence. Every head was bowed, reflecting on the loss of our friends, our brothers. I kept thinking about Ron's daughter and how he would not be there for her as she grew up. A terrible feeling of emptiness filled my heart and knifed at my stomach.

A light mist fell from a grey sky, the color of dingy bed sheets. The sad silence was broken when Tex began asking me questions.

"Just shut up Tex. Let me think," I snapped. "I'll catch you later." None of this was his fault, but I could barely function right then.

As we walked to the hooch, Commando Jerry jumped me with a hundred questions, "What happened? Where's the other crew? Where's Spooky One?"

"I don't really know," I said. "I saw quad fifty tracers coming at us. A sudden flash of light. Then Tricky Misfit said an airplane was shot down. I don't even think the VC were shooting at them. They were shooting at *us*."

The other men gathered around as we sat down in the break area. Someone asked, "Why did the Commander pick you up in the slick, and where did you go?"

Still light-headed, I answered, "Our radios went out for the last couple of hours. So the Commander came to look for us. He was getting ready to take off when we taxied in. Then he decided he was going to take us back to Nha Trang and turn us in for flying too low and firing after daylight. But Ace explained how the other airplane from Pleiku wouldn't go down to fight the target because it was too dangerous. So our Commander flew us all back to Tricky Misfit to see the battle scene himself. He got a report from the C.O. of Tricky Misfit and decided to bring us home. He is flying to Nha Trang, with Ace, to decide what to do about our loss and the chicken pilot."

The hooch buzzed with questions from the other men. I felt dizzy. I went to the showers to get away from the commotion. Commando followed me and stood there in his flying suit while I showered.

"Did Ron and the guys get out?"

"I couldn't see anything where they crashed. I used the best binoculars I could find and couldn't see any evidence of them. Tricky Misfit said they were dead! But how could he be sure? I think Ron and the crew are in the jungle waiting for the Marines to come and rescue them. We should get an aircraft and fly over the area all day, and listen for the emergency radios. I heard an emergency beeper once. They're still alive," I insisted, wanting desperately to believe it.

"I wish they were alive but, I know Tricky wouldn't have said they were dead unless..." My words trailed off. "I hate to admit it, but I think they're all dead."

I continued to let the cold water run on my head. I leaned over to the wall and let the water spill over my body, like a bucket of tears. After a while, I turned off the shower and dried off. I walked back to the hooch, where everyone was still standing around the day room. I shuffled to my bunk to put on my flying suit and a poncho.

Tex came over, and once again, I told him to take a hike. "Not now kid. I just want..." I shook my head and hoped that he understood.

I walked out into the rain, past the row of other hooches, past the guard shack and into the wet street. It was a light rain, just pissing down enough to make you feel terminally miserable. At the mess hall, I went through the chow line, sat down, and just stared at my nondescript meal. My heart wasn't in eating. I kept thinking of Ron, his dreams…

What kind of God could let someone like him die? He had all of the finest characteristics of man. Why had he died . . . while I was still alive? He was a much better man than I. He was going to be somebody, he was going to college. He was going to be an officer, the perfect father and a wonderful husband. There couldn't be a God who would allow me to live and him to die. It made no sense; it seemed so unjust.

My mother always lit a candle in church when something bothered her.

I walked by the chapel, lit a candle and knelt in the back pew. I stayed that way for an hour. I prayed silently. *Please God let them be alive, let them live and I will do everything perfectly for the rest of my life. I swear it.*

I walked back to the hooch, not noticing I was wet. The troops were still moping around in the day room. Someone said, "There's no flying tonight and there is a 1600 meeting in squadron operations."

I lay down on my bunk and closed my eyes to fake sleep. My mind kept returning to the flash of light outside the window of the airplane at the moment they got hit. I drifted in and out of nightmares. Finally at 1500, I heard commotion around the hooch and got up for the meeting. We drove in the rain. Utter silence, everyone afraid to mention the unspeakable.

We sat around for a few minutes until someone called the room to attention. The Commander entered, accompanied by the Full Colonel Wing Commander from Nha Trang.

"At ease, take your seats," he commanded.

We shuffled in the chairs for a couple of seconds; then all became quiet. "I'm sorry to be here under these circumstances, but there are things we need to discuss. You will not be flying tonight. Instead, the

151

other detachments will fly your missions while we determine why you have been losing aircraft and crews. This is the third aircraft and crew you have lost in less than three months. This has to stop immediately!

You're taking unnecessary risks and killing your people. We thought we'd solved the problem by painting the bottoms of the aircraft black, by ordering you to fly above two thousand feet and only at night. But we were wrong. We have not solved the problem and we will not leave here until we do. I now turn it over to your Commander, who has some words for you."

"There's a funeral at 1100 tomorrow in the base chapel. We will all attend. Uniform of the day is flying suits. Now the first sergeant has a few words."

The first sergeant got up and announced, "The following individuals will meet with me after this meeting." He called out names and to my surprise, named me.

The Wing Commander rose and barked, "Officers stay here. Anyone with information about the crash, report to the back of the room to the operations officer. Those called, go with the first sergeant to the next room, and the rest of you are done until tomorrow. Dismissed!"

I stumbled to my feet and walked to the next room, where the first sergeant had packages of paper ready. "You men have been selected as Summary Courts Officers for the deceased, because you were the closest to those who died. We want you to do a complete and respectful job of straightening up their affairs. I have a package of directions for each of you." He called our names one at a time and I was last.

"Gunner, here's a package for Ron. If you have any questions I will be available throughout the night at the orderly room."

I got in the van and rode back to the hooch in silence, barely moving. I sat on my bunk and opened the envelope and found an Air Force regulation stapled to an instruction sheet. The regulation said the Summary Courts Officer was a highly trusted agent for the deceased, responsible for taking care of all affairs of the lost airman. It said to go through everything he had on the base, to look at every letter,

book, notebook and picture in his possession. Further, eliminate un-
savory or improper material and return the remainder to the family,
pay off any debts he had and collect monies due. I had to return all
government items to supply.

I was instructed to write a personal letter to the family and express
the heartfelt condolences of a grateful and saddened nation. I leaned
back, stunned.

*Was this what it came down to? Was this the final result of his life? Was
this the way a military bureaucracy disposed of the destroyed dreams of a
family? What if I wrote a letter and sent it back with his hopes and dreams
to his wife, and maybe she'd find a way to piece her life back together to go
on? Should I send the letters so his daughter can see what kind of man her
father was?*

It was all so trite and meaningless.

I sat on Ron's footlocker. Opened his wall locker and started
going through Ron's unfinished letter. I felt like a spy, as I read the
personal feelings of a young lover and his wife. The letters were filled
with love and expectations for the future. Hopes and dreams and plans
that would never come to fruition. There were little kisses, x's and o's,
to his daughter. These reminded me of my own little girl Cindy, and
brought tears to my eyes, I saw drops on my chest.

I saw the stack of letters from his wife. They smelled of flow-
ery perfume. I couldn't read them. I couldn't go through my
brother's personal discussions with his wife. It was a violation of
his privacy. The manual said I was only to make sure nothing un-
toward was in them. I decided that returning them to the author,
his wife, unread was best. I was not going to betray his trust and
read his private letters.

I bundled up the letters and the rest of his property and took them
to the mailroom. I sent them with a receipt-requested form and returned all the paperwork to the first sergeant.

"Ron would have appreciated your prompt and personal attention. We are having a funeral ceremony in the base chapel at 1100 tomorrow. Be there," he commanded.

I trudged back to the hooch and moped. I had a terrible evening, constantly thinking about Ron's shattered dreams. I was a better man for having known Ron. I would strive to be the best, as he'd expected of me. I would be the best gunner ever, and I would become an officer I swore. For Ron. I swore if I ever got out of Vietnam alive, *I would be a better person.*

At 1100 I shuffled off to the chapel where the whole Squadron was assembled. There were no coffins. The bodies were already sent back to the families in the states. There were seven folded flags, each with a Purple Heart. Moreover, none of these had been won because of a cut from a Goddamned C-ration can.

I kept my head bowed as the chaplain said prayers. The Commander spoke next and I didn't hear a word he said. My mind had fixated on Ron and his wife and daughter.

· · ·

My head spun around and I felt confused, disoriented, and dizzy. Ron was the best gunner of us all. If he could be killed so could I. And if that happened, who would take care of Cindy? How could I leave Toni without a husband? I couldn't fly again. I couldn't risk getting killed. It would destroy my family. I decided at that moment—*I would never fly in combat again.* The Air Force couldn't force me to fly—I'd take the court martial. I couldn't leave Cindy without a father.

I walked up to my Commander as we left the funeral. My head was down and I said, "Sir, I don't want to fly again. Not ever."

He answered, "What's that Gunner? Speak up!"

I almost changed my mind but mumbled, "I'm never going to fly again."

He looked at me and his mouth softened, the rain dripping off his thick beard shadow. "I understand son. You don't have to fly ever again." He put his arm around my shoulder. "What you went through …is enough to rip the guts out of an eagle," he stuttered out the words in a halting voice. I couldn't tell if it was rain or tears coming from his eyes.

Cold, wet, and scared, I walked alone back towards the hooch. I walked past the club compound and thought about Ron's daughter. I thought about my own baby girl, and I visualized them playing together on my lush lawn in New Mexico. I thought about his dreams of finishing college.

It was a long trudge and I thought about everything that had happened. I walked past my hooch. My heart was torn for his daughter, my daughter. I walked by the flight line and saw the three Goony Birds lined up, a space between the second and third one, like a silent, missing-man formation.

When I finally turned back to return to my hooch, the sun broke through the clouds and I felt warmth on my face. I walked on and before entering the building decided that this wasn't what Ron would expect from me.

In fact, Ron would be greatly disappointed to learn that I had quit flying. I heard his voice in my head. *When the going gets tough, the tough get off their asses. Your crew depends on you. You fly tonight! I heard his voice in my head, You're a warrior not a coward, never give up!*

I sat on the side of my bunk with my head in my hands, just weeping. I tried to hold back the sound so that nobody would know. The water on my face was rain, I swear, it wasn't tears. Yeah, right. My heart hurt. Everything hurt. I'd never felt so low in my life.

A noise brought me out of my stupor. Commando Jerry sat down beside me and said, "Gunner, you're off the flying schedule. Go to the club and have a drink on me."

I said, "No way, you're not keeping me off the schedule. I can't let my crew fly without me. It's not safe and they could be killed."

"But ..."

"Ron expects me to learn from what happened. He demands that I fly and go get the people who shot him down. He told me not to quit."

He had a quizzical look on his face as he shook his head and then walked away.

• • •

Later, I heard the crew from Pleiku was exonerated of cowardice in the face of the enemy. I was told they'd suffered combat fatigue. Who knows? I have my doubts.

CHAPTER XXII

ALERT

Two nights later, while preparing the aircraft, Tex said, "Partner, I'm sorry about your friend. I hardly knew him."

"I know, buddy. Thanks. Let's not talk about him."

After our prep work was complete, we went inside the alert trailer and sat around with the crew. I went to a reading corner to study and opened my book to where I was the last time I read it. But all I could think of was Ron and how much I missed him.

I felt insane, like *Yossarian* in *Catch 22*: That the world had conspired to kill me and give me no way out. I decided I would not get close to anyone in the squadron for a second time. It was too painful to lose a friend. I refused to do it again. I'd just go through the motions and never care about anyone in the Squadron.

Around midnight I heard screaming sirens. It sounded like a rocket attack. The alert phone rang and Ace answered it as I ran out the door to our airplane. I pulled out the right main landing gear chock, and Tex got the left. He jumped into the airplane with me. I heard the rockets fall and an explosion next to the long 09-27 runway.

"Arm the guns! We have to be ready to shoot right after takeoff," I said to Tex.

Ace and the rest of the crew ran to the cockpit and started the engines. We taxied toward the runway. I turned all the lights out as Ace spoke. "Rockets are firing from two clicks west, by the old church. The runway looks screwed up, so we're taking off from the taxiway. Hold on."

The engines revved and we accelerated down the taxiway, which was very long but also very narrow. I saw aircraft and helicopters rapidly going by the window as we hurtled down the rough taxiway. Ace kept us in the middle, despite its narrowness.

Something exploded outside the right window. A bright red flash followed by rocket sounds: whish, shoo. Then a yellow flash.

When we lifted off, I connected the electrical plugs and hurried to the left door to look for ground activity.

Ace called out, "Watch for the rocket team, somewhere by the church."

There was an old wooden Catholic church with a white steeple in the middle of the open rice paddies. As we approached I thought I saw something scurrying to the south, into a long drainage ditch.

"Ace, someone ran out of the church and into that ditch," I reported.

I noticed sporadic explosions on the ground on all sides of the church. This is was a new phenomenon to me. *What the heck were the explosions?*

"Warning! Warning! Artillery exploding underneath us," the navigator screamed.

"Control, Spooky. Shut off that artillery immediately. They're shooting right through our altitude. Shut it down or we leave this target!" Ace shouted.

"Artillery shut off, Spooky. Sorry about that. Do you have a target?" Control asked.

We rolled in and fired into the ditch where the shooters had run. There was an orange explosion and fire on the ground.

"We have a secondary explosion; it's the rockets," Ace replied. "Control, is that artillery shut off?"

"Spooky, Control. Roger, artillery is shut off. It's your target, but we haven't seen any rockets since you arrived over the church."

"Roger, Control. We think we got them, but we'll continue to fire until the Marines arrive on the ground."

We kept firing for another thirty minutes, while the rockets burned in the ditch. Finally, six or seven Huey choppers arrived with the Marines. While the Hueys landed, there were two helicopter Cobra gun-ships flying around their perimeter, providing covering fire for the air assault. We stayed above with armed guns as a third level of protection.

In short order, the Marines secured the site. After the all-clear came over the radio we returned to ground alert. When we got back to the trailer, Ace called us all together for a meeting.

"Crew, I want to explain what happened. When the rockets fired at the base, there was an automatic system that sounded the alert horn and gave the coordinates to the artillery, who shot off rounds to suppress the rockets. However, when we approached the target, they were supposed to turn off the artillery fire so they wouldn't hit us.

The artillerymen say 'big sky little bullet,' meaning we should fly while they shoot at the rocket team. We absolutely disagree and do not fly over the target until they turn off the artillery. That was a good catch Nav: seeing the shells landing and having it shut down. To repeat, we will not fly over a target while artillery is firing through our altitude. Got that?"

"Yes, sir," I answered.

• • •

Now that training was over, we were assigned on hard crews. This meant that we flew with the same people on every mission. The hard crew structure allowed us to bond together and to know what to expect from each other during combat. The scuttlebutt around the squadron was that no hard crew, with all members present, was ever shot down. Because of the invulnerability of the hard crew and our trust and reliance on the people we knew, I was very secure with my crew.

Ace, our pilot and aircraft commander, was the oldest and most experienced flyer among us. He had flown the C-47 since the Second World War and had eighteen thousand flying hours in the airplane. He often spoke of flying the hump, the historic missions of flying over the Himalayas to resupply the Chinese army, who were fighting the Japanese during WWII. I had all the confidence in the world in Ace.

Our co-pilot was Zoomie, a brand new first lieutenant graduate from the Air Force Academy. Tall, handsome and very athletic, Zoomie was a fine young officer with the reputation of being overly aggressive and was trying to make general. I liked him a great deal, but I was glad Ace was there to hold him back from getting us killed.

The joke among the enlisted troops was that when we ran out of ammo, young and aggressive Zoomie would want to fly down and hit the enemy on the head with the landing gear.

On the other hand, as the story went, old Ace had just married a twenty-four-year-old virgin before leaving the states and would do nothing to jeopardize his return and consummation of his vows. Ace would always say, "Let's get up to altitude. There are more enemies tomorrow."

My navigator, called the Soarer, like a glider airplane, could find his way out of anywhere, under any circumstances. He was a great guy and had the reputation of insuring the safety of the crew at all times. He was a very logical, deep-thinking Alaskan.

We called our flight engineer and radio operator Roger Ramjet. He was a forty-ish Master Sergeant who was a consummate professional. He had the reputation of knowing everything there was to know about the airplane, having spent almost twenty years flying Gooney birds. Roger was universally liked and respected.

Whitey, our loadmaster, was an older man, of about forty, who kept to himself and quietly went about his business. He had a poor reputation with the flyers, as some men thought he drank before missions. I kept my eye on him even though he was a Staff Sergeant and out-ranked me. If I ever caught him drinking within twelve hours of flight, I would take him apart myself.

That was the essence of a gunship crew. Seven tireless Americans, joined by a random Vietnamese interpreter for each mission. Seven men with dreams and aspirations whose lives were interrupted by this God-forsaken war ten thousand miles away from home. Seven futures, tied together for this short tour of duty, and wholly dependent on each other for life. We lived together. We died together.

CHAPTER XXIII

GROUND ALERT

We seven brothers spent a great deal of time together during ground alert, especially through the rainy season. During times of monsoons, May through September, there was little combat action and few flights. Many nights we did not take off, and instead, spent the hours lounging around the alert trailer. For the duration of these times, I spent all night studying to go to college as I had promised Ron. I still missed him in the deepest part of my soul, but I still had to question the officers to learn all I could about becoming an officer, like them.

Ace was our official leader. I liked his quiet confidence and infinite wisdom. I was sure he could bring us successfully out of any battle or aircraft emergency. I sought his wise counsel and guidance when he was alone. I asked him about his road to becoming commissioned.

"I went through the Air Force Aviation Cadet program during WWII," he said. "We learned to fly and were given a temporary commission as second lieutenants when we successfully completed pilot training. After flying gooney birds during the war, I applied to go to college and received my degree and a permanent commission after I graduated."

"If you had it to do over, would you get a commission?" I asked.

"Absolutely. If you're going to stay in the military, becoming an officer is the only way to go. You know, Joe, civilians work for the Air Force. Airmen are in the Air Force and officers are the Air Force. This is the only service where almost all of the combatants are officers, and all of the pilots are officers. The Air Force is run by and for pilots and officers. Never forget that," he admonished me. "And if you ever want to become an officer, I'll recommend you."

"I don't know if I'm cut out for it. I've taken a few courses but I don't know if I can hack a degree. What do you study to become an officer?" I asked.

"I don't think it matters. Just take anything related to airplanes and finish your degree and get commissioned. What was Eisenhower's major in college? What was General Lemay's major in college? How about the Wright Brothers? Who cares? They did whatever it took to get ahead and never looked back. Just do whatever it takes and don't worry about the minute details," he wisely advised.

"I didn't finish college until after I was commissioned and it didn't hurt me. The point is to do whatever it takes to get where you can achieve your life's work. Let nothing stop you. You can always go back and straighten out anything you missed later, when you have time.

"There are certain milestones of accomplishment," he continued, "that society wants to see before it allows you to assume a higher position in life. One of the most important milestones or hurdles you have to clear is to finish college. Do that just finish college, and it won't even matter if you become an officer. You will have accomplished one of the highest goals society sets for you. Look, Gunner, you can't go to the Air Force Academy like Zoomie did. That is the Cadillac of educations.

"You're married and too old for that, so just take the next best opportunity to complete your college education and you will go far. As a matter of fact, I want you to ask Zoomie about getting an education and becoming an officer. He finished the Academy last year and is up to date on all the requirements for commissioning."

He called out, "Zoomie, come over here and talk to Gunner for a couple of minutes and explain to him about getting commissioned and becoming an officer."

Zoomie came over and extended his hand. I took it and we shook. "I think it's great that you want to become an officer. It's the only way to go!"

"What do you recommend, Lieutenant?" I asked.

"Gunner, the Air Force is run by the officers and we have a brotherhood that is incredible. It's even called the Officer Corps because we are considered, as a group, the leadership of the military. Every military throughout the entire world is led by the Officer Corps. Even between different branches, the Marines and soldiers treat us like their officer brothers and we are a team of leaders working together for a common cause. The finest thing you can do is to join the Officer Corps! Understand: I'm not taking anything away from the NCOs, because they are a vital component of the military. They are the technical expertise and the lower level supervisors, but they do not run or lead the military. The Officer Corps does."

"You sure make it sound like a plum," I said, "but what about the things I have heard about the officers?"

"What have you heard?"

"Oh, you know. That the officers have to totally kiss ass, and that they promote the sons of the rich people. And there is a reduction in force whenever they aren't needed."

"Well, you know, we have to obey our senior officers, but they will always listen to the complaints and ideas of a younger brother officer. You don't often see that because differences between officers are handled discreetly, behind closed doors. If you don't believe me, ask Ace."

"If you disagree with Ace you can question him?" I asked.

"Absolutely, I can question him, but I would never do it in public. Same with him, when he doesn't like what I do. When I make a bad landing, he praises in public and criticizes in private. After a bounce landing I made at Dong Ha, we took out an airplane the next day and he made me practice eight times until I got it right. But, we correct our problems between officers. We never criticize in front of anyone else."

"That's pretty neat," I said.

"As to there being nepotism in the officer ranks, I guess it's somewhat true. The political process and the elected civilians are in charge of all of us and if they want to control the promotion process to advance someone, I guess they can. It is the place of the senior officers to bring abuse to the attention of the appropriate official and correct it. The senior officers say that they serve until they find an important enough situation to resign. Then they take the right action, resign and tell the newspapers about it. That's what they say McArthur did at the end of Korea."

"I thought Truman fired McArthur," I said.

"McArthur went to the newspapers before he resigned and left Truman no choice but to fire him. In any case, he did the right thing as an officer and brought the problem to the attention of the newspapers, Congress and the people. In the final analysis, he did his duty and brought the problem out to the public light."

"What about RIFs?" I asked.

"There are reductions in force required at the end of wars, but the military tries to do it right. First, they never RIF regular and permanent officers, only reserve and temporary officers. If you have followed all the rules and done what's right, they will try never to RIF you."

"Are you a regular or reserve officer?"

"I am a regular officer by virtue of my commissioning from the Academy. Ace is a regular officer because he competed for, and won, a slot. But Soarer is a reserve officer and has a chance to compete for the limited number of positions every year. He just has to beat out the competition, and that is extremely hard. With a good combat record from this tour, I think he will be selected to be a regular officer next year."

"Wow, Lieutenant, that's a lot to absorb. Thanks for the information. Can I ask you more later?" I asked.

"Sure, Gunner. We're crewmates and you can ask me anything at all. In fact, every officer feels responsible for encouraging enlisted members to follow their dreams and get commissioned. If I can help in any way I will be glad to do so."

Later, I had a similar discussion with Soarer and he told me, "Do anything you can to become commissioned. To become an officer is to reach the pinnacle of success. I didn't have the opportunities that Zoomie had. I worked my way through regular college, but I got commissioned as soon as possible. He had another advantage. He was a regular officer upon commissioning, while I have to compete for the honor. I will get my regular commission next year, though, I'm sure, and then I'm home free."

The only negative comments came later, when I went to lie down on one of the cots in the rear bedroom. When I got to the bedroom Roger Ramjet was laying on the cot reading. As I entered he looked up, "Sucking up to the officers, Junior?"

"No, Sarge. It's just that I have never been around officers before and I wanted to ask them some questions about getting commissioned."

"Don't suck up. You're enlisted. Your family is enlisted and you weren't born in the right family to be an officer. They all come from rich parents and live in country clubs and you don't. Who the hell do you think you are, to jump ahead of me by sucking up to the officers? I earned these master sergeant stripes, and I'm your superior noncommissioned officer, and you will do as I say and get those crazy ideas out of your head. You got me, Airman?" he spewed.

"Sarge, you got it all wrong. I'm not trying to get ahead of..."

"Shut the hell up," he interrupted. "You suck-up asshole; just do your job and I'll leave you alone. I'm the senior enlisted man on the airplane, and if you have any questions ask me—not the officers. Got it?"

"I got it Sarge."

I lay down with the light on and thought about what had just happened. Why would my NCO be so angry because I asked a couple of questions? What had I done wrong by asking officers about getting an education? Whom did I hurt?

I decided to get some rest and ask Commando Jerry the next day.

CHAPTER XXIV

WE NEVER LEAVE A BUDDY
ON THE BATTLEFIELD

The jangle of the alert phone jarred me awake. I kicked Tex's cot, ran out to the airplane, pulled my chock and got aboard. After takeoff, Ace got on the interphone and briefed us.

"The Marines were in a firefight in the corner of South Vietnam, North Vietnam and Laos. They thought the firefight was over so they picked up and were flying on helicopters back to Dong Ha. During roll call, they determined a Marine was missing. The entire helicopter force headed back; returning to the battlefield. They requested our assistance. The Marines never leave a buddy on the battlefield. Dead or alive, everyone returns together. We should get there before the Marines, so I want all the guns ready. Sparks, see if you can locate the missing Marine; we have a frequency for him."

"Roger, sir," the radio operator answered.

Then he turned on the radio system so we could hear what he was saying and hearing.

"Alpha 7, Spooky Three. Do you read me?"

No answer. So he called time after time, "Alpha 7, Spooky One-Three. How do you read me?" He continued to call out into the void,

169

but we heard no sound in reply. I strained my ears, thinking I could hear something, when nothing was actually coming over. It felt like a hearing test, when they lock you in the little booth and send in low tones to see if your hearing is damaged. You strain to sense the slightest sound, and jump at nothing but imagined noises.

Then I heard a very low radio call, "Spooky, Alpha 7."

"I got him," the radio operator shouted. "I found him!"

"Spooky, don't shout. Whisper—they're listening," Alpha 7 said.

We sprang to life as Ace called the airborne command post aircraft.

"Cricket, Spooky One-Three. We have contact with Alpha 7."

"Roger, Spooky. Understand positive contact with Alpha 7," the reply came back.

"Alpha 7, Spooky." Sparks said more quietly now. "Understand they're listening. What's your position?"

"Roger, Spooky, I'm two clicks south of the river, under the big tree."

"Hold tight, Alpha 7. The Marines are on their way back to get you."

I watched intently through the back door of our aircraft as the battle unfolded.

High above us was the airborne command post called Cricket. Cricket controlled the entire air battle, as all aircraft reported in to Cricket and were given their assignments. Most aircraft were assigned orbits and holding patterns, awaiting their turn to attack the target.

The operators in Cricket were a combination of aircraft traffic controllers and combat operations officers, and were in constant contact with the ground commanders. The ground commanders requested air support and Cricket directed aircraft in to attack the target. The fighter aircraft came out of their orbits and attacked the target where directed.

As they expended their ordinance, Cricket contacted bases throughout Vietnam and had replacement aircraft flown in to take their position in the battle. That way, the ground commander had all the combat aircraft he needed, under all circumstances, and for the maximum time required.

Cricket was at twelve thousand feet, orbiting the target. Above him were two flights of four F-100 Super Saber fighter jets. These aircraft were armed with two napalm tanks, two five-hundred-pound bombs and four 20MM guns each. Each aircraft could stay in orbit for about an hour before they ran out of fuel or, 'Bingo fuel.'

Inbound were two B-57 Canberra bombers with five-hundred-pound bombs. Also inbound, returning from Dong Ha, was a host of Huey transport helicopters full of Marines. These were accompanied by a large number of Cobra gunship helicopters with rockets, guns and grenades.

Finally, these were followed by a number of Medical Evacuation helicopters called Dust Off.

As the Marines in the Hueys approached the battlefield, they requested that Cricket direct fire on Landing Zone Echo, to the east, and LZ Golf, three kilometers (clicks) to the west. Cricket directed the two B-57 Canberra aircraft to make a pass at LZ Echo and drop bombs to clear the area of any enemy soldiers.

I watched from the open door and saw the top rotating beacons from the two bombers; they did not have their wing tip lights illuminated. The rotating beacon was going so other aircraft could stay clear of their path. We were told by Cricket to remain on orbit, south of the river, to avoid conflicting with attacking fast-movers north of the river, where the LZ's were located.

I watched the two Canberras approach the target and saw an enormous flash of bright white light underneath the belly of the closest airplane. I heard the report over the radio. "Cricket, Canberra had a premature detonation under the aircraft. I have a fire-warning light. Returning to base."

"Canberra, Cricket. I will alert air sea rescue to follow you on radar and have their rescue helicopters enroute to your previous position."

"Roger, Cricket. We're on our way home and seem to be holding together. Canberra, going over to guard channel."

Guard channel was the special frequency used by all aircraft in case of an emergency. It was monitored 24/365 by rescue personnel around the world. It was a good idea, but many people thought the enemy monitored it and used it to find downed airmen.

Likewise, there was the feeling that the enemy knew that we Americans would return to the battlefield when one of our troops was missing, so they used that against us. There were times when they captured an American, put him in a vulnerable location and set a trap for the returning forces. That possibility was on our minds as we attempted to save Alpha 7.

As I looked out at the starlit battlefield, I saw the big "S" curves of the river going from northwest to southeast. Alpha 7 was about two clicks south of the bend in the river. To the north, about two clicks were the two landing zones Echo and Golf. Artillery was shelling Echo in preparation for the return of the Hueys laden with Marines. A mass burned on the ground by Echo, which were the remnants of one of the bombs dropped by the Canberra. In the distance eastward, I saw a long string of red, rotating beacons, which must have been the returning Hueys.

As they approached LZ Echo, I saw a stream of tracers shoot out from the jungle close to the river. "Guns shooting at the Hueys, north of Echo. I have a fix on them."

Ace responded, "We're cleared to fire on the gun that is firing at the Hueys."

A flash of light appeared, as one of the Hueys was hit and crashed to the ground. My attention was back on the enemy gun, for it immediately stopped firing as we shot at it. Another Huey took a hit as it landed at Echo, but I couldn't tell where the rounds were coming from.

Cricket said, "Spooky, there is a request for your guns one click north of LZ Echo, and you're cleared to fire."

We flew up there and fired on the target, without observing any return fire or secondary explosions. As we were firing, I heard that they were landing at LZ Golf. I looked over in that direction and a Huey was burning on the ground. Luckily, I saw the gun firing at the Hueys, so we went over there and shot at it. In the middle of the firing, there was a mighty explosion of white-hot light.

"We got a secondary explosion," Ace reported. "I'll keep firing on that target. It's probably the ammo magazine for the enemy."

"Step back, Spooky. Go to five thousand feet over the river. Fast-movers!" Cricket warned.

We flew over to the river and I could barely make out two F-100s diving from the east by LZ Echo. Incredible flames shot out as one of the aircraft dropped two napalm canisters on the target. The bright red and orange flames scattered over four hundred yards and someone shouted, "Crispy Critters! Yahoo."

We were in a standby mode as the fighters were doing their work. Another fighter flew over LZ Golf and dropped napalm on the western perimeter of the LZ as the Hueys approached to try to land after being beaten back previously. This time they went in with the Cobras flying circles, firing their guns and grenade launchers around LZ Golf. The Hueys landed, picked up the wounded and took off in less than a minute, while the Cobras went over to Echo and started firing.

"Spooky, Cricket. Go to Echo and fire around the south side, as they are sending a recon force towards Alpha 7, accompanied by the Cobras, with you flying CAP over them."

"Roger, Cricket," Ace replied.

A Marine command helicopter radioed in and took charge of the ground forces. "Recon 1, Command. Are your forces assembled at Echo?"

"Rog, Command. Recon all present and accounted for. We have to leave our medic behind to help the crewmen at the burning Huey," he reported.

"Negative, Recon. I'm sending in a dust-off to take care of the crew. Keep your entire team together and head south to the briefed position. I have a force, called Blocker, leaving Golf to support your position from the west. He will be in a position to block the enemy if they try to send in reinforcements. Get moving."

"Roger, sir. We're on our way."

"Command 1, this is Blocker. Assembled and reporting two losses, but able to complete our mission. We are departing Golf now

173

for our position north of the river, between Recon and the resupply route from the Hoi Chi Minh trail."

I looked toward the south from LZ Echo where the rescue recon team was going toward Alpha 1. Two burning helicopters were on the ground beneath me. I looked southwest and saw LZ Golf with two burring hulks, with the Blocking force departing south toward the river. Artillery fired around the river, softening up the route.

Two more fighters screamed down toward the river, released their bombs, and cleared a path for Recon. Meanwhile, I heard over the radio, "Spooky, Spooky, Alpha 7. What's the situation? I hear a lot of movement behind me northeast towards the river."

"Alpha 7, Spooky. There are friendlies enroute to your location. Just keep your head down," Ace replied.

Over the next two hours, Blocker got into position while Recon crossed the river and approached Alpha 7. Recon figured out that a trap had been laid for them — a large force ambush— and called us to fire on the hidden enemy position.

We fired south of the river, between Recon and Alpha 7, and heard Alpha 7 say, "That's them. Keep shooting. I can't shoot or I'll give away my position."

Recon joined the fight and started shooting at the enemy between himself and Alpha 7. Command directed Alpha 7 to get his head down, and called artillery into the fight. We backed off and observed the firefight.

Recon went in, found the missing Marine, and prepared to evacuate. In addition, his force sustained two minor wounds but the men were capable of evacuating. Command determined that they would meet up with Blocker, and both would return to LZ Golf to evacuate, as the enemy had counterattacked LZ Echo.

Blocker reported, "Command, Blocker. Enemy forces coming down the trail towards our position." He went silent.

Hell's door opened on the ground: twenty muzzle flashes fired simultaneously from Blocker toward the west. The radio crackled. "We got them in an ambush, running down the trail towards Recon! Send Spooky."

"On target, and firing," Ace said. We fired on the position, tracers streaming down toward the ground. We were firing so fast that each gun was quickly out of ammo and Tex and I had to load them with a vengeance. Finally, we heard, "That's it, Spooky. You got them. We can handle it from here."

We climbed to five thousand feet, reloaded the guns and watched the evacuation unfold. Recon 1, with the rescued Alpha 7, joined up with Blocker and returned to LZ Golf. The choppers landed and they all started loading.

In the meantime, another chopper, this time a medivac, got shot down over Echo trying to rescue injured Marines. We covered the departure of the helos from Golf and returned to Echo to see if we could help. We began firing around the perimeter as Command directed. At about 0500 hours, the last chopper left LZ Echo with the Cobras behind it and us above all of them. We followed them back to Dong Ha and I had a moment to reflect.

I thought, *what an incredible night of valor and courage and heroism. The entire strength of the United States military was sent to save a single Marine. Unbelievable. We will leave no stone unturned, no expense spared, no effort halted to save the life of a single combatant. Furthermore, we had no proof that the soldier was alive before we set out to retrieve him. We made the entire effort on the chance that we could save the life of a friend or retrieve the body of a fallen comrade.*

I wondered to myself, how could a force with such a noble and moral character ever be defeated? Every American would be infinitely proud of his country and his military if he witnessed such dedication and loyalty.

God Bless America and God bless the warriors.

•   •   •

The Marine was saved.

CHAPTER XXV

FRATRICIDE: KILLING MY BROTHER

The charred hulk of Ron's burned out airplane and the heartache of losing him and his shattered dreams were emblazoned on my mind. They never stopped haunting me for a moment. *Ron's dead, he will never be back to take care of his daughter.*

I kept to myself in the hooch, spending most of my time writing letters home and reading. Having just experienced deep mental anguish from losing my brother, I feared becoming closer to my other squadron mates. The other gunners asked me to go to the club with them, but I waved them off, just laid in my bunk remembering. I kept busy reading *Catch 22;* I was transported away from the war and the terror of flying with the agony and fears of the characters.

I ordered two correspondence courses that counted three credit hours. I did this in guilty tribute to Ron, to whom I had promised to go to college and get an education. I heard him in my mind, 'You can do better than this you're not spending your life just fixing guns.'

Haunted by the thought that Ron would never live the dream, I was determined to do my best to live for both of us. I thought a great deal about him during the slow times of little flying. Every night, in a recurring dream I flew Tricky Misfit and saw the bright flash of his plane being hit. My heart cried to know him better, yet I regretted knowing him so well that I hurt deeply from his loss.

The old question reverberated: *Is it better to have loved and lost than to never have loved at all?* It hurt so much to think about him, I couldn't get the image of Ron's airplane death pyre from my mind.

I became closer to Commando Jerry, he bunked near me. Commando was older and wiser; he understood the crippling effect of Ron's loss. I asked him about the troubling discussion I had had with Roger Ramjet, about speaking to the officers on getting ahead.

"I was asking the O's about getting commissioned and Roger gave me a bunch of grief about it. What gives?" I asked.

"Don't worry about Roger. He's bitter because he didn't take advantage of his opportunities when he was young. He resents you. All the NCOs dislike you young guys for your energy and drive. They feel that you're being uppity. That you feel like you're too good to associate with them. Don't worry about small minded guys," Commando said.

"I'm not worried about him; I just don't want to cause a problem."

"Then shut up about what you're trying to do. A lot of them never had the chances you have. The NCOs have not always wanted their brighter members to try to become officers. To the sergeants we were a different class from the officers; we were the workers and doers. We were the hard-toiling, blue-collar peons while they were the sons of the elite who didn't get their hands dirty and went to Ivy League schools. Go about your business, keep your mouth shut and you'll be fine. Now, let's play pinochle. I want to take a couple of bucks away from those two smart-ass staff sergeants over there."

•   •   •

Later that night, after take-off, we were assigned a target southwest of Da Nang, where thirteen Marines and two dogs were lost, in the middle of the jungle. There was a typhoon threatening, and the Marines radioed they were surrounded by Viet Cong.

"Just what the doctor ordered," Soarer said and then instructed Ace on the exact course to the last known location of the Marines.

It was a very sinister, moonless night and the ground was totally black, with no discernable features. As we approached the target, Sparks spoke to the lost Marine leader.

"Ringer, Spooky. What's your location?"

"Spooky, Ringer. We're one click north of the bend in the river, under the big tree. Got me, Spooky?" I could hear firing in the background.

"Negative, Ringer. They all look like big trees from up here. Give me a terrain feature."

"Spooky, the hills are west of us on a heading of 270. Roger?"

"Negative, Ringer. Any lights?"

"Negative, Spooky. We can't fire at the enemy or we will give away our position."

"Roger, we'll figure it out." More firing came over the radio.

"Spooky, Ringer. One of my guys said he saw a squad put a strobe light in a tree. We are trying to wrap tape around the strobe, so it can't be seen. Then we'll climb up the tree, aim the light straight up. Roger??"

"Roger, Ringer. Are you sure the Cong won't be able to see it?"

"Yeah," he laughed. "I'll be sure, Spo..." I heard a ricochet in the background.

Ace came on the interphone and briefed us. "Watch for a strobe light in the trees, one click north of the bend in the river. When you see it, we will fire one hundred yards north of the strobe and work the rounds in on his direction. Give me a gun."

"Strobe light, ten o'clock, two miles," Tex called.

"Ringer, Spooky. I got the strobe. Where's the VC?"

"Spooky, they're very close to us—mostly north," the firing got louder.

"Roger. I'll fire a short burst. Direct me from there."

We flew towards the blinking strobe light. I thought it was strange, using an emergency light to direct an aircraft.

Ace turned the aircraft into the firing circle and I armed the gun. He said, "One hundred yards north, a one second burst."

BRRRRRRR we fired.

"Bring it in, Spooky," Ringer yelled over the radio.

"I'm firing at fifty yards," Ace said.

BRRRRRRR, the tracers were noticeably closer. The stream looked like a red finger pointing just north of the light.

"Bring it in baby," Ringer called.

Back in the firing circle. A short burst of 100 or 150 rounds — this time slightly closer.

"Bring it in Spooky. You're way past them," Ringer pleaded.

"Listen Ringer, I can't fire any closer," Ace said. "Give me two guns and we'll fire for effect."

I put two guns on the line and we went around the firing circle on the south side — meaning we were going to fire over the top of Ringer. We lowered the wing, aligned the sight, and BRRRRRRRRRRRRRR. With two guns screaming out six thousand rounds of searing lead, all of a sudden the airplane bounced all over the place. The wing went down and we fired straight into Ringer's position.

I held on and was still thrown to the floor. I strained to get up and look out and the rounds were going right through Ringer. The light was shot out. Time compressed in my mind. In less than two seconds, I slapped down the master safety switch and turned off the guns. They had already fired hundreds and hundreds of rounds. I jumped away from the panel and saw a stream of tracers going right through the strobe light. I felt sick. The strobe light was blown away.

Oh, God, we just killed thirteen Marines and two dogs. I squatted down and held my head, petrified. My hands shook. *What have we done?*

Then the radio crackled. My ears perked up, *can they be alive?*

"That's it baby, do it again! Do it again, baby," Ringer screamed.

Ace came over the interphone. "What happened to the guns, Gunner?"

"I turned them off when we hit the prop wash and shot out the strobe. I thought we were killing the Marines."

"Good thinking, Gunner. Scared the piss out of me, but Ringer liked it! Thank God we didn't kill anyone. Let's get back to work. Nav, do you have a fix on his location?"

"Roger, Ace. We don't need the strobe. I'll align us. Tell Ringer to keep his head down."

"Ringer, Spooky. Keep your head down and we'll finish the fight. Where are they?"

"Spooky, we're firing at them now. They're running north. Get them," Ringer said.

We kept working the guns and firing at the enemy, but I was a total mess. The shaking stopped in a minute or two, and I concentrated on the guns. After a while the enemy was routed, and we began flying Combat Air Patrol over Ringer as the team walked toward a landing zone, where they could be picked up and returned to safety.

On the return trip to Da Nang, Ace broke the silence and said what we were all thinking. "Geese, when we shot out the strobe light, I was sure we'd killed them all. Can you believe them yelling, "do it again" when I thought they were all dead? Man, those Marines are crazy."

Later, I would learn how crazy the Marines truly were.

CHAPTER XXVI

FLYING INSANITY

The Sergeant looked up from his *Playboy* and twirled his black mustache that was too long for regulations. "Don't tell me you're ordering another damn course? Where's Ron? Why isn't he ordering classes too?"

"Ron's got shot down," I said, the pain jabbed into my heart.

"Yeah. Too bad. You need those?" He pointed to the stack of forms needed and turned his attention back to his magazine.

"I'm trying to finish what Ron started," I looked down ashamed.

"You're gonna numb your brain with all that studying," he said, without looking up.

"I'm trying to get some classes done like I promised Ron," I said, turning my head so he wouldn't see the tear in my eye. "Just order, the, the course," I blurted and lurched out.

That whole day, I was sick and stumbling around. Heart sick and gut sick, I had some kind of screaming Montezuma's revenge and could barely get out of bed. But I had to fly with my crew anyway. No full hard crew had ever been shot down — only crews with replacements were in danger. There was no way I would let down my crew and not fly. They needed me.

Commando Jerry saw me make a mad dash for the latrine for the fifth time and said, "You better go to sick call before you shit out your guts."

"I can't do that because the medics will make me DNIF (duties not involving flying) and ground me for a couple of days. I can't do that to my crew. I have to fly tonight."

Ace came over to the hooch, very unusual for him, and asked how I was.

"I have the screaming shits, but I can to fly."

"Good. Just get in the airplane. You can sleep on the floor and Tex can handle it. But come with us. Don't let us down," he asked.

"Roger," I answered.

Tex drove the crew van to the chow hall to get the C rats and I went in to sign for them. The place smelled like baking bread. Half way across the big kitchen the projectile vomits wretched my gut and I let it loose. I spewed all over floor, like a flash flood. I grabbed my stomach in pain and the head cook screamed at me. I grabbed the case of C's, with my left hand, ran out the back door, jumped into the van and we sped to the airplane.

That night's mission was to fly to Dong Ha and sit ground alert, awaiting the major attack expected across the demilitarized zone (DMZ). A favorite tactic of the Viet Cong was to sneak-attacked into the south, then run back across the border because Americans were not allowed to cross into North Vietnam.

While sitting ground alert at Dong Ha, we were told to launch and go to the center of the DMZ and report to Waterpipe. Over the DMZ, the radio operator turned the FM radio on so we could listen to what was happening. I heard an odd conversation from an Aussie.

"I'm telling ya' Yank, if you shoot into my position again, I'm callin' artillery on ya."

A meek American voice countered, "Sorry, buddy. Some of the troops were spooked and thought they were being attacked from the east. It was two minutes before I could get them to stop shooting. Won't happen again."

"Better not, mate. We're tired of it!"

The next radio call was for us, "Spooky, Waterpipe. We have North Vietnamese artillery firing into a marine unit in the DMZ. Many casualties. We have to medivac out the critically wounded. Can't get the Medivac in because the artillery fire is too heavy. The cloud layer at four thousand feet. Fighters can't go in. We order you to fly four clicks north of the DMZ and fire on the artillery. Time the shots so the medivac's can go in and get the wounded out. They only need three minutes. Spooky, how do you read me?" *I wish Ron was here with me.*

Ace took a second to respond. "Waterpipe, Spooky. We are expressly forbidden from flying north except in the most dire emergency. Give me a minute and I'll get back to you."

Then, over the interphone system he spoke to us, "Guys, you heard the problem that Marines have. There is no one but us who can go up north of the DMZ and shoot at the arty long enough for them to quit firing and the medivacs to get out the wounded. It is my judgment that we can do it safely at six thousand feet. There is thick cloud cover under us at four thousand feet, so they can't see us. We can fire one burst from all three guns and come straight back south. Now, I won't do it if anyone objects. So think it over and let me know."

I went over to Tex and shouted into his ear, "Sounds insane to me, but one fifteen-second burst of all three guns ought to be okay. What do you think?"

"I'm game if you're game," he answered.

I heard the rest of the crew talking about the mission. I keyed my microphone and said, "Ace, the gunners are ready. Let's go for it."

After polling the rest of the crew, Ace said, "Waterpipe, Spooky. Tell the medivacs to get ready—we're going in five minutes. Can you coordinate everything?"

"Roger, Spooky. We're getting all the helos positioned, and the medical personnel have the stretchers in the doors of the sandbag bunkers, all set."

Tex and I got the guns ready to go. I was in a cold sweat but excited because I had never been north of the DMZ. Ace pushed the throttles full forward, as he intended to go in and out fast. At six thousand feet, thick clouds, I couldn't see a thing as we raced north.

"Hold on," Ace called out. "I'm kicking the rudder and firing now!" I held on to the gun in the door so I could see better as the aircraft rolled left. BRRRRRRR, I looked out as all three guns fired. The red tracers were a sight to behold. You could almost walk on them, they were so thick. The crisp smell of burned gunpowder made me nauseous. But what was that?

What the fuck was that? *Red tracers coming up at us from the ground!, just off the nose of the aircraft about fifty feet in front of us.* A steady stream of large tracers led us in a left hand turn staying exactly fifty feet in front of our airplane and going way over our heads.

"We're taking ground fire," Soarer screamed.

The guns continued to blaze, and I felt the nose of the airplane decline about twenty-five or thirty degrees in a dive, still blazing all three guns. The G's pushed me down, we kept firing with the tracers inches off the nose, our guns still raging. Then the guns ran out of ammo, spinning free, still with deadly enemy tracers fifty feet in front of our airplane. I could almost hear them, like in the movies, pfffft pfffft, pfffft.

"What the hell was that?" Zoomie asked in a high-pitched voice.

"Must be a radar controlled quad fifty that's out of calibration and aimed in front of the airplane," Soarer answered.

The tracers stopped. Ace leveled the airplane and said, "Geeze that was close. Waterpipe, Spooky. We're headed back. Did the Medivacs get the wounded?"

"Roger, Spooky. Thanks the wounded are on their way to the field hospital. Good job."

I was shaken, having never seen so many enemy tracers that close to the airplane.

I thought about the situation that had just unfolded. I knew Ron would be proud that we did what was necessary to save the wounded

Marines. But I didn't think I could say anything back at the squadron; Ace would get in deep shit. Ace did the right thing by asking all of us, but who could say no and chicken out in front of his buddies?

On the way home, we received a strange mission we had to investigate. The radio operator wanted us to work a mission on Monkey Mountain, the famed hill next to Da Nang. Monkey Mountain had hundreds of Marine gun emplacements, helicopter bases and firing positions. It was generally off limits for us to fire at. Roger Ramjet briefed us.

"Controller is located in a command post at the base of Monkey. He reports that a Marine sniper is in a tree, halfway up, and has a ground wire. The sniper is reporting that the Viet Cong are climbing up the mountain towards his position, and he requests fire support. Controller said he will grant us authority to fire but we have to be sure of what we're shooting. We can't talk to the sniper, as the only radio he has is the old-fashioned, crank-handle, wire phone to the command post. Controller will relay messages from sniper."

Ace said, "Sounds pretty complicated, but we have ammo and can help the sniper. Find out where he is."

"Sniper is in a big solitary tree, one click down from the marked LZ," Rodger said.

"Ace, this is Nav. I think I have the position of sniper but cannot verify at this time. Ask controller for more information about his position, like a heading to the top of the mountain and a heading to the ocean, so I can triangulate and figure it out."

Nav said, "I got a fix on sniper. Where does he want our fire?"

Ace said, "Sniper said the VC are one thousand meters north of his position. Down lower on the mountain, climbing up. Controller, tell sniper I am going to fire one aiming short burst. It will be half-way between him and the VC. He can direct my fire from there."

"Roger, Spooky. Cleared to fire," Controller replied.

"Here we go," Ace said as we entered the firing circle and fired off a one second burst.

The emergency radio crackled and I heard a deep voice with a decidedly southern accent shout, "Spooky, Spooky. Who you shooting at, boy?"

I safed the guns as the navigator got on the guard radio and said, "Who's calling Spooky? Authenticate."

Authenticate is a procedure to make sure the enemy hasn't captured an American radio and is using it to have us shoot at our own forces. Each day Intel gives us a new authentication challenge and a response series of words used to verify who is using the radio.

After proper authentication, the radio signaler said, "Spooky, this is Marine First sergeant Striker, from the unit of sniper. Sniper has been up that tree for three days without a replacement. I am bringing his replacement up. Tell that stupid so' o' bitch to sit in that tree for three more fuckin' days—and if'n he eer has a gunship shoot at me again, I will shoot him out of that tree myself. I am calling controller. Who gave you permissin' to fire and why they didn't have me on their order of battle. Striker, out."

What a hell of a situation for the sniper to be in, thinking the enemy was attacking him and having us shooting near his first sergeant. I wouldn't want to be in his shoes.

I was happy to be going home to Da Nang without killing any Americans today.

CHAPTER XXVII

MEETING THE TWO STRIPER HERO

"**H**ave a seat, Gunner." He turned on a tape recorder and asked about the night Da Nang was rocketed and we killed the Viet Cong shooters. I felt self-conscious, like I was pretending to be something I wasn't, by trying to talk about what happened. The Warrior Code of silence kicked in, I lowered my head and felt shy and speechless. There was a secret place in my ego that really wanted to brag, but the warrior code demanded silence.

He said, "The Civilians need to hear what we're doing, it's good for their morale."

That made sense to me and I secretly wanted to tell the world what I had done. So after a few minutes, I relaxed and told my story until the door opened and someone new entered.

The whole atmosphere of the place changed when a young Airman walked in and took a seat at the desk behind me. It was as if a spring sun came from behind the dark clouds and lighted and warmed the room. He was short and gaunt, without an ounce of fat on his 5 foot 8 inch body, 145 pounds and black hair; a baby-faced, Ivory soap kid in a flying suit. He had a square jaw, bright brown eyes and looked intelligent. His voice was young, full of Oklahoma.

The story he told was one of the most captivating I had ever heard and transported me to the battlefield beside him. Jack was a Para rescue man trained in helicopter operations, first aid, and escape-and-evasion tactics. He flew with a Jolly Green Giant helicopter rescue Squadron.

On a recent mission, Jack was sent to rescue a crew of two pilots who ejected out of an F-4 Phantom jet, deep within North Vietnam. Flying to the pickup point, they avoided thick killer flak to fly where the downed pilots were escaped and hiding. Jack's pilot hovered above the downed pilots and Jack descended on the tree letdown device, finding the first pilot with a broken leg. He'd started to apply a splint to the leg when enemy rifle fire broke out. There were rounds pinging off the chopper. Then he surprised me to the max.

In combat, the first rule of the warrior code is never leave a buddy on the battlefield. Under no circumstances will an American ever leave another American on the battlefield, even if he is dead and the only hope is to recover the body. This is such an important rule that one night I saw seven helicopters shot down trying to rescue one missing Marine. Under *NO* circumstances do we ever leave a buddy on the battlefield.

Then Jack knocked the wind out of me when he said, "The helicopter left with me on the ground!" My heart was in my mouth and beating at the rate of a machine gun. *They left him in North Vietnam ON THE GROUND!*

I couldn't imagine, the crew abandoning Jack while he was trying to rescue the pilots. Jack said the chopper had to depart immediately or risk being shot down and would lose the chopper and entire crew. His pilot retreated to a safe distance then called Jack with radio instructions to depart south with the downed pilots. Then, when it was safe, the Jolly Green would return once every twenty-four hours. Jack applied a splint to the downed pilot and noticed that the other pilot had head injuries and was blind. He hoisted the first injured flyer over his shoulder in a firefighter's carry. Then he unraveled a gauze bandage so that the blinded pilot could hold on to it, like a leash. Them Jack led them away south before the enemy forces could kill them.

After an hour Jack and his two wounded pilots were discovered by a couple of enemy militia. Jack started running, firing his M-16 behind him, and killed both.

He ran on for about an hour until they came to a canal, where all three Americans lay down behind the embankment, caught their breath and waited for dark.

After nightfall, Jack hoisted the crippled pilot over his shoulder and slogged through the rice paddies and jungles south. When the sun rose, he found a thick jungle area and they settled down to rest and prepare to fight their way after dark.

At the second nightfall, an enemy soldier again discovered them. Because there were enemy searching all around in the jungle, Jack silently killed him with his K-bar knife. He picked up his pilot and started trudging south again. He struggled on for seventy-two hours. Finally, on the last night; the Jolly Green returned, found them and rescued the three worn out warriors. I smiled a big broad grin and silently cheered at his success.

Jack was making a tape to send home because his unit had submitted him for the Silver Star for heroism—bravery above and beyond the call of duty.

I had a guilty image flash through my mind of me riding in a 57 Chevy convertible with Miss America. We were sitting on the open top and I was wearing a Silver Star in the Fourth of July parade. My chest was puffed out and all the little boys saluted as we went by. They looked like John-John when his father's casket passed.

I found this story miraculous. In fact, the sergeant conducting the interview and I stopped talking while Jack recounted his story. When he was finished, I introduced myself.

"Hi Jack. You the man! I'm proud to meet you."

"Hi," he looked surprised while shaking hands. "I'll give you a ride back," I said.

We drove off in the crew van and made plans to meet the following night when we were both off from flying.

Jack lived in a hooch, five or six away from mine. On Friday night I walked over and met him. We sat around for a few minutes and discussed his life in para rescue. He was nineteen and looked twelve. I was very respectful of him. I had never met any other flying enlisted man who was combat capable.

I told Jack, "My teacher Ron wanted us Airmen to be the best we could. He pushed me to go to school and have good morals and values." I told him about Ron and his dreams and aspirations for all airmen. We discussed taking correspondence courses and going to college after getting out of Vietnam. He said, "The system was designed to use young airmen. The system sucks the life out of airmen, and if one of us wants to advance, he has to do everything himself." He thought superiors, the noncommissioned officers, showed no interest in helping airmen advance. In fact, a number of them were antagonistic toward any airman trying to better his education or outwardly attempting to advance.

My heart still fills with joy because many of the real heroes were the youngest warriors, the airmen. I have often read about various Pentagon Generals receiving honors and medals from the president. I never met any of them on the battlefield—on the front line I saw only men like Ron and Jack.

I met some real heroes on the next mission.

CHAPTER XXVIII

"THEY'S MORE HORSES ASSES
THAN THEY IS HORES"

My insane life was punctuated with tremendous seconds of terror through a veil of academic work and days of tedium. I flew deadly combat missions every moonlit night and studied my academic courses during high temperature daylight like a scholastic vampire. Somehow, deep in my heart I knew that I had to change my world of death to a world of life.

Waking up, I thought about Ron, and remembered. I felt like I was punched in the stomach and needed to vomit. Ron and his destroyed dreams and life. I walked around listlessly, in a constant funk, staying mostly to myself, afraid to make friends in case they were killed and their loss would add to my stomach pains, heart aches and hatred of the Viet Cong.

On Friday, I received a package from home. My aunt Rose and teen-age cousin Donna sent me a "care package." In the foot square grocery bag wrapped box were a world of goodies; homemade cookies, current magazines, beef jerky and powdered ice tea. Aunt Rose and Donna always seemed to make the world brighter for me and I wrote back my loving thanks. I don't know how they came up with the powdered iced tea idea, but it enhanced the flavor of the local piss water.

My mother sent me books, and the one I gained the most from was *THE POWER OF POSITIVE THINKING by Norman Vincent Peale*. Every time I felt down thinking of my Ron or Toni and Cindy, I opened this great book to gain strength and to buck up my spirits.

I was ordered to fly with other crews when a gunner was sick, wounded or indisposed. I found these flights frightening because I was not with my most trusted crew members. We never lost a full crew, unless a replacement was on it. The next crew I flew with helped be.

Billy seemed old, like fifty, for being just a Captain, but he was a trusted aircraft commander. I heard his lead Gunner say, "Man that cat's cool under fire. Nothing rattles him. And he has that sensible old knowledge that always knows exactly what to do under the most hazardous situations." So when I pulled ground alert with him, I went to seek his wise counsel and seasoned advice.

I walked into the room in the back of the trailer, where he was seated alone near a wooden table lamp, with a yellowed shade and a book in his hand. He looked to be about a hundred to my young eyes, with grey hair and a receding hairline. He had a weathered face but always a smile on his lips. He exuded an air of self-confidence and conducted himself like an officer and a gentleman so I had no qualms about speaking to him.

"Captain Billy, can I disturb you for a minute?" I asked.

"You're not disturbing me, Joe," he replied. "Have a seat."

"Thanks, sir."

"What's on your mind, son?" he asked.

"Sir, I am looking for advice about becoming an officer and one of the other pilots suggested I speak to you about it."

"Why do you ask me?"

"I heard you were prior enlisted. I wanted to know how you did it and how you would advise me to go about it."

He leaned back in his chair and gave me a long assessing stare. Then, in his nasally southern drawl, he related his tale to me. "I grew up in the old south, the son of a share cropper. We were dirt poor, but honest folks. I am the first person in my family to finish high school. Shoot, I'm the first person to *go* to high school. You see, all my family had to work the dirt.

"You know, son, a share cropper is as po' as they come. We don't even own any land. We work on another farmer's land and get our share of the harvest. That's how we live," He closed his book and put it on the table.

"I went to a dirt-floor, one-room school house where all of the grades were together in a single class room. We tended to our studies in the morning and the farmer's crops in the evening, and studied the Holy Bible at night. Like I say, we was poor but honest.

"When the war came along, people said they was looking for soldiers and I went down and signed up. I was so happy. The recruiter said I would get to be a soldier and be issued uniforms and boots. Man, I was in hog heaven!

"The next week I went off in a Greyhound bus, to Fort Dix, New Jersey for boot camp. Boot camp was great three hots and a cot— we called it. All you could eat and a warm bed. Hog heaven, I say, hog heaven. Anyway, after a couple of weeks they gave us all kinds of aptitude tests. When the tests came back they called me in and said that I could become an aviation cadet and fly airplanes." He paused and shook his head. "Hell that was my first trip on a bus! Imagine being told I could fly airplanes. So I jumped right in and signed up to be an aviation cadet."

They sent me to Bainbridge Army Air Field in Georgia for my flying training. There we flew an airplane called a BT-13 and after just six hours got to solo and fly by ourselves. I was in tall cotton; loved every minute of the school and especially the flying. I finished basic flying and was then sent to McGuire Air Corps Base in New Jersey and got to fly Gooney Birds. I flew supply missions in North Africa and on D-Day I delivered gliders full of soldiers to France. Man that was great flying.

After that, I flew supplies to Patton in the Battle of the Bulge and had a grand old time. When the war was over, they had too many pilots so they RIF'ed me back to private and made me a mechanic. I still loved it because I got to work on airplanes and didn't have to plow behind that ole mule my Daddy had.

Then two years ago, there was a recall because they needed Gooney pilots for this here gunship program, and I ran down to the personnel office and volunteered again. Man, I'm back in pig heaven, walkin' in tall cotton, a pig in slop. I just love it.

"So, that's my story, Joe. Any questions?"

"Tell me about being an officer. Do you like being an officer more than being an enlisted man?"

"Joe, there's no comparison. Man the whole service is designed to make life better for officers. WE officers have the easy life and all the benefits. Like we used to say, if screwin' your wife was work, I'm sure the officers would have us doing it for them!" he laughed. "If you ever get a chance to get commissioned, jump at it."

"But Captain..."

He interrupted, "Call me Billy!"

"But Billy, what about the kissing all the senior officers' asses? We don't have to do that as enlisted men."

"Bull hockey. You obey your orders, or you're in jail. You're kidding yourself if you think it's any different for you than for me. Anyway, that's just an excuse for people who don't have the gumption to go for it. Some people are always gonna stay down on the farm and don't have the courage to go for the big leagues. You are a smart fella, Joe. You can make it. You just got to have the guts to go for it."

"If I can make it, then anyone can make it. So go for it, son," Billy continued. "You know Joe, they is more horse's asses then they is horses. Just deal with it and you'll be okay. The horse's asses are the people who tell you not to take a chance, to stay on the farm and not stick your head out. My Pappy used to say, don't stick your head out or you'll get it chopped off like a chicken's. Well, my Pappy is still tilling dirt back on the farm. Walking behind that same dumb-ass mule. And I'm here on an all-expense-paid vacation to a tropical paradise." He laughed and laughed at his joke.

I walked away feeling very confident and reassured. Few officers spoke to the enlisted men with such understanding and optimism in their voices. Fewer yet encouraged the men to try to advance to join their ranks.

CHAPTER XXIX

INJURED ON THE HOI CHI MINH TRAIL

The next night I was in for the fight of my life; a badass shoot 'em up over the trail. The trail was a series of roads running along the border between Vietnam and the two neighbors to the west, Laos and Cambodia. On rare and particularly violent occasions, we were ordered to fly over the Hoi Chi Minh trail.

As one of the most heavily-defended targets in the war, mention of the trail brought up hackles on my neck and a cold sweat to my palms. Because of the intense anti-aircraft guns and numerous missiles, it was rare to send a low and slow gunship. Our squadron had hundreds of harrowing stories about flying the trail.

In fact, a new gunship, Specter, was built specifically for this mission. This AC-130 had bigger and more powerful guns, defensive electronics, and an ability to fly much higher than the Spooky gunship. The Specter had a fighting chance against the Anti-Aircraft Artillery.

We approached the trail from the east with all concealment, quietude and haste. This tactic minimized our exposure to enemy fire and our risk of death. We scooted in, shot a burst and then rushed away east. We recovered and did the same thing again. Rushed in, fired a burst with all three guns, then zoomed out to safety.

On this trip, for some reason I was not paying much attention to what was going on. I was taking care of the guns but had my head in the clouds, thinking about my wife and daughter back in the "Land of the Big BX." I was carrying a can of ammo to the back of the airplane when I heard the Load Master shout, "Break right, break right, enemy missile!"

My legs flew out from under me, the ammo can seemed to float over my stomach, and the airplane dove to the right. Within seconds, I crashed to the floor with the ammo can boring painfully into my chest. My ribs and neck didn't appreciate the acrobatics, either.

"That was damn close," the navigator spoke out. "Did you see the missile?"

"Yeah, it was a SAM 7," the loadmaster said.

I had seen a flash by the cargo door but could not determine that it was a missile, just an intense brilliant white light. But damn, my neck hurt.

I got up off the floor, collected my thoughts and slid, rather than carried, the can of ammo behind the gun. Ace asked, "Everyone okay back there?"

"I flipped onto my ass, but I'm okay," I answered.

"That's enough for tonight. Let's RTB and get a night's sleep," he said.

The next morning I woke with an incredibly stiff neck—rigor mortis stiff, hard dick tight. I could not turn my head from side to side at all. I checked in with Commando and he said to go to sick call and have it looked at. "But don't let them ground you."

At sick call, the corpsman filled out the medical forms. He asked me what happened and I told him that I'd fallen when the missile was shot at the airplane and the can of ammo landed on my chest, hurting my neck.

A young doctor came in, examined me and determined that I would live. He told me to get a heating pad from medical supply and not to use my neck too much.

The corpsman gave me a heating pad and a prescription to go to physical therapy to have my neck massaged. Then he said something that surprised me. "I have to fill out the forms for the Purple Heart."

"What Purple Heart?" I asked.

"You were injured in combat and I have to fill out a form for you to get a Purple Heart."

I found this very surprising. I said, "I thought you got a Purple Heart for being wounded by the enemy, not for falling down and hurting your neck."

I was appalled by the idea of getting a Purple Heart that way. *That's what they sent Ron's wife and mother, a Purple Heart.* I couldn't take one. It would be an insult to Ron, and a greater insult to the medal and to all soldiers and airmen who had ever honestly earned one. *Not me,* I thought, *never.*

"No, thanks, Corpsman, I didn't earn a Purple Heart, and I won't take it."

"Yeah, you did. You met the criteria and I have to fill out this form for you to get one."

I closed the matter definitively by saying, "Listen, buddy, I'm a gunner and gunners don't get Purple Hearts. We *give* Purple Hearts— to the Cong."

CHAPTER XXX

GASH IN THE GROUND

Ope and all the most beautiful round eyes in the After I shaved in the morning, the smell of Old Spice after shave stimulated my memories back to a happier time, when Ron was still alive. It seemed forever, but it was just three months earlier. It was on my first trip to the Marine Base Exchange, on the other side of Da Nang, Ron had pointed out a long line of road graders going up an almost vertical road.

"Man," he said, "I think they're taking away the mountain. I heard that after they return from a month in the field they come back here and start digging this gash. The funny thing is, some believe it's to make room for an officers-only swimming pool."

Though he was kidding, I looked up and saw a red scar in the mountain that reminded me of pictures I had seen of pit mines in the old West. They had removed an area so large it looked like a fifty acre sinkhole in the side of the dirt hill.

"How long have they been digging?" I asked.

"For months. They've nearly removed one whole side," he said. "Even the Marines don't know why they're digging. Some say they have run out of salt peter in the mess halls and use the hard work to keep their minds off women. In reality, we don't know why they're doing it. It's a deep dark secret."

During that first shopping trip to the MBX, I picked up paper and pen to write my family, a lamp to dry my locker, and a copy of *PLAYBOY* to ogle the girls. Ron, for some reason, bought a kitchen broom. I asked him why.

"I've been reading a book called *THE UGLY AMERICAN* that said older Asian women have permanently stooped backs because they use short reeds for brooms and the constant bending disfigures their spines. I bought this broom for Mama San, so she won't get a humped back," he answered.

I found that very revealing.

I looked from the broom to my copy of Playboy, and back to the broom.

That evening I was scheduled to fly the first mission at 1630. After taking off we circled back over the base, and I purposely looked down to see what the mountain looked like from above. There on the backside of the base I saw a peak shaped like Mount Fuji in Japan. On the side of the peak facing Da Nang, there was a large red blotch, the color of a fresh facial scar or a Rosetta birthmark. The long line of olive-drab road graders looked like a giant caterpillar feeding on the open red sore of the wounded mountain. In this verdant tropical world, the red blotch reminded me of the largest bomb crater I had ever seen, a scar on the beauty of the earth.

Over the next month and a half, there were many sightings and discussions about the true meaning of the sinkhole of Da Nang. Some people said they were building an underground bunker to house all the important generals and civilians from the state department. Others said the Marines were building a secret underground base, like the one in Korea.

Every evening, after take-off, I looked for it and it seemed to grow larger by the day until it scarred almost the entire side of the mountain. The big scar, as I had taken to calling it, remained a mystery for many months. Then a strange rumor began to circulate: The Marines were building an arena and stage for a USO show.

I was transported back to stories my uncles told about WWII. They had loved the USO shows with American movie stars, and most importantly, beautiful round-eye showgirls. It was the highlight of every year. As excited as I was, it was impossible to believe that they would come here, because the heavy combat in the area would be a danger to the cast. However, I kept my hopes up.

Finally, a month later, the First Sergeant came to the barracks at noon and asked for everyone to assemble in the day room. When we were there he said there was a secret event the following day that could not be revealed, but we were all eligible to attend.

"Commandos, tomorrow at 1400, line up outside the orderly room and pick up tickets to a special event. If word gets out it will be cancelled for security reasons, so keep your mouths shut," he said.

I could hardly sleep all night. I had recurring dreams of Marilyn Monroe, Joey Heatherton, and another beautiful blonde with perky breasts; her big headlights calling me. When I closed my eyes, she was on a deserted beach, wearing a tiny bikini and a come-and-get-me grin. There was a fire in my nether regions and lust in my heart. After lights-out, I heard someone snicker, "Thinking about those beautiful girls just started the launch sequence for my nocturnal emissions."

We were all excited the next day. Walking to breakfast in the chow hall, Commando said, "That Joey Heatherton is the prettiest girl in California, and that makes her the prettiest girl in America." An argument ensued about where the prettiest girls were from and we all became immersed in the discussion. I had the jitters in my legs. Barely able to contain myself, I bounced around all morning. I told Commando, "This is the first show I have ever seen. I can't wait!"

By the time we all got in our bread trucks for the two mile drive to the orderly room, I was a sad case of jitters. Commando said, "Quit fidgeting in your seat—you're acting like a pimple faced teenager."

We called it the Hollywood Bowl West as we got in line at the orderly room for tickets. Standing there with seventy-five or eighty Squadron mates, everyone was guessing at what the show could possibly be. Out of nowhere, the First Sergeant pointed to me and said, "Not so fast, Gunner. Where do you think you're going? Didn't you see the assignments? You can't make the show, you're flying."

"What do you mean, First?" I asked.

"Because so many Marines will be concentrated in one area, a great target for the enemy, we're going to have maximum air cover. You're flying the cover."

Jeez, I thought. *Finally some entertainment to break the monotony and I can't go.*

An hour later, we took off and flew the entire afternoon over the Bob Hope Show, with guns ready and a disappointed crew who did not get to see the great man. But in a way, we did get to see him. From three thousand feet, as we flew overhead, he looked like a miniature ant crawling across the stage.

CHAPTER XXXI

THE GREAT DON COMES TO DA NANG

To piss us all off, Air Commando Headquarters began annual re-certification check rides and a program to standardize the crew duties between the five detachments. We had heard rumblings of that nature, but we were so far from HQ that we felt insulated from their bureaucratic machinations. Little did we realize how wrong we were.

Commando Jerry announced a gunner's meeting for 1300 that afternoon. I ran into the operations briefing room to hear him out. He strolled up to the podium and told us that we were going to receive check rides from a newly appointed senior gunner.

"The chief check gunner, Don, will be here next week and will fly with each of us to certify we are following safe practices and procedures. In preparation, I want you to pay particular attention to following every single checklist, step by step. I cannot emphasize enough that you must faithfully follow your checklists and memorize your emergency procedures. Now, are there any questions?"

I started to laugh to myself, imagining Don as the head gunner for the entire squadron. *He couldn't fly right if God himself gave him wings!* I thought *I heard about a Wing and a Prayer, this was a wing and a joke.* The least competent gunner in the world was the HQ check gunner. I laughed to myself for hours.

We returned to the hooch and I jumped Commando to give him what information I had on Don. I went up to his bunk, "Commando, I know Don. He was in my gunner's class and with me in survival school. If he's qualified to be the stan-eval gunner, then I'm the Queen of England!"

"You know him?" he asked.

"Sure do, buddy. And a bigger chicken shit never lived. I called him a Detroit yellow back because he was scared to come to Da Nang."

"Well, he's coming to Da Nang next week to fly with us. Do you want to be assigned to fly the first mission with him?"

"Sure do. There is nothing he can ask me that I can't answer. In fact, I would love to ask him some questions of my own," my arrogance kicked in.

"Don't be a smart ass, Joe. Just do your job and fly your check ride and we'll be fine. I heard he's a killer on emergency check-list procedures so you had better brush up."

"Gimme a break," I answered.

"Don is coming with the new Wing Commander to inspect our detachment. We are having a reception and party for them and you're in charge of doing the gunner's part of the party. It will be on Saturday at 1300, in the base recreation area by the lake. We'll have a barbeque and you'll be the one to set it up."

"Can do, Sarge," I answered in mock sincerity, and began making plans for the big day.

In the meantime, I had befriended two Marines at Dong Ha who wanted a bottle of Seagram's 7 and a case of 7-Up. The Marines were not allowed to have alcohol, so they tried to get everyone who flew in to bring them some. My plan was to trade them the 7&7 for a case of big juicy steaks for our party.

I went to the class VI store and bought a bottle and a case of soda for ten dollars. I stowed them on the airplane. When we arrived at Dong Ha, I found my combat weary friends, gave them the contraband, and got back my ten dollars, plus a case of 120 T-bone steaks for the party. The Marines took great delight in telling me that the cook had hidden the steaks in the back of the cooler for a special 'Officer Only' party scheduled in a next few weeks. I was in heaven, knowing we got the contraband from the officers and that our party would be a great success.

The following Saturday, Commando, our detachment commander, and I were all assembled at the flight line to meet the visiting dignitaries. Standing at attention in our newly cleaned and pressed flying suits, we were a scene to behold as the slick C-47 pulled into the gunship ramp.

I took Don on a tour of the gun shop and bomb dump, where he played the visiting potentate to the hilt. He acted like a movie star, strolling up the red carpet on opening night. He strutted with his head held high, giving interviews to all the fawning fans. He clearly relished the spectacle of the troops scurrying around, showing him their newly cleaned, painted and polished shops.

I shook my head and frowned at the dog and pony shows. These shows always felt artificial, synthetic, and like mock displays. It had become a cause célèbre; combat units were forced to focused on body count and spit-and-polish as a measure of their success, rather than on doing a competent job. I felt that putting on shows for visiting dignitaries was weakening our combat forces. These displays emphasized "Style over Substance." The real measure of our worth was how we flew, how we operated our guns and how we protected our American troops.

Don and all the other headquarters types smiled and strutted during the show and even brought a photographer along to document his war effort for the relatives back home. Most of the time news reporters came along with the potentates to write stories from the front to show the incredible heroism of these desk jockeys.

After visiting the shops and making the required rounds and introductions, I took Don to the base recreation area. Commando and the other senior NCOs grilled the steaks on a barbeque pit they'd built by cutting a fifty-five-gallon drum in half, the long way, and welding a grate over the bottom half. They really put on a show and had beer and chips for the entire squadron, but of course, because I was flying that night I didn't drink.

I was having a great time, lazing by the lake. I had a big T-bone steak, drinking Coke, and playing volleyball. Across the lake from us, the Marines were doing the same thing, and someone challenged us to a flag football game.

While the game was on, the Marine commander, a full colonel, recognized our wing commander, also a full colonel, as a classmate from the National War College. They renewed their acquaintance and we had a great time losing the game to the Marines.

The Marine colonel spotted our steaks on the barbeque and re-marked that they only had hot dogs and hamburgers to eat. "The Air Force always had it easy," he said, referring to the steaks. Not to be out-classed, our wing commander picked out the biggest and juiciest T-bone and gave it to the Marine colonel as a reward for winning the football game. I resented that he had given back the best steak. After all, I had worked hard to hornswoggle the damn things.

Later, there was an uproar coming from the Marines by the lake. It looked like they were throwing rocks at someone who had jumped into the water and was swimming our way. When the figure finally came into focus, we saw a dog with something large in his mouth, paddling for all he was worth. The Marines were yelling and throwing rocks and the dog swam like a hairy dolphin.

About halfway across the lake I recognized the dog. It was the mangy face of our mascot, Spooky, who was now out of range of the Marine's rocks. His head was mostly dry from the customary big grease spot and his mouth was wide open. I swear that he was smirking from ear to ear.

As he got closer, we saw a piece of meat in his mouth. Someone shouted, "Spooky got the steak back from the Marine colonel!"

As my favorite mutt climbed out of the lake, I heard a chorus of, "Here boy. Good boy, Spooky, nice steak." He did his dog-shake to get the water off. Then he lay down under a tree to eat his hard-won prize T-bone.

By this time, some of the Marines came around the lake to take care of that 'mangy mutt,' and were confronted by Commando who said, "Come on boys, he's just a dog. We'll give you another steak."

He walked over to the cooler to get them a replacement T-bone. However, they had all been eaten and there were no more to give the Marines. We stood around laughing while our wing commander took delight in telling the story about how Spooky got the last steak from his classmate.

We had a great time patting Spooky and laughing at the Marines eating their hot dogs and hamburgers while we ate the finest 'Marine' chow in all of Vietnam.

Near the end of the party, I asked Don a question.

"Are you ready to fly with me tomorrow night and get a real taste of real combat?"

"I would love to fly with you Airman," he lied, "but the wing commander and I have been designated critical personnel. That means that we have been ordered not to fly on combat missions. I will fly to the training area tomorrow afternoon and give you your check ride there."

I couldn't help rubbing it in. "Stay tomorrow night and fly with me. I have a great mission north of the DMZ where the radar-controlled quad fifty is out of calibration and misses us by a good fifty feet. It's sooooo cool."

"I would love to go, but duty calls. See you tomorrow afternoon. The wing C.O. and I have to go to a reception with the base commander, now, so I don't have time for your petty games." He dripped with snobbery and disdain.

The next afternoon I had a flawless check ride with Don, in a combat-free zone over the China Sea training area. During the flight, Don felt the need to say to me: "You're always going to be just a gunner; meanwhile, I'll be the chief gunner of the Air Force."

211

Joe Berardino

I couldn't help it. I replied, "I always *wanted* to be 'just a gunner, to protect my crew and the marines. That's enough for me. I don't have to be a high and mighty chief to prove my self-worth."

He looked at me with a sneer on his face and said with scorn, "You'd better remember your place, Airman. We senior NCOs are the backbone of the Air Force and we have seen many smart-assed airmen come and go. If I hear one more insubordinate comment out of you, I will flunk you on the spot. I am the Stan-Eval gunner, and if I say so, you are grounded and will never fly again. You'd better show me some respect and remember your place. I've heard how you've been undermining the authority of the senior NCOs, and I will not stand for it. Obey my orders, do your job and quit this nonsense about going to college and getting commissioned. If I ever hear you're undermining the authority of the NCOs again, I will personally end your career there and then. You got it, Airman?" I had to swallow my pride, and it was a bad moment. "I got it, Sarge. Sorry if I offended you. I meant nothing by my thoughtless comments."

I certainly felt put down. I had been insubordinate to Don and not shown him the respect due to his rank.

I put my ego in check and acted the humble Airman. But the humility sure tasted like a shit sandwich.

During the check ride the wing commander was along, and wanted to fly over the battleship New Jersey. He said, "There are only two battleships in the fleet, the New Jersey and the Iowa. They are the finest ships ever built. I studied them in the War College and the NJ has a sixteen-inch gun that fires a bullet heavier than a Volkswagen."

He spoke to the controllers and received permission to fly east, near the great ship, and observe it firing. I watched out of the door as the behemoth positioned herself and fired a mighty salvo. The three guns exploded, and I felt the percussion in the airplane from a mile away.

An enormous cloud of smoke came out of the barrels and three two-thousand-pound rounds propelled over twenty miles to hit their intended target.

The mighty New Jersey was an incredible sight.

. . .

After his theft of the Marine's steak I found a great love for Spooky the Wonder dog. Even more remarkable, he found a new respect for me. I started a food saving bank where we put all our ham and lima beans C-rations and daily served him a warm can for breakfast. He became my great friend and constant flying companion.

CHAPTER XXXII

THE MONSSON MISSION

I got up early and my mind was still hazy. Walking around in a trance, I needed a cup of coffee so got ready to hike to the chow hall.

It was raining, light and misty, I put on my poncho, one of those big green ones that fit like a tent and had a large hood. With the hood up, it was similar to being in a tunnel, I could only just see straight ahead and nothing to the sides. Even the sight in front was fuzzy and indistinct.

The dark clouds made me smile because we often did not fly when the weather was bad. Monsoon season, in early June, always caused a lull in the fighting. I knew the Marines would be happy about the lower chance of being attacked. They could use a break.

As I walked past the Guard Shack, in the entrance to our compound, the clouds separate and a ray of bright warm sunshine blazed through. The bright light illuminated me and I took down the hood and walked and basked in the fine morning.

•   •   •

While sloshing through puddles, my mind remembered that it was my last mission. And like everyone else, I started to shake and secretly choke up with joy. *I go home tomorrow!* Death on my 'fini flight' would be a great pity, for I had almost made it. We often heard stories about a soldier who had almost made it; but, tragically died on his last mission. A heightened foxhole mentality, fear and anticipation, gripped me. But, the night finally arrived. The words, 'last mission' hung ominously over my heart.

Tex and I went out to the airplane to preflight. After tonight, he was going to be on his own, and I thought he was ready. Previously, he had taken the lead when I was hurt one night and performed admirably. Later, I was out sick, he was given a new airman to train and Ace said he was "terrific." He had developed so well that Commando Jerry asked him to be a lead gunner. Tex took me by surprise when he said, "I can't wait to be a lead gunner, but, I want to fly the last few missions with my old trail-mate, Gunner Joe."

I watched in amazement as Tex went through his check list. He was methodical, detailed and careful as he examined each gun. He went to the extreme of taking off every feeder and cycling it through watching and listening for any glitch or hitch in the smooth operation of the unit

Ron used to tell me the only real safety margin we had was crew coordination. And that Tex and I had developed by flying together with our brother warriors.

I felt honored that Tex wanted to fly with me. He added to my pride when he told me that he conveyed the wishes of all the enlisted flyers that I get home safely, get a degree and get commissioned. Sounding like Ron, he told me, "It is your responsibility to become the best and most that you can. You represent all of us now."

Though elated about leaving, I felt an elephantine weight; a fear that something would happen to my crew without me there to fly with them. I had an overwhelming feeling of impending doom. "Tex, you're a fine Gunner and will lead your new second gunner with bravery, wisdom and distinction," I told him. "I will be with you every night. Protect my crew, our airplane and yourself at all times." I almost sounded like a referee in a boxing match.

I looked for Ace, found him reading by himself, and asked for his final words of wisdom. He told me, "Everyone will be against you and will try to dissuade you from going after your goal. Never let them talk you out of it. You can accomplish anything you want to, with enough hard work."

"I promise to work hard and never become discouraged. I will represent this crew and make you proud of me," I told him.

I saw Zoomie and asked for his advice. He told me that everyone would be against the young guys getting ahead. "They fear that you will succeed and show them up, so they want you to fail. Don't let them see you fail. Older folks had their dreams crushed so they resent your aspirations and will put roadblocks in your way. It has been this was since Aristotle, but the old folks can't stop the march of youth."

Soarer had been a great friend and counselor to me as well, often advising me on what courses to take and even helping me with difficult college assignments. I would miss him enormously. He said, "Joe, you are like a son to me. I want the very best for you. Keep the fire in your heart and the pep in your step and nothing can stop you."

The phone rang and before the first ring had finished Ace picked it up and signaled to us. I ran out, grabbed my chock, got in the airplane and began arming the guns as Tex got in and helped me. We fast-taxied out to the end of the runway and took off.

Soon after takeoff, Ace got on the interphone to brief us. "There is a Marine platoon surrounded near Hue Phubi that needs our immediate help. There is no other aircraft available, we've been elected."

"Nav, what's the route and weather we have to penetrate?" Ace asked.

"Pilot, Nav. Take a heading north by northeast, and I will get a better weather report. Right now they're saying overcast, with the cloud layer at 1,500 feet. It doesn't look like we can do much to help the Marine platoon."

This was a common weather pattern during monsoon season. Rain, winds, mountain and clouds made it almost impossible to descend low enough to help Marines under attack and in peril.

217

"Okay, Nav. Get us the best report you can. We need to help these guys!"

A minute later, Soarer came back over the radio and reported.

"Pilot, Nav. Cloud cover to 1,500 feet. Large hills, up to 3,500 feet, surrounding the platoon and no navigation aid to help us let down in the vicinity of the troops in contact."

"Roger, Navigator. Get us over the South China Sea and I will let down safely over the water. Over the ocean, we can't hit any hills. When we are low enough, we will visually find the mountains and fly inland between the hills. I know it's scary, but, the Marines are in critical condition and need our immediate assistance."

"Roger, pilot. Understand, just wanted to point out the inherent danger to the crew and airplane using that tactic."

"Got it, Nav. We have to try to help the platoon," Ace replied.

We flew northeast, found an acceptable place to let down, and started our descent. I told Tex, "You look out the right side of the airplane and I'll look out the left, to see when we can locate any discernable ground or water reference position. Keep your eyes open and report anything you see."

Ace began the descent, and after two minutes, I was just able to make out the shoreline from the open cargo door.

"Tally ho on the surface. Nine o'clock a couple of miles away," I reported.

"Roger that, gunner. Now look for the mountains to the south," Ace ordered.

We strained our eyes in the dim light to see any single feature that would indicate an open path inland, towards the embattled Marines. Zoomie cried out, "There's a break in the mountains at two o'clock. Can you see it?"

"Roger," said Ace. "Nav, get a LORAN fix on it, to use as a way point."

He was referring to the Long Range Aid to Navigation system that used ground reference beacons to broadcast signals that could be homed in on to triangulate a position. Soarer answered, "Got it, Ace.

I can find our way back out to here if we get disoriented. By the chart, we can proceed inland from here between the mountains, where there is an open space between hills. We can orbit and shoot from there. If this ceiling holds, we should be okay."

We flew in between the mountains with enough clearance that it didn't seem a problem. We found the platoon and began firing for position, so they could see where we were and guide us, prior to firing for effect. I had the guns on and stayed in the doorway to watch the action. After firing the first burst for effect, we were back in the clouds and I couldn't see a thing.

"Where the hell are the mountains?" Ace yelled.

"Break left, descend," Zoomie said. As the airplane banked left and dove down, we momentarily broke out of the clouds, and I saw the mountain to the left.

We passed in and out of wispy, misty air, losing sight of the ground and the mountains from minute to minute.

"This is insane," Ace said. "We can't all watch the target or we're going to hit the mountain. Here's how it will work. I'll fly as close to the clouds as I can, and Zoomie, you watch out front and to the right. Gunner, you watch out to the left and behind. Nav, you keep our position with the LORAN and I will work the target, with Tex working the guns. We must keep track of that mountain at all times or we will hit it and kill ourselves."

"Got it, sir!" I answered.

We entered the firing circle again, this time at around 1,500 feet, very close to the clouds. I didn't know which was more likely to kill me, the enemy or the pilot. We fired again and I fixated on the mountains.

On the next circle, I was watching the mountain when we once again got into the clouds. Ace yelled, "Where the hell are the mountains?"

"Dead ahead. Break right!" Zoomie shouted. We made an emergency hard-right turn, away from the immediate danger. The hackles raised on the nape of my neck as I held on for dear life.

"Son of a bitch," the navigator said. "This is impossible. Ace, you're jeopardizing the entire crew and accomplishing marginal results. I think it's time to return to Da Nang."

"Negative, Soarer. You have been through hell with me before and we can make it this time, if you will give me your full attention on keeping us out of danger. Crew, keep one hundred percent alert. We will make a couple more passes and then RTB."

Again we went into the firing circle and absolute blackness surrounded me. I couldn't see a thing. We were back in the clouds and Zoomie shouted, "Mountain ahead, break right!" The airplane jerked hard right and I fell against the cargo straps. I jumped up to stare out of the open door, unable to see a thing but thick clouds. Then we broke out of the darkness. Ace jerked the airplane to the left, and I could see the ground rushing by the door.

"Damn, that was close," Ace said. "I'm climbing back to altitude to see if we can find a hole in the clouds to shoot through."

We climbed in a tight left hand circle, slowly gaining altitude, with moment-to-moment reports about the location of the dreaded mountain. After a few minutes, we broke out on top of the cloud layer.

I was exhausted, almost entirely spent. I felt like a runner at the end of a marathon, having put forth maximum dash-speed for the last mile. I had never felt such exhaustion. I wanted to get a drink of water, lie down on the floor and close my eyes. The incredible tension of watching for the mountains had nearly killed me. Finally Ace spoke. "That was a hairy one, crew. We're done. They are sending in ground reinforcements to relieve and evacuate the platoon. We think the enemy has stopped firing and departed the area. We're going back to Da Nang. Good job."

Later, after landing, he said, "I'm sorry to make your last mission the most exciting of your life Joe, but, it couldn't be helped."

He was wrong. My life had many more exciting episodes to follow.

CHAPTER XXXIII

WHO CAN DIE ON A MILK RUN

A dark cloud hung over me. It was overpowering. A feeling of impending doom. My thoughts were full of sadness. Every night I saw again Ron's airplane shot down in my horror dreams. Vivid crash scenes woke me in a cold sweat. The bitter taste of tears clouded my coffee every morning. I couldn't shake the pains in my stomach or the downs. My constant companions, sadness and grief were like open sores on my heart.

I couldn't stand being at Da Nang; everywhere I looked reminded me of pain and death. Yet, the thought of leaving my brother warriors made my hands shake and my head break into a sweat. The obsession continued to haunt me; we had never lost a crew and airplane when the whole team was together. Leaving felt like abandoning my brothers, exposing them to death.

How could I leave them? But, I had to leave some day, I reasoned. My family needed me back home and I damn sure needed them.

So I said my pained goodbyes and turned away. I was ashamed that I felt weepy. I had a hollow feeling in the pit of my stomach.

With head down, I caught a hop to Nha Trang to out-process from the squadron and catch the freedom bird home. After landing, I met Don at the NCO club. He couldn't wait to tell me how wonderfully he lived as a senior NCO. He wanted to rub it in that he had a beautiful girl in a villa in town. He bragged that he flew the safest missions, and got the best medals. He went on and on about the hot and cold running girls in his palatial villa. I tried to blow it off, but my face turned hot whenever he bragged. I actually dreamt about him being killed by walking into the propeller of the airplane. The whole talk with Don made me sick to my stomach.

Don was not the first to take advantage of his rank and position. He was just the latest person to point out the utter unfairness of life in the war zone. The difference between the combat grunt serving his honorable duty and the politically motivated sycophant self-serving his time to advance himself was a stark comment on the failures of the American system.

Honest heroes like Ron, Jack, Tex, Zoomie and Ace slugged away, risking their lives, while pretenders and cowards hid in headquarters and rear echelon bases.

• • •

At 7:00 P.M., some other Air Commandos joined us. I recognized a couple of them and we spent the next hours telling war stories. I wondered about my old crewmate Whitey. He had some problems at Da Nang. He told the medics that the fear of dying caused him to pass out drunk, every night. So, they sent him to Na Trang to dry out.

"Hey, Sergeant Que. Where's Whitey?"

"Your old Load Master is doing fine. You know, he's flying tonight," Master Sergeant Cubrandich said, sipping his beer.

"I heard he quit drinking."

"Whitey made a complete turnaround when the Commander ordered him to dry out. You know, he was a paranoid nervous wreck flying at Da Nang. When he got into rehab he became a changed man." Cubrandich smiled warmly.

"That's great. I always loved him as a human being. But, honestly, we all hated him as a drunk," I said.

"You know, he even volunteers to help out at the chapel," Que said. "Bullshit."

"He is a sober changed man, you know," he said shaking his head.

"Man, at Da Nang, I never saw him drink before he flew, but we were all suspicious that he was half shit-faced when we took off. Flying in combat is tough, but flying with a drunk just turns the odds completely against you."

"You wouldn't recognize him. Once he got away from the pressure, you know, he quit drinking, stopped smoking, straightened out his uniforms and volunteered to help anywhere he could. He's a model NCO and we're proud of him," he glowed.

"Wow, I'm amazed. I guess the fear of combat is too much for some people," I said, putting my thumb up to my mouth and turning it up as if it was a bottle. In the back of my mind, I thought I was drinking way too much myself and would have to kill that monkey when I got home.

"Well, here's to Whitey." I raised my bottle of Bud and everyone toasted and banged bottles with me.

Like good Air Commandos we drank at the club until they threw us out.

. . .

I woke to a gorgeous orange and rose-colored sunrise. I even heard a bird chirping at the open screen of the hooch where I crashed. My heart raced, *Today I will see Toni and Cindy.* I smiled as widely as possible. I put in a new blade and shaved so close I nicked myself and couldn't stop the blood dribbling off my cheek. I slammed on my clothes, jerked closed the lock, hefted my duffle, and lurched outside to rush home to my beloved family. But, I did have to stop at the orderly room to pick up my pay records before going to the passenger terminal and strapping on the freedom bird.

I hoisted my duffle over my shoulder. Man, it felt unbelievably light. It was so light, I felt I could carry it the ten thousand miles to

Miami if I had to. I never felt happier in my life, I whistled *We're off to see the Wizard, the Wonderful Wizard of Oz.*

I must have looked a spectacle, jogging to the Air Command compound. As I floated along, my heart was full of love, my mind full of happiness, my face full of smiles and my step full of skipping. *What could be better?*

Rounding the corner, I gathered myself to add a little dignity as I walked between the ten foot high walls and through the gate into the entrance of the compound. Something was wrong. The sight didn't register for a moment. Something looked out of order. The white gravel driveway was still pristine and brilliant, the shiny Jeep was parked in the place of honor, the two propellers lined the entrance and the captured AAA gun was still pointed to the enemy. But something was strangely wrong.

My shoulder hurt. I put down the heavy duffle. I rubbed my shoulder where the straps dug in. I looked over the scene. *What's wrong with this picture?*

Then I saw it. I stopped breathing. My mouth dropped open. I put my hand over my heart. The flag was at half-mast. *I hope President Johnson wasn't assassinated. What if my crew got killed last night after I left them. Ace, Zoomie, Tex, Roger, are they okay? Please God, Please...*

A fog slipped over my heart. My mouth gapped open. Suddenly I felt cold, my stomach sank and I wanted to run to the airport and escape home. My hand trembled and darkness came over me. I took a deep breath and crept in the screen door.

The First Sergeant and Commander were standing with heads down. They were whispering in hushed tones with Sergeant Cubrandich. The room felt sad and almost crying. Cubrandich looked at up with a frown and sad eyes. Speaking in slow motion, he said, "We lost an airplane last night. The whole crew was killed. Whitey is dead."

CHAPTER XXXIV

THE JOY OF LIFE; GOING HOME

As we broke ground in the Boeing 707, a cheer went up from the hundreds of soldiers in the airplane. The airplane smelled clean and fresh and the aroma of fresh donuts and coffee made my mouth water. A tall soldier wearing a white bandage wrapped around the top of his head yelled, "Let's sing a hymn."

All the other soldiers sang out, "Him, him, fuck him."

I didn't know what it meant but I laughed anyway.

Time after time, they went over the same song. The elation at leaving the country that had been our prison made all of us smile and laugh without provocation.

I looked out at the South China Sea and thought what I learned about Whitey's death. They were flying base CAP at seven thousand feet and just disappeared off the radar. There was no evidence of enemy fire or any misdeeds. There was speculation that a wing broke off. The crash was being treated as an accident. The irony wrapped me like a blanket in the cold.

To distract myself, I opened the *How to Win Friends and Influence People* and started reading the ebullient and bolstering words. I had never heard such a positive voice in my life and it gave me hope and encouragement to dream for my family's future.

On the final leg to Miami I finished the great book. A feeling of hope overwhelmed me. A cloud had been removed from my head, *I made it.* I was bolstered with positive thoughts: that I'd escaped the hellhole of Da Nang and face a new future of great adventure and success. *All will turn out well.* As we circled to land I was thinking Miami was a green and beautiful tropical wonderland, which I will appreciate all the more for having been overseas. The curtain was opened and the Wizard revealed. The poncho hood was pulled back and I could see all the way to forever.

I had an incredible reunion with my wife and was reminded of why I loved her. Her dignity, elegance, purity, kindness and infinite patience with our daughter amazed me. I was filled with love, respect and admiration and wondered how I got so lucky as to have married her. She gave me courage to be a knight in white armor and I wanted to be worthy of her. She represented all that was good and noble in the world and I made a silent commitment to be the same for her and Cindy.

We had a great leave time and spent our days on the beach. The smell of the salt air and the sound of the waves cleared the stench of death and sound of guns from my head forever.

We whiled away the hours during the day and spent the nights visiting relatives. Of course we spent most nights drinking, partying and making love. But, most of the relatives were positive thinkers and encouraged us to work together as a young couple and build our life.

The real stick-in-the-mud was my father. He was a proud six foot tall, thin man with a perpetual tan and caustic attitude. He wanted me to get out of the service and work with him in Miami. He was a staunch liberal and hated war and feared that I would have to go back to Vietnam in the future.

"Get out of the Air Force, Joe. You don't need to be around those war-mongers," he said. "You can have a great life here, in beautiful Miami."

"Pop, I'm staying in the Air Force and going to college. I'm already taking college courses and there is a program where I can become an officer," I told him.

"Don't be so stupid. That is a trap where they keep enticing you with benefits and use up your life going to war. We are hardworking, blue-collar people who are honest. If you try to become an officer they will trap you in their politics and turn you into a war-monger. Is that what you want?"

"No, Pop. You've got it all wrong. They are honest, like we are, and they will help me get ahead. My pilot Ace was a major and as good a man as you will ever know. You don't know officers. You have prejudices based on your experience as a mechanic in the Army."

We were drinking at his local watering hole. After quite a few, he asked me, "Were you shooting at children and women?"

"Of course not!" I said in horror. "I only shot when an American was in danger. We were incredibly careful to make sure we didn't kill civilians."

He pulled his trap closed by asking, "What if it was a kid shooting at the Americans at night? Didn't you kill him then?"

"I would kill anyone who was trying to harm Americans."

"Then you're a baby killer!"

"I never knowingly shot at a child in my life. If that's how you think, then we are having the last conversation of our lives," I shouted in disgust.

"Calm down, Joe. I'm just making a point. The war-monger Pentagon leaders trap you into positions that are against what you stand for. I don't want you getting those stupid ideas in your head about becoming an officer. They are not our kind of people."

I couldn't sleep all night, thinking about my father's anti-war feelings. His belief that American warriors could be baby killers made me toss around all covered in sweat. I finally fell asleep thinking I would disown my own liberal father. *I think I'm defending the women and children of America and he thinks I'm a war criminal.*

·   ·   ·

The next day, my mind was clearer, and I let my concerns slip away. Toni was incensed though, and felt my father was abusing me. I drove her over to see my mother.

227

Ma' and her new George were having breakfast when we arrived. We sat down at the kitchen table and had coffee and Danish as we discussed our plans with them.

"Mom, we have to leave next week and go to Ohio, my new duty station," I said. But we have some exciting plans and we'd like your blessing.

I am going to try to finish college and get a commission as an officer. We know it will be hard, but we want to try it. What do you think?"

"I always knew you had it in you to make something of yourself. You have the brains of my side of the family and I always thought you should be an officer. I am so proud of you! I want to tell everyone I know," she said.

As I knew she had a flair for the dramatic, I learned to take every word she said with a grain of salt. I thought to myself, *she exaggerates to a fault and goes on longer than is comfortable, but she is the smartest person I have ever known. If she really thinks I can do it, then I think I can, too.*

We departed Miami on the following Monday to drive to Columbus, Ohio. Columbus was known to us as the home of Ohio State University and, more germane to my life, the home of gunship training for Vietnam.

CHAPTER XXXV

COMBAT CREW TRAINING

"We're forming a Combat Crew Training Squadron, the 4413 CCTS. We'll train aircrews to fly in Vietnam. We are building brand new gunships out of Korean War vintage C-119 Flying Boxcars. You are part of the initial cadre who will work with the Fairchild Hiller Aviation to build the aircraft. Then, you'll write the courses for the gunners who will be arriving in a few months. We have one other gunner, two pilots, and several navigators, loadmasters, and engineers who will arrive over the next week. In the meantime, go and get your family settled and report back here tomorrow morning at 0600," my new Commander ordered.

"Yes, sir!" I saluted smartly, about-faced and left

The next day I reported to the orderly room determined to build the finest training in the Air Force. I would teach my gunner students to be the best they could be and live up to Ron's high standards. I went over all the lessons Ron taught me and decided to incorporate them in what I wrote for the new students.

I first called Hulbert Field in Florida to talk to my instructors. I asked them what they had done to set up their program, and if they would send me copies of the training literature they had produced.

229

I set up a temporary classroom where we could begin training. In addition, I called all my weapons friends around the Air Force to get help finding training aids. I needed dummy ammo and demilitarized weapons, as well as training films and a host of other items to adequately train gunners.

In the afternoon, I went to the base education office to see what classes I could enroll in. It was July 1967, just in time for the beginning of the first semester. The education officer interviewed me and recommended I take the SAT, get transcripts from my previous schools and start classes that night.

I filled out all the paperwork, took the SAT, and sent in my application to be a temporary student, then awaited my transcripts and test results.

My wife was definitely excited about my classes. She had grown up in a family that stressed education and her parents always regretted that she couldn't get a college degree. She was giggled that I was pursuing one and greatly encouraged me.

"You go to school, darling. I will keep the home fires burning," she said. "You're doing this for all of us, and we are behind you 100 percent," her British accent still wowed me. "If you complete your degree, we will have many more opportunities for advancement. You won't have to be a gunner or a bomb loader for the rest of your life."

That night I attended my first class: Economics 101, Macro. My professor was from Ohio State University. I was amazed that, although the class was on base, the majority of students were civilians.

During the first break in class, we all stood around the hallway and introduced ourselves. A man who seemed to be around my age caught my attention. He had bright eyes and used a very large vocabulary.

"I'm Joe, and new to Ohio. This school, aaah, how is it?" I asked.

"I'm Rick," he answered. "It's okay, but this professor has the reputation of being a ball breaker. Have you had any econ before?"

"No," I answered. "But it's the only course I have the prerequisites for."

"What's your major?"

"Engineering, for now, but I have a while before I have to decide. What about you?"

"I'm doing pre-med, so I have to take everything that's hard," he said. "This is the first class I have taken on base, and you're the first military man I met. Is that your uniform?"

"Yeah, it's called a flying suit. I just came from work, so I kept it on."

"Do you fly?" he asked.

"Yeah, I fly a gunship."

"You're a pilot?"

"No, Rick, I'm a gunner—a member of the crew. Without the gunner, a gunship is useless. The pilot is like a very skilled taxi driver, and he takes me to the target."

"That's interesting. But why are you going to college at night?"

"I want to become a pilot someday, or at least an officer. I want to get a degree and do something with my life other than work on guns. What about you? Why are you in night school and not going full time?"

"I have to work all day in an electronics factory to afford school. But this way I don't owe anyone anything when I graduate. I'll do it all on my own."

"That's what I'm doing," I said, looking with wide eyes. "Working all day and going to school at night. I didn't know civilians did the same thing. I thought Daddy paid for all of you to go to school," I spread my arms out.

He laughed, "And I thought Uncle paid for you to go to school." He had a gleam in his eye.

We had a great hoot and chuckle about our mutual misperceptions..

. . .

The professor had an ass-kicking capacity for economic theory, causing me to study hard every night. I loved the class and the opportunity to better understand capitalism and the other schools of economics.

However, it was apparent that my math skills weren't up to standards. After class, I asked Rick, "Do you guys ever have study groups? To compare notes and prepare for tests?"

"Sure do. Want to join one I'm starting for this class?"

"Great! I don't know if I can add much. But I'll work hard as I can," I said.

I went home with my latest inspirations—a shiny textbook, a new friend and a rekindled spirit for the future. I was so excited, I stayed awake most of the night studying my textbook and adding to my limited knowledge.

The next evening, I drove off-base to Rick's apartment. I met his three other civilian friends and we studied for a couple of hours.

I left our session with a newfound respect for my friend Rick. It was a revelation that the civilians were studying very hard and trying to achieve worthwhile goals without a military or parental structure guiding them. They truly were self-motivated and dedicated to earning an academic education. Meeting them gave me great confidence in the determination and resourcefulness of the American youth.

The following night I had another eye-opening course, philosophy. Once again, armed with a knowledgeable professor, aided by great books and motivated by a love of knowledge and desire to advance, I entered the battlefield of academia.

Thus, I entered one of the most enlightening and exciting periods of my life. Every class, every study session and every night spent memorizing my text seemed to double my knowledge and awareness of life through education. In essence, this was my academic water shed, the time when my love of learning came to fruition.

The light went on; the clouds rolled back, Socrates awaited me.

CHAPTER XXXVI

FLYING THE BOXCAR GUNSHIP

"Son, I was a gunner before you were born," Chief said. "In the B-29 we fired the guns ourselves without the pilot pushing the trigger."

"I'll bet you saved democracy and the western world, Chief," I jibed him.

I never spent any time with a Chief Master Sergeant before, so I was glad to meet the highest-ranking gunner in the Air Force. He was my same height, six foot; a little heavier, maybe two hundred pounds; and a lot older, perhaps fifty with a round red face with busted blood veins in his nose and thin wispy grey-blond hair. He was my new boss.

He was the leader of all us enlisted personnel. To make it better, he was a gunner even though he had not flown in over twenty years. Chief was tough, old school, brash and headstrong. He knew everything and was a take-charge kind of guy. Like most of us he had an ego and didn't mind telling me what he knew and what he had done. He loved to tell me he had fought the devastating Germans with modern weapons, while I had only fought tribal warriors with spears. All day long he would pick my brain to find out how he could be a better gunner.

The next crewmember to flash into our lives was Big Turkey. He was my pilot. Big Turkey was a huge man, larger than a tank and louder than a cannon. He walked big, he talked big and he acted big. He had thousands of flying hours and countless combat missions.

He was chosen because of his vast flying experiences. Though not a recent Gunship pilot, nonetheless he was confident that gunship flying would present no problems

Next to arrive was Finder, a real brain. Finder was assigned as my navigator, but this position was much more than that, as the navigators were expected to evolve into weapons control officers and sensor operators. These had to be highly intelligent individuals to develop the requirements and implement the systems.

Finder was a hell of a guy and acted as my academic adviser and counselor. He even went to the extreme of checking my homework. He was a hard working father of four and I had the greatest respect and admiration for him.

The last enlisted crew member to join us was Joe, the illuminator operator. The illuminator operator replaced the load master in the Spooky Gunship, as this aircraft had a gigantic spotlight as well as a flare dispenser. Using a small jet engine, or an auxiliary power unit (APU) as an electrical generator, the aircraft could shine a bright light on the target. The light could be used in infrared mode so we could see the target but the enemy couldn't see the airplane. This large complex light system needed a full time crewmember to operate. Joe was the first illuminator operator in the history of gunships. He was going to college at night himself and was helpful in my endeavors.

The first assignment for our dauntless crew was to go to the factory where the airplanes were being modified to make them into gunships. We went there to give our input to the company writing the flight manuals.

We took a commercial flight to Hagerstown, Maryland and drove out to the Fairchild Hiller aircraft factory. This was my first sight of the airplane and I was as wide eyed as I'd been the first time I saw a Mustang car, sleek, powerful and shiny. I stood there like a teenage boy, admiring a mechanical thing of beauty.

The AC-119 was a modified, Korean War, flying box car. It was a lot bigger than the AC-47 and had twin booms from the wings that supported a T-tail. In our discussions, I learned that it was a 43,000-pound airplane and had bigger and much more powerful engines than the Gooney Bird. The cargo compartment was very roomy and had four mini-guns installed on newly constructed pods. These pods sat under the gun and had electric feeders, so there was no more manual loading of the guns. Everything was new and clean. I felt great walking around the airplane like a kid with a new car, I wanted to show it off.

One day we had a chance to fly with the factory crew. Big Turkey was excited as hell to be flying the gunship and wore a cowboy hat for the inaugural flight. He cranked the huge 4,360 cubic-inch engines and we blasted off, with Turkey singing his heart out.

"OFF WE GO, INTO THE WILD BLUE YONDER, FLY-ING HIGH

INTO THE SUN, WE LIVE IN FAME OR GO DOWN IN FLAMES, HEY,

NOTHING CAN STOP THE US AIR FORCE."

CHAPTER XXXVII

GIVE YOUR ALL

I would stand back and watch Ron loading his guns when he didn't know I was. I acted like a fly on the fuselage observing my teacher, so I could get a better understanding of why he was so much faster. It gave me a feeling of confidence to watch Ron because he attacked loading a gun like a professional wrestler attacked his opponent. He jumped in with the greatest amount of energy he could muster. He clinched the gun, spun the barrels with amazing gusto, connected the ammo belt with perfect fluidity and he drove the loading handle like a tornado spins around a trailer park. In a flash, Ron was finished and his gun was firing, saving Marines.

He held nothing back; there was no reserve, no tomorrow, no power for a sprint around the arena. When he loaded a gun he did it with every ounce of energy in his body. When he finished he looked spent, weak, depleted, used up, and exhausted. Yet his recuperative powers were immense; he was like Popeye, life was his spinach and he took a breath of life and was renewed and fully able to repeat the performance minutes later.

"Don't do anything half-assed," Ron said. "If you are loading a gun, do it as fast and efficient as humanly possible. If you are

237

studying for a test, do it with the same gusto, energy, and enthusiasm that you load a gun. Don't slow leak your crew; give your all every time."

When I saw the adulation in others' eyes for Ron my chest swelled and I had a lump in my throat. I wanted to be like him. I watched, plotted, and practiced so I could emulate my teacher. Really he took on religious proportions; Ron became my Guru, the airplane my Ashram, the gun my Buddha, 'You can do it' my mantra. I studied and practiced his way in every aspect of my life. This included college studies.

•   •   •

After being gone for two weeks at the Fairchild Hiller factory, I went to Rick's apartment. "How you been, buddy? What's going on? How's school?" I asked.

"Everything's good Joe, but I have decided to speed up my graduation. So I am taking the College Level Examination Program (CLEP) tests."

"What are CLEP Tests?"

"They're tests you take and if you pass, the exam counts for the credit hours the same way as if you took the course."

"That sounds good to me." I said, as a picture of Ron came back to me. He looked in my eyes and said, "Why slow leak education when you could attack it and finish sooner and achieve your life goals that much earlier?"

I was left to ponder the essential questions of academic life. What was the purpose of an education? Merely egotistical, to be one of the educated few who had greater opportunities? Was the purpose of an education economic — to make more money? Was the purpose of an education status-seeking? To change one's rank and become an officer rather than an enlisted person? Or was the purpose of an education grander and bigger than the individual, as Rick suggested?

Then another thought crossed my mind. The real purpose of getting an education was to fulfill a promise I had made to my dead friend Ron, to be the best I could be.

Those thoughts turned each class into a combat mission. I had unsurpassed situational knowledge and awareness. I was on edge to harvest new knowledge; I had a new clarity of thought, and couldn't wait for class every night. I was consumed with my newfound love of learning.

Throughout that semester, I spent countless hours learning my lessons and thinking about the larger question of my purpose in getting an education. It was only later that I found the true purpose in my life was to fulfill Ron's dream.

CHAPTER XXXVIII

HATE RETURNS

In the afternoon of a fine, crisp Ohio day, Chief called me into his office with an announcement. "Joe, we have a new head gunner coming in today. His name is Don and he worked with you in Vietnam."

"Chief, are you *shitting* me?" I asked.

He shook his head. "He's going to be at the NCO club after work today. He said he knows you and was a friend of yours. Let's go later and meet him."

"Well, I know him, but he was never a friend of mine."

"What does that mean?" he asked.

"He has always lorded his rank and position over us airmen. He acted like he was better than the rest of us."

"Don't start out negatively. You have to work with him. He's Master Sergeant...leader of the gunners. Get used to it," he ordered.

After work, I scrambled into my red Volkswagen Beatle and raced to the club to meet Don. I forced myself to act happy to see him. I smiled, shook his hand and sat down with Chief and a couple of the other instructors and hoisted a few. We welcomed our new head gunner in the Air Command tradition; alcohol and war stories.

Halfway through the evening, after we were reasonably well-oiled the situation turned ugly. Chief was like an Irishman on St. Paddy's day, shit faced. When I returned from the men's room, Don and Chief were missing.

"Where are they?" I asked one of the other instructors.

"Don said Chief was over the hill and not flying in combat like he had. Well, Chief was pissed and invited Don outside to see what a real man was made of. They're on their way out back now."

I jumped up and darted to the back door. I saw them with their sleeves rolled up ready to fight. I grabbed Chief and said, "No, you don't, soldier. You are not hurting my newest gunner tonight. If anyone gets to fight the new guy, it's one of the young instructors who have never been in combat. They need the experience of fighting a real warrior like Don."

Chief pushed me away and said, "Get out of the way, Joe. I'm not taking shit from this asshole!" He had wide eyes and a frown of hate on his face.

"Chief," I said, "he didn't mean anything by it. Give us a break, leave him alone and let's get back to drinking. Somebody told the Sergeant at Arms we were coming out here and he called the cops. Let's get back inside."

"I ain't drinking with that fool," Chief retorted.

"Let's get in my car and I'll drive us to a nice, quiet bar off base," I said.

He swung at me and missed, spun around and I got him by the back shoulders and guided him to my car. He cooled down and I drove to my local watering hole.

Later that night, I called Toni and Chief's wife and told them where we were. After a couple more drinks, I dropped him off at his house and left.

The next day there was hell to pay. Chief called me into his office and read me the riot act for interfering with senior NCOs. He told me to give Don all the required study materials and to prepare to certify him within the month. I said, "Certify him as a gunner?"

"No, he has to be a fully certified *instructor* gunner in one month," knowing that was twice as hard as certifying as a gunner.

I went to Don's office to see him. I gave him the study materials and told him what Chief said. "You know that's a much higher standard than just being a gunner."

"Yeah, I know Joe." He looked at me sarcastically, "Don't worry about me, I can do it. Now you're dismissed. Leave me alone, I have an important meeting with the commander."

I went to the other instructor gunners, those who would eventually work for Don, and told them, "You'd better schedule him to fly every night. Chief will review my check ride results and won't tolerate any slack. You'd better make sure Don is good to go or there will be hell to pay."

I and the other check flyers worked for the check pilot and not for our area specialists. So I worked for Big Turkey and reported to him, not to the head gunners, Chief and Don. That way there could be no conflict of interest when I was required to evaluate one of the gunners.

A couple of weeks later I was meeting with our college study group in an empty classroom during lunch. We were discussing a midterm exam when Don walked in.

"What's going on?" he asked.

"Sarge, we're in class together," I said. "We have a study group that meets during lunch time. We're working on preparing for our mid-term."

Don exploded, "The NCOs have been telling me that you guys have been neglecting your duties to spend your time on frivolous crap, to impress the officers. I want this shit stopped immediately," as spit shot out of his mouth. "I forbid my instructors from meeting during duty hours to go over unnecessary school garbage. I'll assign areas of their *jobs* for them to study. Now, break it up and get out of here!"

I stood up and answered, "We're only studying during breaks. We are not neglecting our duties. In fact, going to college makes us all better and more pro…"

He stopped me by shouting, "Get out of here and back to your duty station! I warned you about your insubordination, airman." He stomped away.

We gathered up our books and left the classroom and returned to our respective duty areas. I stopped by Big Turkey's desk and told him what had happened.

"There are always old timers who resent young guys trying to get ahead. You just keep doing your job and keep me happy and you'll be fine," he told me.

• • •

It came time for Don's check ride. Prior to receiving his evaluation from the squadron, he had taken a practice check ride with his instructor. Then the results were evaluated by a second instructor. So, for all practical purposes, his official check ride should have been a mere formality. We never put a crewmember in the position of failing without adequate preparation.

That afternoon I had his evaluator, Jerry in to my office to discuss his written evaluation. "How did he do?" I asked.

Jerry looked away, lowered his head, and said, "He's okay."

"What do you mean, he's okay?" I asked. "Okay is not good enough. Didn't you train him? Didn't you get him up to speed?"

I looked at his evaluation forms. "You rated him marginal in a couple of categories, so what gives? You know we don't check ride someone unless they're fully qualified," I said.

He hemmed and hawed, "Joe, we tried to fully train him, but he only flew with us five times. He wouldn't study, and any time we tried to tell him something, he told us we were wrong. He writes my promotion recommendations, so I can't shoot him down."

"That's not good enough," I said. "We have to train him until he's fully qualified. I'm going to see him and get this straight."

I went down the hall to Don's office and asked for a minute of his time. "Sarge," I said, "I'm worried about this check ride. I'm going over your records, and you haven't flown a lot. Your pre-evaluation was marginal. I want to postpone this check ride until next week, after the instructors have more time to do their jobs. I don't think they have…"

"Listen, Airman," he stood up and looked directly in my eyes. His voice was shaky. "I'm the judge of who's ready for a check ride and who's not. You just do your job and don't try to run the instructor gunners. That's *my* prerogative. Now, we're having this check ride tonight and I will pass. Do you understand?" He pointed right at me.

I understood his implied direction immediately and answered, "Sarge, I have to evaluate everyone up to Air Force standards. We make exceptions for no one. Chief has to meet the standards; I have to meet the standards; every instructor has to meet them. So there's only one standard I evaluate by and I'll use it tonight."

He spat back, "Don't get on your high horse, college boy. We're just gunners around here. I'll pass the check ride or there will be consequences to pay. Get out of here."

I left and returned to my office to ponder my predicament. After a while, I went to Chief's office to ask his advice.

"Chief, I have to check ride Don tonight and I'm worried."

"What's the problem?" he asked.

"The evaluators say he hasn't flown enough and he's not ready. So I went to see him to delay it, to give him time to get ready. He told me that I *would* pass him and threw me out of his office. I don't like it."

"What do you want to do?" he asked me.

"I want to delay the check ride for a week; give him a chance to get up to speed."

"You gave him a chance to delay, and he didn't take it. I say give him enough rope to hang himself and check ride him tonight. If he flunks, it's his fault, not yours."

"Chief, that's not how we've done it in the past. We always gave a guy the chance to get fully prepared before we evaluated him. I think it's only fair."

"Joe, you gave him that chance. If he's too hard-headed to take it, then you've done your duty. Give him the check ride tonight. In fact, I'm so concerned about him trying to intimidate you to give him a passing grade that I'm going to fly with you tonight. I'm evaluating that you are fairly and properly executing an instructor's check ride. Any questions?"

"No, Chief. We take off at 1900 hours," I replied and left.

At 1800 hours, we assembled in the operations briefing room: my entire standardization evaluation crew, the full student crew, Chief and Don.

The pilot being evaluated by Big Turkey gave the mission brief. "We take off at 1900 hours and fly to the gunnery range in Indiana. We ingress the target and locate a Special Forces combat controller who will direct our fire. We will expend fifteen thousand rounds, twenty-four flares, and use the illuminator, all on target. We will depart the target at approximately 2300 hours and RTB. Are there any questions?"

After that, we went out to the assigned aircraft and began our pre-flight. I asked Don to recite his emergency procedures checklists. He stumbled and mumbled and it was obvious he didn't know them. I left him sitting on the ramp, and told him to study the checklist for fifteen minutes while I checked the other gunner.

Chief asked me why Don was sitting on the ramp. When I told him the reason he was irate and said something about giving special privileges to a friend.

After checking the other gunner's emergency procedures, which were flawless, I asked Don if he was ready.

"This isn't necessary," he said. "I'm in charge. I don't fly with students, so it's ridiculous to expect me to know every single check list item."

"It is a requirement of being a gunner to know your emergency checklist," I said. "I cannot pass you unless you recite it from memory."

The Chief came over and verified what I had said and listened in while I quizzed Don. Don was barely able to recite his procedures.

Chief asked me, "What are you gonna do?"

"He can't operate even as a student gunner if he doesn't know his emergency procedures. He fails on the spot, puts on his parachute and takes a passenger seat. He can stay on the flight, but he will get no credit for acting as a gunner."

"Do it. Inform Don and his pilot."

I told Don, "Your check ride is over. Put on the parachute and have a seat."

He glared at me. "I'll get you, Joe. You have had it in for me since we first met. You can't do this to me," he said, but he didn't see Chief standing behind him, who heard every word.

Chief broke in and said, "Don, shut the hell up. Joe told you that you weren't ready and tried to postpone this check ride. I only came along to see if he had the balls to flunk you and ground you. If he didn't flunk you *I* would have. And I would have fired him as the standardization gunner.

If you want to be pissed off at someone, be pissed off at me. I'm enforcing the gunner requirements and I'm insuring that you fail this check ride. In fact, it's a bigger problem than that. I don't like your whole attitude about gunner standards and the role of the check ride. I will discuss this further with you and the commander tomorrow morning. Now put on your parachute and have a seat."

Don did as instructed and we flew the rest of the mission without incident. After landing, I gave everyone a thorough debriefing and Chief and I retired to the club for a cool one.

Chief explained the entire situation to me at the club. "I flew tonight because the commander asked me to. He was concerned about Don's attitude. Don has not taken our flying requirements seriously and has been a bone of contention for all the gunners. I've asked the commander to send him to the gun room as the head mechanic and take him off of flying status. I'm tired of Don and so is the commander. We will take care of all of this in the morning."

The next morning, I reported to duty as always, and Big Turkey asked me about what had gone on. I explained it to him and he then said the commander wanted to see me.

I reported and he asked the same questions and informed me that a 'Flight Evaluation Board' was convening that afternoon to consider what had happened. The board was composed of the commander, operations officer, standardization pilot and Chief.

At 1300 I reported to the board.

"Sir, Airman Joe, reporting as ordered." I saluted and stood at attention.

My operations officer spoke first. "Have a seat, Airman. We are here to determine what happened on your check ride with Master Sergeant Don last night. There have been allegations of favoritism, cronyism and pay-back and we would like to determine if it is true."

He then asked me a series of questions and determined that I had known Don for a couple of years and had been through gunner's school, survival school and Vietnam with him. "It was alleged that you harbor some antipathy against Sergeant Don because he received the best position in Vietnam. Was it true that he got the better assignment over your objections?"

"No, sir," I answered. "I didn't care where I went in Vietnam, but he made a big deal about not wanting to go to Da Nang. In hindsight, I'm happy that I went where I did, and harbor no ill feelings about our assignments at all."

"Is it true that you have an intense dislike for Don and want him to fail?"

"No, sir," I answered. "I wanted him to pass. As a matter of fact, I told the other instructors to make sure he practiced enough to ensure he passed. I tried everything I knew to guarantee that he had enough training and practice."

"Thank you, Airman. You're dismissed," he replied.

I stood, saluted smartly, did an about-face and left the room. I returned to my office. About an hour later, Big Turkey came in and said I was off the hook with the board.

After lunch, there was a mass meeting of the gunners in the operations briefing room and I attended. The commander and the chief came in and the chief began to speak.

"We are concerned that the instructor force has not been taking their responsibilities seriously enough. This will stop immediately. We are engaged in the most significant flying training you will ever have during your careers. We are training aircrews to go into combat. We must individually maintain the highest standards in our flying duties, and we must demand the highest standards in our trainees. If you are unwilling or unable to do that, raise your hand now and you will be excused without prejudice. But if you are to remain a member of this squadron, we will not tolerate the slightest slip in professional standards. Now I'll turn it over to our commander for further comments."

The full colonel walked over to the podium, adjusted the microphone, and then addressed us. "I know you gunners have not spent a whole career flying like the pilots and navigators have, so I feel that I should tell you some of the requirements that we have not stressed enough in the past. To be a flyer in the United States Air Force requires the highest individual standards. First, hundreds of people want to fly in the Air Force and you have been competitively selected from among all of those people.

"We selected you because we thought you were the best in all categories. You have worked the hardest, you have studied the longest and you have performed the best under pressure. Because you have this incredible opportunity to fly, you have become a representative of the Air Force to everyone who sees you. This is an enormous responsibility, as you project the image, heritage and history of the Air Force. I require that every flyer in my squadron project the highest image of professionalism, accomplishment and dedication. If you fail to do that for one second, I will cut you out of this squadron immediately. Any questions?"

Chief answered, "No, sir! Squadron, atten-hut."

And the commander marched out, leaving us standing.

"At ease," Chief said. "Take your seats. Do you see how seriously the commander takes our actions? We have not lived up to his expectations, and that changes this minute. You will never send an instructor for check ride who is not fully qualified. If you have the slightest concern, don't let him check ride. Everyone who fails to meet the highest standards of excellence will be sent to the gun room immediately and grounded for a minimum of three months. You may also never get to fly again. Do I make myself clear?"

We answered in unison, "Yes, Chief."

He left the room and we stood around for a few minutes discussing the situation.

Almost everyone thought Don had been fired and sent to the gun room because he failed to take the flying standards seriously. I thought it was also because he always tried to make himself look good, to the detriment of the program.

Needless, to say we felt sufficiently chastised to re-examine our standards and take every action as seriously as possible.

• • •

Big Don did not take demotion to the gun room very well. He became very intolerant of all the gunners and avoided us like we were anthrax. As soon as he could he planned a cataclysmic retirement party for all of his Detroit friends. I happened to see him at the party at the club and tried to talk to him. He was wearing his old flying suit, and as I approached, he turned away and started laughing with his friends.

He retired to Detroit and we never heard of him again.

• • •

Don had always been a challenge to me, but I had bigger challenges to come.

CHAPTER XXXIX

SELF INFLICTED WOUNDS

"Gunner, where the hell are all those stray rounds coming from?" Turkey screamed over the headset. "This is freekin' insane!"

"I don't see them, sir." I knowingly smiled at the students. "Everything looks fine back here." I said looking through the window of the dark airplane. I walked around the cargo compartment giving check rides like I was the king. I was the center of attention showing the student how to disassemble the gun in the dark. I talked with my chin held high and my nose in the air. In truth, I couldn't see the left engine housing, or nacelle, where he thought the ricochets were coming from. But, having flown the aircraft twenty times over the last year, I felt certain that the rounds were not hitting it.

"Every time we fire number one gun, stray tracers shoot off toward the front of the airplane." Big Turkey sounded pissed.

I got down, squinted my eyes like aiming a rifle and sighted down the barrels of number one gun into the pitch-black night. It was aligned close under the left engine nacelle. But, there had always been just enough clearance to be safe. "It's perfect. Nothing to worry about. Maybe some bad ammo causing stray rounds," I winked at the student and shrugged.

"You better make absolutely certain that weapon is firing a safe distance under the airplane. It would cause a catastrophic explosion if one of the rounds went into the fuel tank." I never heard Turkey sound so serious. I strained my eyes down the barrels and looked again. *There must be enough clearance; I flew this plane only yesterday. No problems.*

We rolled into the firing circle, left wing down, ROOOOOMMMM. "You gunners, did you see the stray rounds shooting forward?" The student pilot's voice was screaming and shaky.

I was in charge so I answered, "No, pilot, nothing wrong back here."

"Check out the left side. Big Turkey's coming back to look."

I leaned over the gun and Big Turkey, the senior pilot shined his little pencil flashlight out but we couldn't see a thing. "I can't even see the wing or the engine nacelle," I said, straining my eyes.

"Okay, but it's your ass if there is something wrong with the guns," he said with a stern voice and hard look on his jaw.

I decided to stop firing number one and load all the ammo in the other guns. We didn't have any more problems. The other gunners came over and fiercely peered out of the window but couldn't see any problems.

•   •   •

"Gunner, get up. There's a truck load of officers who want to see you," my roommate said shaking my bunk the next morning.

I rubbed the sleep from my eyes, the clouds from my head and the lead from my ass and hustled outside. They had an extended cab truck and Big Turkey was driving. In the rear seat, I recognized the pilot from the previous night and there were two other officers.

Turkey introduced them, "Joe, this is Major Jordan the Flying Safety Officer and his Assistant Captain Curry."

"What's up, sir?"

"There's a problem with the plane we flew last night. We're investigating what happened and sending a report to higher headquarters," he had deep furrows on his brow and seemed serious. I held my breath, *What happened last night?*

Off in the far distance I could see it. There, in the explosive loading ramp, where it couldn't threaten other aircraft, was my plane, parked all by itself. As we crept up to it, I could see the lonely machine was surrounded by a barrier of flaming red tape with ACCIDENT INVESTIGATION slashed across it. The airplane looked like a quarantined diseased buzzard, fenced away from the rest of the flock so as not to infect them. Like maggots on the corpse of the injured and dying bird, there were a gaggle of fifteen mechanics under the left engine nacelle. They had ladders and maintenance stands all around the wing and three other mechanics were on top, examining it.

We parked and joined the maggots and looked up at the bottom of the black widow airplane. The nacelle door had a gaping open wound eighteen inches long, five inches wide and five inches deep. It looked like a slash from a giant knife. The gash of aluminum was shot away, the ragged edges were torn and frayed, like exposed flesh that I would have to suture closed. It looked hideous with uncovered hydraulic lines, rivets, wing spars and fuel lines open to the decaying elements.

Major Jordan said, "This is a very serious aircraft incident that requires a full investigation. Gunner, you need a lawyer."

I felt dizzy. I could hear Ron in my head: 'You ain't Doris Day—you should have stopped this. You can't go through life 'Que sera, sera. You are the master of your destiny, take charge and make it right.'

I shivered in my skin. I felt cold and alone looking at the airplane. I had caused the guns to shoot up our own airplane and could have killed everyone. I hung my head and thoughts raced through my mind: *If I ever get out of this predicament, I will never fail to follow Ron's example.*

After taking pictures and examining every inch of the tear in the aluminum skin we finally left the flight line. I couldn't have hurt more, there was an ache in my stomach and fear gripped my ribs. I was disappointed with myself. I saw red. Anger and pain flowed through my veins.

I drove to see the Area Defense Council, my lawyer, to find out what to do. He told me we had to wait until the investigation report came out. I felt alone for the three days it took to get the report. I went to his office every day and was told not to contact anyone who was on the airplane or might have information about what happened. I was alone—like my plane.

•   •   •

Friday the report came out and I went to the ADC's office to read it. The investigation exonerated me. The accident board determined that there were insufficient procedures to insure the gun had adequate clearance to safely fire under the nacelle. It was the fault of the engineers at Fairchild. From that day forward, gun stops were installed on all aircraft.

I thanked God. I thanked Lady Luck. I thanked Ron for the great lesson. I swore to follow his example every day of my life.

CHAPTER XL

SPOOKY ONE IS DOWN, RON IS DOWN

"**Y**ou're like a one legged man in an ass kicking contest," Chief said.

"Man, you know it. I don't have time to smell the roses," I said as I looked around his small efficient office by the flight line.

"Yeah. But do you have to take so many classes at night? Three nights a week doesn't leave you enough time to fly," he said.

"I have to finish thirty hours so the AF will send me full time."

"You have a bigger problem. One of the students saw a crack in the airplane wing. Go check it out with maintenance." Chief had a frown on his lips.

I went out to the aircraft parking ramp. Six airplanes were lined up, the first one was a shiny new AC-119K. She took my breath away; twin engines, twin booms, twin 20MM cannons and twice as large as the AC-47. This beast was a sight to behold. The airplane was painted deep black so to be unseen at night. The troops called it the black widow or the black scorpion because it was the most deadly airplane in the gunship fleet. Secretly it had a bad reputation for killing American paratroopers when they crashed in Korea. The soldiers called her the black widow because, 'She kills the men who ride her,' they said.

I had my first new instructor gunner with me, Jerry. "The damn airplane is trying to kill me," he said.

"Nobody gets killed in Ohio," I reminded him. "We're just in training."

"Joe, that airplane has an enormous crack in the wing and it's going to kill me. Remember the airplane from Nha Trang; the wing fell off and killed everyone." A cold chill came over me as he spoke of Whitey's death.

The crew chief put a stand up to the wing and we climbed up. "Right there," Jerry pointed an eight or nine inch long crack in the skin of the wing. "That damn wing is gonna fall off and kill everyone on the airplane," I nodded in agreement.

"Crew Chief," I waved my arm and shouted to the Crew Chief below us on the ground. "Have your supervisor come out here and look at this with us."

In a few minutes, a Master Sergeant came out and climbed up the wing stand. "My mechanics saw this last week and we drilled a hole to stop the crack growing. The crack went past the stop drill hole so we will have it evaluated by the engineers."

"Man that's dangerous as hell," Jerry said. "We have twelve people flying on that airplane every night and firing the guns. If there's a wing crack, it could break and kill everyone."

For a month, Jerry had warned us about the wing cracks, but maintenance had done nothing to fix the aircraft. There was some macho arrogance among the veterans that caused us to minimize the danger. In our minds, the missiles and bullets from the Viet Cong were going to kill us long before a broken airplane. Perhaps it was our egos but we were willing to live with the problem. It was a different story for the students. Four or five National Guard students went to the base Inspector General and complained that they were afraid to fly, terrified the wing would fall off and they would die even before arriving in Vietnam.

•   •   •

"Squadron, Attennn-sion," the First Sergeant screamed as he marched up to the front of the base theater.

We all jumped up and stood rigid still. I glanced out of the corner of my eye as a two star climbed on the stage. He was wearing a dramatically pressed flying suit that looked a little crispier than ours, a little sharper, a little nicer. Knife edged creases in the legs, shined silver stars on his shoulders, a chromed pearl handled .45 strapped to his hip. I thought he looked like the Air Force version of General Patton.

"I was sent here by headquarters to get to the bottom of your problem," he bellowed out, standing at rigid attention. He pointed directly into the audience and right at us. "You're too chicken to fly these brand new airplanes! What the hell is wrong with you? Are you cowards?" I was stunned into silence.

"You fly the broke ass airplane," someone behind me shouted. "Yeah you fly the fuckin' widow maker. We heard it was called the Paratrooper Killer, shit box in Korea." Shouts came from everywhere.

The first sergeant approached the podium; he held his hand upraised and apart. "The engineers checked the airplanes and there is nothing wrong with them."

"You and the engineers fly them, we don't have to fly," a voice behind me again.

"I know you enlisted flyers are only here for a tour or two. Your officers are in for a career of flying and they jump right in the airplanes. You can do it. There's nothing to be afraid..."

"Him, him, fuck him," a bunch of voices broke out behind me, from the Reservists students.

My face turned red and was very hot. *Who the fuck was he calling a coward?*

I vowed *I will never let that airplane kill me. I will stop flying. I'll never get in the C-119 Widow maker again!*

CHAPTER XLI

LEAVING COMBAT

"Joe, you simply can't risk it, darling," my wife came over and placed her hand on my forearm.

She had frown lines on her mouth and furrows in her brow. "You cannot fly that killer airplane ever again," Toni said.

"I can't be a coward. The men, they depend on me."

"Joe you have a daughter and wife who need you. All us wives live in constant fear like when you were in Vietnam." She looked so hurt; her eyes were sad and downcast.

"Pauline says the wing is going to fall off and kill the whole crew. The wings are cracked and ready to break," she shrieked. Then she turned away crying and ran off to our bedroom.

Her words pinged my heart. I felt a pained tug, when she looked miserable especially because I caused her the pain.

Suddenly, a knot grabbed my stomach as the memory of the scorpion black colored, widow maker airplane flooded into my mind. I saw Whitey's plane falling to the ground with one wing broken off, like a black and white film of a WWII bomber spinning down, out of control, to its death. A tingling went up my spine and I had a cold sweat going. I felt dizzy and didn't know what to say.

I went to the couch cuddling my baby girl, Cindy. I closed my eyes and quietly thought about the things a man shouldn't think about. The forbidden path, the path I could not take, my father's stepping over the line. *How can I quit? I'll be a coward like my father.* The night in Vietnam flooded into my mind, the night Ron died. I saw his airplane exploding in the sky, then burning on the ground, and then an image of his wife and baby daughter over the smoke of the shattered airplane. His daughter had Cindy's face. I tried to hold them in but they seeped out. Like Ron's dreams seeped out. Tears and dreams fell to the ground and were gobbled up by the dirt and dust of war.

Toni came back into the room with a tearstained face, "Sheila told me that when Dwight departs next month there is an opening as a classroom instructor." She clenched her fists, "Everyone would understand why you would take that assignment with a baby on the way," she pleaded. "And I was going to tell you later. We're having a baby."

"We're having another baby," I smiled and put my arms around my wife, she smelled like lavender. I hugged Cindy tightly. She squirmed in my arms and smelled like baby powder and felt as soft as the clouds in heaven. She made quiet cooing noises and I loved her.

I smiled so wide my jaw hurt. *A baby.*

.   .   .

"We have a real dilemma when Dwight leaves," the bright, crisp captain said.

"I'm sure I can teach his gunnery classes, I been on the gunships four years," I said.

"Will the flying squadron release you to a classroom slot?"

"Sure, the gunners rotate every other year for a tour back in the war so I would be leaving next July anyway. I'll ask my commander today."

"Our classroom slots are protected with assignment deferment for three years. That way you would be here when your wife has the baby."

I raced to our squadron building to see the Commander. I had to wait a few minutes and was let in. I marched in and saluted, "Sir, Gunner Joe reporting with a request."

"At ease, what gives Joe?"

"Sir, my wife is having a baby and I want to volunteer to teach in the ground school."

CHAPTER XLII

GUNSHIPS ARE FULL OF HEROS

"Do you know the difference between a fairy tale and a war story?" Bruce asked.

"No, man," I grinned.

"A fairy tale starts: Once upon a time. A war story starts: Man, this ain't no shit."

"Yeah, yeah," I laughed.

"Well, this ain't no shit." He made a flamboyant wave of his arms. Bruce had just returned to the land of the big BX and was telling us what had happened since we left Nam.

"Last month," Bruce said, talking about February 1969, "from their hiding places deep in the jungle, the Viet Cong launched a massive attack on the outpost at Long Binh. Just after 11:00 P.M., Spooky Seven was circling overhead after fighting the VC for four and a half hours. The enemy was all around the army outpost and the guns of Spooky Seven were hot from the thousands of rounds already fired. The threatened soldiers on the ground cheered every time Spooky Seven shot into the charging bodies of the Viet Cong. Time after time, the fearless men of Spooky Seven turned back the onrush of the VC."

Bruce continued, "Airman John Leetow was the Load Master inside Spooky Seven. The VC used the night darkness to hide their evil

263

intentions. John was throwing out magnesium flares so the soldiers on the ground could see the massing VC and turn their killing fire on the enemy hiding in the shadows. Near midnight, the soldiers directed Spooky Seven to fire on three mortar positions. After destroying two, the huge airplane turned to attack the third. An enormous explosion rocked the aircraft wildly, shaking and lurching from side to side and blew a devastating three-foot-hole in Spooky's right wing. They had flown directly into the path of an enemy mortar. Thousands of pieces of shrapnel tore into the airplane and into the bodies of the crewmen. While the pilot struggled to control the airplane the four men in the cargo compartment were dazed and unconscious, violently thrown to the floor from the devastating explosion."

"John shook himself to clear the dizziness from his head, while blood poured from thirty shrapnel wounds on his right side. He felt like he had been hit in the chest with a baseball bat. He saw an unconscious gunner lying by the open cargo door and perilously close to being flung out from the wild gyrations of the airplane. John dragged his bleeding body to the door and heaved the gunner forward to safety."

"Then he shook himself to clear his mind and remembered that when the enemy mortar exploded, John was standing in the doorway with a flare connected to the activation lanyard, ready to be launched. The concussion of the rocket knocked John down; wounded him, blasted the flare forward into the cargo compartment and pulled the lanyard activating it's timer.. The flare had a thirty second delay fuse for the canister to blow off, and another ten seconds before the flare lit. When lit, the flare burned at four thousand degrees, was three million candle power bright and gave off toxic fumes."

"Recognizing the danger, John could have jumped out of the airplane with his parachute and saved himself. Knowing the rest of the crew would die if he jumped, he struggled to save his crew. With shrapnel injuries caused him excruciating pain, and almost losing consciousness, he crawled forward and looked for the flare. As it rolled around the wildly careening airplane in the pitch dark of night, John hurled his body on the flare and captured it. John cradled the ticking time bomb, crawled to the back of the airplane, dragging his wounded and bleeding legs."

"When he got to the open door, the flare in his bear hug, with the last ounce of strength in his body he tossed the twenty-seven-pound bomb out. Just as it passed his fingers it exploded and ignited its skin melting light. But it was outside the airplane. His heroic action saved the lives of his entire crew and saved the airplane from certain destruction."

Bruce told us that the squadron had submitted John for the Congressional Medal of Honor. It came as no surprise to us that the great hero of that gunship was a lowly airman and one of the youngest members of the unit.

My heart swelled and I almost cried thinking of the other most important airman in my life: Ron. He would be, and I was, chuffed, of Airman John and reveled in his valor and bravery.

• • •

Two weeks later, I was summoned to the Orderly Room. "Gunner, get in here," he hollered while I waited reading my book in his outer office.

"What's up, First Sergeant?" I asked while looking around his office. He had two Japanese Samurai swords hanging from one wall, a picture of himself with boxing gloves on in the ring with Muhammad Ali and a plaque proclaiming him BADDEST DUDE IN TOWN. The place smelled like a cheap stale cigar; the braggart's artificial testosterone. Everyone knew he was just a high ranking clerk in a combat squadron so he did everything to win the respect of the warriors and to fit in with them.

"Some dopey ass Load Master is being reassigned to our Squadron from the hospital at Wright Patterson. I want you to go over and pick him up. Bring him here, first thing." He put his thumbs under his arm pits. "Did you see that they are having the base boxing championships and I want you in the combat arena," he threw left and right air punches.

"No, thanks. First, you're too tough for me," I joked, feigning a punch at him.

He took the boxing stance. "Come on kid, I'll give you a lesson."

"No, thanks, where do I pick up the new guy?"

I ran outside and got in my car and drove the sixty miles to Wright Patterson. I pulled up to the side of the hospital, parked, found the lobby and was sent to go to the third floor.

I went in and his room saw a very young airman sitting, watching the T.V. He was baby faced, had thin lips and a slight grin. His wry smile was endearing and it seemed like he knew a secret that no one else knew. He had bright eyes and dark hair, and I liked him a lot.

"Where's your duffle and stuff?" I asked.

"They're sending it to me." He shrugged his shoulders. "I was Medevacked out of Nam and didn't get a chance to pack my stuff. I'm lucky to be here. They'll send it later," he said. "I appreciate, you picking me up."

His flying suit was all ripped and torn with holes in it and dried crud on the chest, legs and shoulders. "Where are your boots and hat?" He looked funny in the blue hospital slippers.

"Still back in Nam. When I get paid, I'll buy new ones or someone said they'll issue them to me. Hell, I don't even have my wallet, money or ID card. Will you help me get them?" he asked. He smelled all antiseptic and pine cleaner.

"Sure, buddy, after we check in the orderly room." I laughed, "We'll have to go to supply and get you a new flying suit; the one you're wearing stinks. But, first I'm going to buy you your welcome home all American meal."

"I owe you for helping me and I can't tell you how much I appreciate it," he said with humble downcast eyes. He whispered under his breath, "I'm so lucky."

He ravished the Big Mac, fries and large milkshake; like a bear after starving all winter. He refused when I offered him an apple pie. The smell of the hot pie baking got to me so I walked up and bought him one anyway and he licked his lips and ate it very slowly like he was savoring every bite. "I'll never be able to thank you enough," he said. "I'm lucky to have you for a friend," he said. He looked very serious for one so young.

He was pensive and quiet as we drove back to Lockbourne. He just peered out of the car window watching the farms go by, his eyes filled with delight and tears. He looked into the clear sky and pointed out the cottony white clouds. A couple of times he mentioned how lucky he was to be an American.

I parked by the orderly room, went around the car and got in front of him so no one would see that he didn't have a hat. We slinked in with him following close behind me. I banged on the frame of the First Sergeant's door and he shouted, "Get in here, Airmen."

I felt under attack. He yelled, "Stand at attention. What the hell are you doing coming in here in that filthy flying suit and wearing those pansy-ass slippers?"

I was astonished, my eyes grew large and my heart raced at sixty knots a minute. I stammered, but before I could speak he shouted at my friend, "What kind of kid comes into this squadron of combat heroes and wearing hospital slippers, no hat and a filthy flying suit? Are you totally out of your mind or are you just stupid?" He waved his fists.

I stepped back behind the new guy, where he couldn't see me and waved at the First Sergeant. I shook my head and mouthed the words 'No, No, No.'

But he was on a rant to end all rants. He called it a Come to Jesus Meeting; a session where he tells the Airman who cuts the corn.

I waved like a madman and couldn't get him to stop. "This is entirely disrespectful to the gallant warriors of this combat squadron. You have no…"

"First," I shouted over his voice. He looked wide eyed like I slapped him, "He was Medivaced from Vietnam. He was flown out without picking up his gear. He couldn't even get his wallet. That's dried blood on his flying suit—this is Airman John Levitow."

CHAPTER XXLIII

A CHILD MAKES A MAN

January 1970: A new year, a new decade and a new world because Toni went into labor. It began at 0400 A.M., after she had been awake all night, with a burning need to use the bathroom. After a hundred "no tinkle" close calls, I screamed on the phone at the Base hospital. "Bring her in Right now," the maternity nurse yelled back in frustration.

I drove as fast as I could. Hit sixty getting out of my street. Two wheels around the corner. Skidded over the icy road by the base chapel. Spun around the end of the flight line. Zipped by the corner of the ammo dump. All of a sudden there was a flashing red light behind me. *Thank God, the security cops are going to escort me to the hospital.*

I waved for them to get in front of me. They wave excitedly and stayed close behind. But, we were near now and I didn't need an escort. I raced ahead.

Why did they turn on the siren?

Skidded into the emergency entrance and waved at them. Went around and pulled Toni's door open and there was a hand on my shoulder. I looked back and the aero cop had his pistol drawn.

"Hands up! Why did you run from me?" he asked.

"My wife is having a baby, I thought you were escorting me," I said breathlessly. I held Toni's hand and put my left hand behind her back to help her. She was enormous and had trouble getting out of the seat. *Be gentle*, I thought. Finally, after great effort on her side, she waddled out. Then she noticed the gun and her eyes got as wide as baseballs.

"Put that away Airman, you might hurt someone," I said. "Grab that suitcase and help me get her in the hospital; we're having a baby."

He looked dumbfounded. He grabbed the suitcase and we three walked through the double doors. As the door closed behind us I saw two other cop cars race up with their lights blazing.

In the hospital she was in a standard green room with a drip attached to her left arm as the nurses hovered around, getting her ready. After a while, they told me to go to the father's waiting room and they took her away to have the baby. I kissed her on the lips. She seemed so small and fragile and I was very fearful for her safety. The last scene from A Farewell to Arms went through my head, *is she gonna die? Is my wife going to die?*

I went to the expectant father's waiting room. I was extremely tense, and tried to study my textbook but couldn't. I looked around and saw the standard furnishings and dog-eared magazines: a year old *Field and Stream*, last month's *Time*, and Methuselah's *Newsweek*. It was dark, with subdued lighting and the walls were painted pale blue. Felt calming to me. There was only one other person present in the thirty-foot square room. He was a black Technical Sergeant. He sat alone, directly across from me, his head down. He looked as if he was in prayer, so I turned back to my book and did not bother him.

To take my mind off of my fear, I wrote a list of people I had to notify when the baby arrived. The only paper I had was the back page of my economics textbook. There, I listed my mother and father-in-law, my father, my brother, her brother and a variety of friends in both England and the United States.

I was sitting there pondering the concept of birth, and thought: what an incredible event! A child was born; life was renewed; hope sprang eternal. There was a chance for a new human being to make real progress in the world. My mind naturally turned to Ron. He would have had another baby by now.

What was it about the birth of a child that immediately renewed my faith in mankind?

It defied logic; if I, a fully functional adult man with all the power in the western world, could not affect real change for the better. Why did the birth of a child, weak and frail and unable to fend for himself, make me think that he could make a difference?

I heard a fumble as the double doors swung open to my right. Slowly a tall lanky man drifted in the room. He was wearing pale green scrubs and an operating room mask. His head was down and he slowly slid his feet over to where I was sitting and stopped in front of me.

"Mr. Brown?"

"No, I'm not," I answered.

The Technical Sergeant stood up. "I'm Brown."

The doctor went over to him and placed his hand on his shoulder and said, "Mister Brown do you have other children?"

"Yes, we have six boys and girls."

"Good," the doctor said. Then he guided him over to the corner farthest away from me and they huddled together and whispered in hushed tones. I couldn't hear what they were saying but I knew it wasn't good. I heard the word 'stillborn' and was overcome with a cold chill and fear greater than I had ever known. I thought, *I would rather face thousand VC than have my frail wife go through that kind of brutal pain.*

I tried to hear, but could only catch whispers that were meaningless. My mind went into overdrive and I began to think, *what if he got the name wrong and it isn't Brown he should be speaking to, but me? Maybe it's my baby that is stillborn, maybe my child is lost.*

I had a gigantic hole in the pit of my stomach and fear embraced me. I slowly resigned myself to the loss of the baby and just wanted my wife to live. I prayed to God; *let her live.*

She's blameless. I have done everything wrong, not her. Let her live and I will do better. I will be a perfect person in the future if you let her live. We wanted this baby but we can adopt—just let her live.

I was beside myself. I was sure the doctor had gotten the name wrong. It happened all the time, especially in military hospitals. There were even cases where they sent the wrong baby home with the wrong family.

But, wait, poor Brown was leaving. The doctor looked my way. A cold shudder danced down my spine. Fear gripped my chest. I held my breath. Then blue stretch went out the doors. I averted my eyes, half afraid that he'd turn back and come over to talk to me.

Just go away.

At last, I was alone with my fears and doubts.

Why wasn't I perfect? If I was, I could be worry-free and expect to have a perfect baby.

I left to go to the canteen to get a cup of coffee. But I didn't want coffee. I wanted the agony to end.

I went out into the lobby and called my brother in Florida. He had just had a child and he would understand. He'd talk to me at this ungodly hour in the morning.

"Hello?" he answered.

"Hey buddy; it's me, in Ohio." *Was my voice shaking?*

"Hey," he shouted. "How's the baby? How's the wife?"

"Nothing yet," I reported. "I'm still waiting. I'm nervous." I swallowed, with difficulty. My mouth felt like the Sahara. "How long does this take?"

"It takes as long as it takes," my brother said. "You can ask the nurses how it's going, and they'll tell you. Just relax and it will all be over in a few minutes. You can't rush mother nature."

It was hard to accept that I could stare death in the face during a fire-fight, but I was helpless and terrified in the face of a birth.

"Okay, buddy," I said, exhaling slowly. "I think I'll go out and get a paper. I'll call you when it's over."

"Relax, okay?"

"Relax? Are you crazy?"

On the other end of the line, my brother chuckled. "Talk to ya' later."

I got a newspaper from the rack and returned to the waiting room to do the crossword puzzle. These have always distracted me and made me forget my troubles.

But I couldn't concentrate. My mind returned to the scene in *A Farewell to Arms* where Frederick is in the hospital and hears that Catherine has died. *God, let this be over soon.*

I was sitting there quietly; a bundle of nerves, when the double doors opened wide and the doctor danced in and said, "You have a new healthy baby boy! Congratulations, a healthy baby boy."

Dumbfounded, I stood up. I felt light headed, shook the doctor's hand and blurted out rapid-fire questions. "Thank you. What a relief. How's my wife? Is she okay?"

"She's fine. Just a little tired. You can go in to see her in less than an hour. In the meantime, you can go to the nursery window and see your son. You can see your baby boy!"

I followed the doctor to the viewing window, and saw three nurses in the back of the room, huddled over a bassinette and cleaning up a baby. They had a rubber bulb, ear swabs, washcloths, towels and little blue clothes. They were working deliberately and when they finished, I caught a glimpse of my boy.

They rolled the bassinette over by the window so I could see. What a magnificent sight he was, all swaddled up in a blue blanket and wearing a blue skullcap. He looked wonderful.

I remembered how my father described me as a bloody mess, looking like a wet chicken. My son looked nothing like that. I would never describe my son like that.

He was dark-haired, calm and quiet. He looked so peaceful and serene. The nurse picked him up and the blanket fell away, and I could count the fingers and toes on each of the little hands and feet. He looked perfect.

He's perfect, my prayer worked, he's perfect.

273

What a great sight—and a wonderful relief—to see my perfect son. My heart swelled with pride and joy greater than I had ever known. I felt an instant love and bond to this little mass of humanity; a great love. I needed to see my wife. I was so proud of her. I prayed that she, too, was fine.

My son, my son. What a joy to behold, my son.

I tapped on the glass and the nurse came to the door and cracked it open. I asked her, "How is he? Can I see my wife?"

"He's perfect, just perfect," she answered, "You can see your wife in about an hour, all right? We're cleaning her up now."

I stood by the window, wanting to go and call my in-laws in England, but I was unable to take my eyes off of my son. I kept repeating the words to myself: *My son. My son.*

I stood there for an hour, until they came out and told me that my wife was ready.

I went out the door to the nurse's station and they pointed me in the direction of the room where she was recovering. I ran down the hall but slowed as I approached the room. I entered quietly to see her asleep, curled up in the hospital bed. She looked so serene, so peaceful. It was hard to imagine what she had just gone through.

As I stared at her, my mind turned to the meaning of it all and I thought, *she did this for me.* She did a braver thing than I would ever do, and she did it for me. I didn't think I could do something like that for someone else. I was too self-centered.

I remembered I had loads of people to call and notify of the successful birth of my son.

I went to the pay phone in the lobby, armed with a pocket full of dimes and quarters. I first called her parents in England. They were "over the moon" with delight, and my father-in-law said, "This is my first grandson!" He was beyond happy.

I called my family and told everyone that mother and child were doing outstandingly well. Everyone was happy for us.

After checking that my wife was still asleep and taking another peek at my son, I drove to the Base Exchange to get presents for all.

I bought roses and a Cadbury's chocolate bar for my wife, some cigars with blue bands to give to our friends, and a baseball glove and ball for my son.

I returned to the hospital. My wife was awake and had my son in her arms. She was feeding him. I gingerly leaned over, kissed her and looked at him. His eyes were open. I stared into the eyes of my son for the first time and saw an awareness that I was unprepared to see. He looked me straight in the eye, and I loved him. I was simply captivated by his eyes. I remembered a poem from long ago:

'I looked into my baby's eyes and glimpsed the face of God.'

I saw dreams and hopes in his eyes. Perhaps, my own dreams and hopes, but they were there.

I told my wife that I loved her, and was proud of her. I asked how she was.

Ever the practical mother, she waved that aside. "How's Cindy? Did you phone my mother?"

I answered that I phoned her mother and Cindy was fine. Toni gave me a couple of minutes to appreciate him and then sent me packing.

I did as told and finally arrived at my squadron operations building, armed with my box of cigars. I went to Chief's office first and he had already heard the news, as the wives' scuttlebutt network worked twice as fast as the men's.

"Congratulations, Gunner. We are very happy for you." He then told me, in excruciating detail, the story of the birth of his three sons. I half-heartedly listened, while fidgeting in my chair, trying to figure out a way to escape, see the rest of my friends and get back to the hospital.

Finally, his phone rang and when he answered it, I slipped out. I went to the gunners' office to see all of the troops and hand out cigars all around. I next went to the standardization evaluation office where I resided, my crew having recently been elevated to that grand position, and told my crewmates the great news. Finally, I escaped the office and returned home.

At 1900, visiting hours started and I was standing with the other new fathers at the entrance to the patient rooms when the head nurse entered and allowed us to go to see our wives. I went into Toni's room and saw that she still had my son cradled in her arms. A smile cracked my lips and my heart, what a beautiful sight – a woman and her newborn son. *I'll keep this vision in my memory for my entire life.*

She asked about Cindy, the relatives and our home. My mind was on my son. I could not stop thinking about him and what he represented to me. She handed him to me and I sat down in a rocking chair and held him cradled in my arms.

I saw the past, I saw Ron in his eyes. I saw the future in his calm, pure face. *His will be a life of accomplishments. He will do everything that Ron and I were unable to do. He will have every benefit, and he will have the finest education and the greatest opportunities in the world.*

Then I realized that I had to change significantly if I was to be in a position to afford him all the opportunities that he deserved. I would not have listened to Ron if he had not lived the role of accomplishment. Ron inspired me because he lived the life he expected me to live. Now, I had to live the life I expected my son to emulate.

What would I become? What would I accomplish? What would be my opportunities?

Here was the great epiphany: I was the key to his life. If I wanted him to be educated, I must be the role model of education. If I wanted him to be hard working, I must be hard working. If I wanted him not to smoke cigarettes, I must quit smoking cigarettes. And I promised him that I would do all of those things. And I promised him I would be all that I could humanly be.

Furthermore, I promised him that I would finish college, I would get commissioned, I would work hard and I would be a man of character, integrity and honor. I would do it all because I wanted *him* to do it all. And I promised him that nothing would stop me. And I promised him, nothing would harm him, and he would grow to be big, strong and great.

I will name him John Robert for my inspirations; the Kennedys.

CHAPTER XXLIV

SOMETIMES WE GET LUCKY

I stood in the doorway glaring into my classroom. My friend Charley, an instructor in the classroom next to mine told me that loud shouts were disturbing his students. The young gunners were playing tag around the eight-hundred-pound 20MM Gatling gun, mock up, sitting in the back of the room on casters. Three young airmen were on the side by the window, two of them wrestling on the ground while the biggest one was on the far side feigning to go after them. One student ran to the front of the room where the green boards were full with my lesson about emergency procedures still chalked on the board.

"If you don't have the maturity to treat this class seriously, I will throw you out immediately," I shouted at my six rowdy students. The class leader jumped up and brushed off his green flying suit, lowered his eyes in a humiliated look and answered.

"I'm sorry, Gunner, we were acting the fool," he looked humbled.

"Let's get back to our studies and stop all this childishness, you guys fly tonight. You can rest assured the Viet Cong gunners aren't playing grab ass, they're practicing to kill you." I looked stern and sounded like Ron.

I had settled into classroom teaching and no longer flying every night. The steady hours gave me time to focus my energies on my family and my college studies, ever mindful of my promise to Ron to go for the degree and the commissioning.

• • •

Two weeks later I received a page over the classroom interphone. "Come into the office. You have a phone call from a civilian at the Air Force Institute of Technology.

"Airman, I am Mr. McCarthy from AFIT. I have your application for the Airman Education and Commissioning Program." He was soft spoken and sounded like a grandfather type with a kind voice. My heart raced as I had never heard back from my college application.

"Nice to meet you, Mr. McCarthy. How is my application going?"

"You have been selected to go to college in the fall."

"I've been selected to go to college in the fall?" I was dizzy and a smile cracked my face.

"Yes," he said, "but I have another offer to make to you."

"I'm going to college?" I must have sounded dumbfounded.

"Yes, you are," he said with a little laugh in his voice. "You can wait and start in September in the normal class system. However, if you can start class sooner, next month, I have an immediate slot in Packaging Engineering at Michigan State University. But you have to start in June."

"What's Packaging Engineering and where is Michigan State?"

"I don't know either answer, but you can get the school catalogue from the education office and call me back tomorrow with your answer."

"Mr. McCarthy, let me get this straight. I can go to college in September in Physics, or start in June in Packaging Engineering?"

"That's right. Call me back tomorrow with your answer."

I felt my heart soar, it was racing. *I can't wait to tell Toni.*

I called her immediately and she almost jumped through the phone with delight. "Oh, what a marvelous dream come true," she said. "I shall call my parents and tell them they'll be ecstatic."

I drove to the Flying Squadron looking for Finder. I wanted him to know what an inspiration he'd been to me. I found him and told him the news.

He was as happy as I was. He told me, "Go home now, and discuss it with your wife. Don't make a hasty decision because you want to go to college as soon as possible. But frankly, I would take the earliest start date to avoid any problems. Once you get to school, you're safe from the war. By the way, it doesn't matter what your degree is in, you will find your own level when you get commissioned."

I raced home in a cloud.

I ran in and met my wife. I was shaking. I said, "Sweetheart, we're going to college."

Her mouth dropped open. "We are going to college? Where? When? How do we get there?" She had a thousand questions. I told her what Mr. McCarthy had told me that we could go next month to MSU and I could study Packaging Engineering or wait until September, and I could study Nuclear Physics.

Her response was immediate. "Let's go next month. The Vietnam assignments are due out any moment; the wives are all walking on eggshells hoping their husbands won't be chosen. I can get ready and pack up the house and babies, and we can be on the road in two weeks. You won't have to worry about Vietnam whilst you're in college. Oh, what a dream come true!"

She ran to the phone and, despite the exorbitant cost, called her mother in England to tell her the great news. I spoke to her and my father-in-law and they were unbelievably excited, more because I wouldn't have to go back to war for a couple of years rather than I was going to college with the potential to get commissioned.

We busted our asses, as they say, over the next two weeks. We were ready when moving day came. As we drove off the base, it was a beautiful early morning in June and the sky was clear blue with puffy, cotton-like, white clouds. An AC-119K gunship landed into the rising sun. We were entering a new world for us with different enemies, bigger guns and life altering challenges.

CHAPTER XLV

MICHIGAN STATE UNIVERSITY

'Off we go into the wild blue yonder,' should be our family motto, I thought, as we sped to East Lansing, towards my first day of college. We were two adults, two kids, a Guinea pig, and a car full of our worldly possessions, racing up the peninsula towards a new life; a life significantly different than we had ever known. This became a time of enormous adjustments, the like of which I would never see again.

Orders in hand, I reported to the ROTC detachment, which was in a Quonset hut on the back of the campus. A full colonel introduced himself as the detachment commander. There were four other airmen there, getting their initial briefings, who were introduced as my fellow AECP brothers. I joined John, Nick, Cliff and Chuck.

The Colonel stood. He was wearing civilian clothes with a sports jacket, he looked like a college professor. "You are stationed at a civilian college, but you are expected to maintain the same standards that got you here. You are to conduct yourselves with honor, dignity and military bearing at all times. Step out of line and you'll be spit shining dirty jets in Kunsan, Korea," the Colonel said. "There is a mandatory monthly meeting."

Chuck asked about haircuts. "Don't stand out from the civilian students but don't get so out of control that I want to ship you out to

Vietnam. Stay away from the War protesters on campus." That was the first I had heard about war protests.

"Your main job is to complete all assigned course work and stay in good academic standing with the university. Your initial matriculation will be Saturday in the field house, be there at the designated time."

My first major adjustment was the next morning. I was at the field house at 0700, ready to go. Unfortunately, it didn't open until 0900. I had not adjusted to the civilian time yet, so I went for a cup of coffee until then.

At around five minutes till nine all chaos reigned as thousands of students piled out of all the buildings, looking like cockroaches when you turn the light on at night. Like the gay pride parade in New York, they were dressed in everything from pajamas with footies like little kids, to formal tuxedos as if they just rolled in from a black tie dinner. I thought, *Man Ron would have loved to be here. I wish you were here buddy.* I dried my eyes to get rid of the Raid and ran in with the rest of the roaches.

It looked like the mad rush when they gave out three day passes at the orderly room. The field house had hundreds of folding tables around the perimeter of the basketball court, each table with a sign for the course it represented. I had a list which included English 101, so I went to that table first. I lined up and some pipsqueak of a slight girl punched me in the ribs and said, "Hey, I was here first."

"Fuck off, kid," the guy in front of me said, "That shit won't work here, you used it last semester." There I received an IBM computer card with the course I wanted and the section or time requested. I received English 101 M-W-F at 0900. So far, so good.

Next, I needed pre-algebra. I went to the math table, but the only classes and sections available were at the same time as my English class. So I took the math class and had to return to the English table and get a different class and section. The process continued all day until I had the eighteen semester hours the Air Force required.

Around noon, I met an airman from the AECP program who introduced himself as John. He had been at the school for a week so he was more settled that I was. He suggested we go to the student union.

At lunch, we called our wives and decided to have a barbeque at his apartment that night. My family was still in a motel, so it was good for us. John had been an OSI agent in the Air Force so he was like a mini James Bond. His wife Shirley was a southern belle with the sweetest silky drawl I ever heard. They had a son and daughter, like we did, and this would be a friendship made in heaven. Our families instantly bonded and we even rented an apartment in the same building.

Monday morning, classes started with a vengeance. I carpooled with John and he showed me around campus. It was summer and most of the students were home for vacation, so we parked in the center and walked to the student Union and our classes. The first was inorganic chemistry.

It was hard for me to imagine, but inorganic chemistry was taught in a gigantic auditorium larger than most movie theatres I had ever been in.

The guy on the podium had his academic lineage on the board, tracing it from the Nobel Prize winner, Pasteur. Pasteur taught one Professor, who taught the next, who taught the next, who taught him. That was how he established his academic credibility with the students.

"Every single student in this auditorium is the valedictorian of their high school class except you and me," John said sweeping the room with his arm. So we were in a room with three hundred valedictorians, competing for a grade from a professor of Nobel lineage. This was quite a change from gunning in Nam!

I said to John, "Man, this is impossible. How can we compete with all this talent?"

"Thank God they're young and get distracted easily, so they won't focus for the entire semester. We can work harder, concentrate better and enjoy our stable family lives, while they will be out partying. We'll get our share of good grades."

I stood on the top tier of an indoor, stadium-like room with fifty rows of chairs down to a podium and chalk boards where the professor stood. He got right into the lesson.

Life was not only academic; there was the need to keep up our physical shape. That night we played our first intramural flag football game. It was a welcomed break from the relentless studying. I was a wide receiver and had a great time catching the ball. Afterwards, we went back to the student union where I showed my wife and children around. What a great environment to raise them. How could it get any better than this? This was the American dream.

The flag football team was the only distraction I allowed. I focused on studying, in order to get the best grades and learn the maximum amount possible. It was my routine to arise at 0500, put on the coffee and go to a little room and study. I did this until the family arose around 0800. We ate together and then I drove to campus. I went to my first class, or the library, and stayed there all day going from class to library to study hall and then on to the next class. Usually, I would return home at 1900, after all the classes, and spend the evening with the children, except when I played flag football.

I loved the flag football team, the joy of releasing pent-up physical energy, running around a field. We played against fraternities, clubs and other school organizations. After the second week, they appointed me the quarterback. I didn't like the position, but we didn't have anyone who could throw any better, so I was elected. We were doing spectacularly, winning all our games, until that dreadful night when we had to play the Gay Liberation seven.

I looked across the park and saw a cacophony of color next to the field we were scheduled to play on. There were fifteen or so big men in pink hot pants dancing around the side line. They had their own cheer leaders, twelve guys and girls jumping around spinning pink pom-poms singing 'Go Gaaay Lib, ahhh, Go gaaay lib.' They were smiling and singing the entire time, prancing and dancing to their own music. One of them had a snare drum and another had a kazoo and they laughed and danced playing their go gaaay lib song.

Everything was going fine until the Gay Lib scored the first touchdown. We responded and I drove my team down the field and we scored. For the rest of the first half, we traded punts a couple of times. In the second half the Gay Lib drove down and scored again. We got the ball back and I passed our team down and finally scored again to tie it up.

With two minutes to go, their quarterback, JOE LAYMITH, completed a pass into the end zone and took the lead. My heart sunk but they punted the ball back to us. John got the punt and ran it half-way back. I called a passing play, got the ball, fired it over the middle and hit the wide receiver in the end zone for a touchdown. Then for the point after, I called for John to go to the right corner of the end zone.

The center hiked the ball to me and I dropped back and looked left to distract the defense. As the rushers approached I looked right, saw John, miraculously all by himself and fired off a great spiral. All of a sudden, the biggest guy, half ballerina and half gazelle stepped in front of John and intercepted the pass. The game was over and the Gay Lib beat the Air Force. What humiliation! What utter defeat. The strength of America's manhood beaten, should I say humiliated, by the gays.

I was immediately deposed, fired, removed and ejected as quarterback and even my manhood was questioned. The team was in utter chaos and feeling like a squashed bug. That was my last stint at quarterback. I went back to studying all day and the occasional play as a wide receiver.

Despite my football failure, I was surviving in all of my classes. The most heartening part of the experience was the amount of personal encouragement the Profs gave us. They related to us students and gave a warm caring atmosphere to every class.

During my third semester, I finally realized how dramatically my world had changed when the anti-war protests came to Michigan State. There were marches all over the campus. There was a parade down Main Street with posters and banners everywhere. We Air Force men maintained a low profile, as we didn't cut our hair short or advertise that we were members of the military.

There was a strong antimilitary sentiment on the campus, as most of the students were eligible for the draft. Students could avoid the draft by getting an educational deferment. They had to take a minimum of twelve semester hours and get passing grades in all their subjects, or they would be immediately drafted. We had a joke among the military students: when the grade reports cards came out, Greyhound ran a special of a box lunch and one-way ticket to Canada for $19.99.

On one particular grand day of protests, all classes were cancelled. A billboard in front of the school advertised for the Air Force. It was a picture of a C-9 aircraft and it said, "NURSE, THIS IS YOUR WARD" as a recruitment inducement for flight nurses. Someone had climbed up and erased the D so it said, "NURSE, THIS IS YOUR WAR!" The campus was all a-twitter with anti-war excitement.

John and I decided to go to the parade on Main Street and to the rally in the quadrangle. I don't know why we wanted to attend. Perhaps it was morbid curiosity or plain boredom. In any event, we attended these and everything was fine. Then there was a rally planned in the school auditorium.

We went there and sat in the middle, listening to all of the speeches. I felt like a military spy invading a civilian stronghold. There were all kinds of groups making accusations against us in the military, from Black Panthers calling us racists to feminists calling us male chauvinists, to the gay lib yelling that we were homophobic. Since I'd always considered it an honor to serve my country, something to be proud of, I found the slurs most disconcerting. To me, it was almost an out-of-body experience.

Then someone began a slide show of battle scenes from Vietnam, with all kinds of pictures accusing us of being war criminals and baby killers. I took it all in stride until they showed a picture of Jane Fonda sitting on an AAA gun in North Vietnam with an F-105 Thunder Chief, superimposed over the gun, in a nose dive burning in the back ground. When the students saw this photo they started to cheer.

I couldn't believe what I was seeing! These people were cheering an American being shot down. Here was a true hero, my brother in combat, protecting these kids in college, and they *cheered* when they saw him being shot down. How atrocious. How dared they?

My face turned red and I flushed with anger. I started to jump up and, thankfully, John grabbed my arm. He said, "Don't take it personally. They don't know what they're doing."

I answered, "I'm getting out of here. I've seen enough."

We got up, left the auditorium and went home. I was disgusted by the misguided, childish students and never returned to another demonstration.

CHAPTER XLVI

HONOR AMONG WARRIORS

"You were given a zero on your lab report," the graduate assistant told me as I picked our report from the stack.

"What do you mean a zero? John and I busted ass to get that right," I scowled at him.

"You had the same answers as Chuck and he told me you copied."

I felt flushed and pissed, "I never copied a thing. That moron is behind me in grades, how the shit would I copy from him?"

"Well, it's a zero unless you want to challenge it before the academic board."

Shaken, I went back to our station and saw John there wearing lab glasses and an apron. "That dip shit gave us a zero because we had the same answer as Chuck. How did that happen?" I asked.

"Lord God," John said, "Chuck asked to borrow our report and I lent it to him so he could check his work," he looked pained with a grimace on his face.

"You better check with Chuck and get this straight," I yelled at my best friend.

He marched off looking for Chuck.

I sat on the stool stunned. This could cause us to fail the lab.

John came back, "He won't tell the Grad student he copied our answers. We have to live with it."

• • •

"Joe, some captain from the Air Force called and wanted you to call back," Toni said.

I was put through to the Captain in charge of us students at MSU. I started casually with the normal "hello." He surprised me with his comments.

"Joe there is a shortage of gunners in Vietnam. I am thinking about pulling you out of school and shipping you over." My heart sounded like a bongo drum in my chest, I was dizzy and my face felt hot.

"Captain, you got to be shitting me," I stuttered out.

Apparently I yelled because Toni came around the corner and mouthed, "What's the matter?"

I placed my left hand over the mouth piece and said, "They're thinking of sending me back; there is a shortage of gunners."

"We'll go to Canada," she whispered.

Insanity flashed through my mind. There was any number of my classmates who were only in school for the military deferment. When their deferment ran out, many of them went to Canada and just avoided military service. I could see an image of us wearing tattered clothes trudging through the snow going to some soup kitchen. I would never allow my family to go through that much less let down my mother, let down Ron or fail President John F. Kennedy.

"Come on Captain, really?"

"Listen, I heard you were getting a 'C' in chemistry," he said chuckling.

Maybe it's a sick joke.

"A 'C' in Chemistry, man they call me the chemist. I own Chemistry," I said.

In fact, I was not getting a great grade because of Chuck. Chemistry was as hard as Chinese Calculus for me but work and good study habits kept me above the failure line. I vowed, *I'll study every second to make sure I get a 'B' or better.*

Before hanging up he asked, "How's your buddy John doing in Chemistry?"

"John is my lab partner and they're thinking of offering him a scholarship in graduate chem," I lied. Then I thought of a way to get him back, "Captain, I heard Chuck is thinking of dropping Chemistry," I lied.

I called John, told him what the Captain had said and we formed a pact to study every available moment that semester until we were solid as a granite mountain in the wind storm of life. We studied, learned, crammed, revised and educated ourselves that semester so much that Shirley and Toni complained that we were never at home.

Hard work and John's dedication led to us getting a B that semester.

$$\bullet \quad \bullet \quad \bullet$$

As graduation approached, I was filled with a combination of delight and joy but also a feeling of anticlimax. Was this all there was to it? I felt there was more to do and further to go.

This was interrupted by the overseas visit of my father-in-law from England. He had always been an intellectual inspiration to me because of his strong military and science background. He had been a radar operator on a secret site during WWII. After the war, too poor to attend college, he became a chemical engineering technician at Courtland's fiber manufacturing in England. In this position he studied a great deal of chemistry and other sciences. In fact, he and I often spoke, and I wrote to him with science questions.

Seven years earlier, while on temporary duty to Libya I tried to study a book about light. I did not understand the use of the symbol Lambda and wrote for his help. By return mail, he explained that it was used to define wavelength in all equations, thereby solving my dilemma.

During his visit, he accompanied me to class on a number of occasions. He particularly appreciated my science classes. After an intense astronomy class, he explained the differences between the British and American educational systems.

He asked, as we walked from class to my car, "Do you know the differences between our systems, Joe?"

"No," I replied.

"Your system was designed to make you a success, whilst mine was designed to hold me back and make me a failure."

"How so?" I asked.

"Your military has helped you go to school and the university has assisted in every way they can to impart knowledge to you. My military prevented me from going to university and the universities are so rife with nepotism that they would not even hear my appeal to attend," he answered.

I always regretted he did not have the opportunity to attend university on his own behalf. In any event, his guidance and prodding greatly improved my own education.

As the end of my academic experience approached, I was doing better and better in my classes, to the point that I was offered a position and a scholarship as a graduate assistant to complete a master's degree. When I broached the subject with the AFIT controller, he only laughed and said he required me back working for the Air Force as soon as possible.

My mother came to East Lansing to attend my graduation. It was her belief that I had finally vindicated her; made up for the slight she felt at being unable to attend college herself. She felt that the G.I. bill, after WWII, gave all of the higher education opportunities to the military men returning from war, and prevented the women from attending. I was her substitute as the first in my family to complete a college education.

On the day of graduation, we all dressed up and prepared to attend the ceremony in the football stadium. My mother was in hat and gloves for the first time in her life. My wife was in her church dress, John in a suit and Cindy in a formal. What a sight as we drove to the stadium.

I took my place among the five or six thousand graduates sitting up front. I looked at the doctoral and master's graduates and dreamed of doing the same someday.

As the graduation speaker began, I took time to reflect. This was not all my doing. It was Ron who gave me the spirit of accomplishment; it was Soarer who gave me encouragement; Ace who was my inspiration; Chief and Finder who found an ability to guide me over hurdles I couldn't overcome otherwise; my father-in-law; my wife; my brother and my mother; who stood by me through the most difficult times imaginable. All of them shared in my accomplishment. All of them deserved to wear my mortarboard and gown.

I did not graduate alone.

The spirits of so many people were with me.

The dreams of an entire family rode on my shoulders.

The hopes of all the enlisted people who reached for a diploma, and the drive and dedication of my friends and family had given me the ability to make the mighty trek up to the stage and receive my diploma.

As I walked up to the stage, my heart filled with joy, my eyes with tears. *If only Ron were with me.*

The stage was a blur as lightheadedness overcame me, and I felt as if I were floating. I took the diploma from the president of the university, looked out over the long line of graduates and saw my family.

The admiration and pride in my son's eyes lit up my heart, Cindy beamed with pride and my mother and wife were screaming so loud I could hear them from fifty yards away. I was overcome with humility and cried the entire way across the stage.

CHAPTER XLVII

OFFICER TRAINING/IS RON HERE?

"You're going to be a ninety-day wonder!" was the way my father put it when he learned I was going to Officer Training School. "Ninety day wonders are known for their stupidity and lack of common sense. I knew them in the Army and they were the dumbest people I ever met."

His words kept going through my mind as I flew to San Antonio, Texas to begin a three-month course of training that would lead to a commission. Half way across the country, as I looked out of the aircraft window at beautiful white clouds, my thoughts turned to my friend Ron and how I wished we were sharing this dream together.

The stewardess delivered lunch and asked, "Are you all right?"

"I just got something in my eye," I choked out.

After landing, a number of us got on the bus marked OTS and took the bumpy trip out to Medina. When we arrived, we were sorted into groups and training officers came up and introduced themselves. I was assigned to a group with Captain Bob as the tactical officer.

He had a relaxed attitude and a carefree style that belied his intensity about the school's curriculum. His favorite expression was, 'It only lasts a lifetime.' Our group was called a flight and given a number, Cool 32. We laughed at the other flights and the more 'up tight' tactical officers. Bob said they "had bugs up their asses." I laughed a great deal.

Bob particularly disliked the uptight T.O. of Flight 36, Captain Perfect. He was a golden haired Adonis with a weightlifter's body and a mosquito's brain. Captain Perfect was an Intelligence enforcement officer who reveled in catching Bob's students in minor infractions. Like a spy, he often slunk around, waiting to pounce on the smallest violation. He also lived to beat Bob's students in sports competitions. So to Bob, surpassing Captain Perfect's students was a lifetime goal.

Our first classes taught by Captain Bob were on the requirements of officer integrity. I had always tried to emulate my father and his honesty and conduct myself with integrity, as do most airmen, but the officer corps took integrity and honor to a whole new level. We swore not to lie, steal or cheat, nor allow among us those who did.

Captain Bob explained it in light of the recent Air Force Academy cheating scandal, when over 120 cadets had been expelled. He said that only two cadets had participated in the cheating on a physics test, but the other 118 people had heard of the cheating and had not done anything about it. He explained that the theft of the physics test was an act of commission, but permitting a cheater to remain in their presence was an act of omission. In a similar situation, by failing to act, we would be letting cheaters succeed and become part of the officer corps—and that would not be allowed.

I have never forgotten the lessons of Captain Bob and actually had an occasion to use them during my training. On one occasion, I was taking a major test in the auditorium, where every other seat was filled. For some reason, I looked around. Horrified that someone would think I was cheating, I turned over my answer sheet and wrote, "I am on question number 95 and the answer was A. However, I will not answer this question because I looked around and someone may construe that I looked at another paper for help. I did not look at any other answer sheet."

I formed great friendships in OTS. My closest friend was a former enlisted Marine named B.J. He was one hell of a man; strong, dedicated, intense, and full of integrity. I was sure he would be a great officer. My second friend was F.C. F.C. was a southern gentleman from an old and wise family which had educated him thoroughly. He had great strength of character and fit in extremely well with all of us.

B.J, F.C. and I were married but none of our wives were in Texas with us. I called my wife and asked her to come down to Texas and stay with me for the last six weeks, as I missed her and the children terribly. My friends arranged to have their wives join them for graduation.

Though my thoughts were mostly on friends and family, I still had a number of challenges to overcome and classes to master. Our days were full of early morning wake-ups, barracks clean-ups, marches to chow, classes and physical training. It was at PT that our flight excelled but our nemesis, 36, always seemed in the way of us becoming the champs and having the special 'Champions' gold streamer flying from our guide on.

"Today you are going to learn the beauty of Flicker Ball," Bob said one morning. The sports field looked like the grid iron with white stripes every ten yards. However, at the ends of the field were two vertical goalposts six feet apart and eight feet high. There was a piece of plywood bolted between them. In the center of the plywood was a three-foot rectangular hole with a net behind it. That was the goal, sort of a drunken basketball hoop lying down sideways.

"The rules state that there is no running forward with the ball and no contact," Bob said.

"What power hungry, demented bureaucrat invented this bastardized version of football?" B. J. whispered.

"You can't run forward with the ball?" F.C. asked incredulously.

"No. When you catch the ball, you must stop within two steps— or it's like traveling in basketball. After you stop, then you can throw a forward pass to a teammate," Bob said.

The Grouse was a flight member universally celebrated for complaining about everything. He said, "I can see this will be a real joy to play—how could the Air Force suck the pleasure out of football, basketball and rugby at the same time?"

"Try it, it only lasts a lifetime," Bob said.

"I think my leg hurts," said The Grouse. "I'm going to sick call."

Brian, the tall football quarterback from California, had a different slant on the game. "Listen, boys. I can pass this pumpkin fifty yards down the field if you guys can run down there and stop. That's the reason I wasn't drafted to play in college—I could hit the stationary practice dummy but always overthrew the receivers when they were running."

"Screw that. It's too hot to run," said the Grouse.

"Let's try it," B.J. said, giving the ball to Brian and tearing off down the field. He stopped forty-five yards away and Brian hit him in the center of the chest with a perfect pass.

"This game has possibilities," The Grouse said.

"*Flight 32, you'll get the screw, we will beat you black and blue.*"

Captain Perfect's flight marched by, singing to us in unison. "Jody call, and a challenge," B.J. said.

"Aren't Jody calls what the Army yells while they're marching?" I asked.

"Yeah, and they're so arrogant that they're actually challenging us," Brian said.

"Let's make their shame only last a lifetime," Captain Bob fumed.

So, after losing most sports competitions to Perfect's clones, we plotted to beat them once and for all.

F.C. took our lessons of the desert tactics of Patton, combined them with the Indian's maneuvers that beat Custer, used the wisdom of Grant, and devised a war plan to annihilate Flight 36. Late at night our whole flight assembled in the basement to go over the plan. We had a sand table, used by actual Pentagon tacticians, and had drawn out an exact replica of the Flicker ball field, complete with goalposts and chalk lines. Brian was our sports captain and he showed us his Statue of Liberty play.

The next morning was bright and warm as we assembled at the field for our fateful showdown with 36, for the championships. With

Bob leading, we marched in, all businesslike, pretending to be very military and in command of ourselves. I was chewing gum and feeling jumpy, as were all the others.

"Write two gigs each for chewing gum in formation," Captain Perfect shouted at us.

"That son of a bitch needs to die," B.J whispered to me.

"I will make sure we win," Brian said.

The game was close throughout. They scored first, and as the first half ended, Brian hit The Grouse with a thirty-yard pass which he threw through the hoop for a 7-7 tie. "We won't use the 'Statue of Liberty' until we really need it," Brian said during halftime.

We started the second half with a great drive that scored a goal. Then 36 came back and scored. Next they stopped us and the Grouse was beaten on a long pass. They scored, but in the following series we stopped them dead.

It was 14-14 with two minutes to play and Bob called a time out.

"If it ends in a tie, they win," he said. "Because they beat us at softball, they will be the OTS champs. We have to score in order to win."

We raced out to the five-yard line to receive the kick off. It was a high kick which came down to me, and I got ready to catch it and throw it to B.J. The ball hit me square on the right thumb, which felt like a gigantic knife stabbed into the base of my hand. I dropped the ball and fell to my knees. Thank God Brian jumped on the ball so the other team couldn't recover it and score.

"Can you still play, Joe?" Brian asked.

"I can, just give me a chance to stick it to 36," I said.

"Receivers deep thirty-five yards and buttonhook; I'll hit you," Brian said.

"Incomplete pass," the referee said, after the play.

"Try the same one again," Brian said.

"Pass interference," claimed The Grouse.

"It only lasts a lifetime," Bob shouted over from the side line.

"No interference, incomplete pass," the referee announced.

"Okay, *Statue of Liberty*, just like we practiced it last night—only thirty seconds so make it good. Joe make sure you catch the ball," Brian said.

The play started, and I ran down thirty yards. Flight 36 saw me holding my thumb so they didn't cover me. Brian threw a great pass right into my chest and I held on. B.J. raced past me, down the field like the wind. Brian ran up and I lateralled the ball to him. He reared back, eyeing B.J., nearing the goal line. Flight 36 was on to Brian and three of them headed to get him. Two guys were covering B.J. as Brian let the ball fly while B.J. was still running. The clock ticked down to two seconds. . .one second. . .and the ball hit B.J. in the chest—just as he fell over the goal line and scored the winning touchdown.

We all ran down and circled him. We picked up Bob and carried him on our shoulders past Captain Perfect, who, naturally, had his entire team doing pushups.

.   .   .

Despite these diversions, classes were still most important to me. There was a rumor that those finishing in the top three percent would be designated Distinguished Graduates and offered a regular commission. As Vietnam was drawing down, there were rumors of a reduction in force, or RIF, in the officer ranks. Regular officers did not get RIF'd. So I made a great effort to get the best grades possible, in order to be a D.G.

A system of demerits, or gigs, was in place for when an officer trainee made a mistake. Gigs were given for anything from a uniform out of line, dirty rooms, and lateness to class, talking in formation or almost anything the instructors wanted. One day, on my way to class, I decided to get a drink of water at a fountain that had a line.

True to his deserved reputation as a real horse's ass, Captain Perfect shouted out, "All of you thinking about getting a drink of water write two gigs for being late to class."

I was faced with another moral dilemma as I went on to my class.

I really had been thinking about getting a drink of water, so technically, I must write two gigs. However, my family was arriving that Friday and I wanted to leave base.

If I had two more gigs, I'd be restricted. I decided to make an appointment to talk it over with Captain Bob, who would advise me on how to handle the situation.

I entered his office and explained the situation, "Captain, on the way to class the horse's ass said anyone thinking about taking a drink of water must write two gigs for being late to class. I was thinking about taking a drink of water. Do I have to write them? And can I march them off at the drill pad?"

"Don't be ridiculous. He can't assign gigs because you were thinking about getting a drink of water. Forget about it and if he asks you about it, tell him to see me," Captain Bob said.

Friday, after six weeks of me being alone, my family arrived and checked into a motel. I got a pass to go off-base to see them. What a joy to spend a couple of hours rolling around the floor playing with my little girl and boy.

This was why I worked so hard: for them. . We went to dinner at the officer's club, where there was a party celebrating our promotion to the second phase of OTS, the last six weeks of the program.

During the second phase, the upper class took over running the place. We replaced the previous upper class, and a whole new lower class entered the barracks. Each of us was assigned a specific position and assumed the temporary rank associated with that position. F.C. became the wing adjutant and a temporary Lt. Col, B.J. became the temporary captain and flight leader of the lower class, and I became the inspector general and a temporary captain as well. We each enjoyed our new status.

Every morning it was my job to inspect two rooms of the lower class to ensure they maintained the proper standards of health and cleanliness. B.J. told me which room he wanted inspected, and randomly chose the second one. Three of us assembled in the hall, in a triangular shape.

Then the call went out: *The Wedge is Alive.* The three of us, me in front with the two behind me side by side, marched down the hall to the appropriate room and I called "Halt." Facing the room, I ordered the inspection to begin.

We entered with a two-foot-long ruler, two-sided tape and white gloves to inspect from top to bottom. We only inspected for one minute and left. B.J. and the lower class stood at mock attention during our ritual as we repeated it every day.

We were now just two weeks from graduation and F.C. asked B.J. and I to meet with him in the day room for a private conference to get our advice. I got there at 1900 and the two of them were sitting in the corner at a small card table.

"Guys, I have serious reservations about the war in Vietnam," F.C. said. "I don't think I can support a military service that is engaged in a war that violates my moral values."

"O-kaaay. Did you just come up with that revelation or have you been harboring it the entire ten weeks we have been here?" I asked.

"No, I've had doubts the entire time we have been here, but now it's hitting me that I might have to work to kill an enemy I don't believe deserves to be killed."

"Man," I said, "It's like buyer's remorse. As we approach the last day we all have doubts about what we're getting into. Hell, I've been to Vietnam and so has B.J., and we have doubts, too."

"It's not like simple remorse. I have seriously thought about this since our ethics classes. I do not think I can help to destroy human beings whom I think are only trying to protect their homeland. Ethically and morally, I think I have to resign."

"My God," I said, "don't do anything that drastic without taking some time to deeply and seriously consider the ramifications."

B.J. chimed in, "Make sure you talk to Captain Bob. Are you thinking of taking a Self-Initiated Elimination as a conscientious objector?"

"Exactly. I will SIE because, in good conscience, I cannot support the war."

We left the break room and my head was spinning. First, so close to graduation, how could he even consider quitting after he had passed all of the difficult tests and was on the verge of being a distinguished graduate? Second, what a decidedly moral and ethical thing to do to recognize that he was on the wrong course and make the right decision to stop immediately. Third, what a brave act to face all of his fears and all of his class mates and take the honorable course of action, despite the impact to his future and a group of people who would try to talk him out of it.

F.C. went on to SIE for conscientious objector reasons. B.J. and I often spoke of the bravery, honor and courage of our civilian friend.

Despite that loss, I was extremely excited about graduation. We practiced marching in parade formation for days on end to ensure it would be error free.

My mother flew in to be part of the graduation festivities. I could not help but think that to some extent this was also her graduation, as she beamed with pride every time she saw me in uniform. She could not help telling everyone how proud she was of her first college graduate and first officer in the family.

Chief surprised me and came to Medina on some trumped up excuse of a mission. It was apparent that he too felt like part of him was graduating. He and my mother spent a great deal of time congratulating each other for getting me through. I was full of gratitude as we went to the obligatory parties and receptions prior to the actual graduation.

My wife, son and daughter attending graduation were a source of pride to me. They were the ones who'd followed me all over the world and sacrificed their own safety and comfort to chase our dreams.

When the day arrived, we assembled in our dormitory and marched to the parade grounds. Standing in formation, I could not help but feel a great deal of pride combined with humility. I stood there in a formation of graduates and listened to a colonel giving the commencement speech.

I had the strange feeling that there was a second formation surrounding me. There was Ron at my side inspiring me. Zoomie, Finder, Soarer, Chief and Ace were in line behind me pushing. Rick and my professors were ahead lighting the way.

I heard a drone in the background that was eerily familiar. I could not turn to look toward the sound, as I was facing the reviewing stands, and all the guests would notice our slightest waver.

My eyes began to tear up—perhaps it was the wind. Then I saw, way off in the distance, a small airplane flying across the sky. It was a C-47 with the left door removed. Someone was standing in the doorway in a flying suit.

Maybe it was Ron. To this day, I wonder. He should have been standing there, instead of me. He'd had the dream and passed it on to me. He'd earned the right to be here more than I did.

I took a deep breath. Head up, chin back, stomach in.

That's Ron in the C-47 flying by to make sure you don't chicken out at the last minute.

I said out loud, under my breath, "I swear to you buddy, I will never chicken out and I will always make you proud. I wear these bars for you."

As I left the parade grounds for the last time, now as an officer, I remembered the fine old military tradition of giving a silver dollar to the first enlisted man to salute a new officer. I had the silver dollar in my pocket, as did all the other graduates. It had been arranged that a very needy and worthy Airman be the first to salute our class. I saw the line in front of a young senior airman, selected because he had a two-year-old son, the same age as my son, but his son had leukemia and required expensive treatment.

Dignity and pride prevented the Airman from accepting actual donations, but this way, by acknowledging his salute, we could contribute our small part to the future of his son.

I stood in front of him and he saluted. I returned his salute. He looked at me and my line of ribbons so he knew I was a prior Airman. He said, "Sir, I hope to get commissioned someday. How did you do it?"

"Take care of and love your son, first. Second, listen to those who give you encouragement and above all never give up, never give up. You are an Airman, like me and my inspiration Ron, and we never gave up. You can make it."

I gave him the silver dollar, looked to the C-47 above me and silently vowed once again, "Ron, I will never let you down, and I will never quit."

CPSIA information can be obtained
at www.ICGtesting.com
Printed in the USA
LVHW08s2137230918
591138LV00023B/384/P